Reno
Sept 2010

ATLANTIC CREOLES IN THE AGE OF REVOLUTIONS

Jane G. Landers

HARVARD UNIVERSITY PRESS

Cambridge, Massachusetts
London, England

2010

Library of Congress Cataloging-in-Publication Data
Landers, Jane.
Atlantic Creoles in the age of revolutions / Jane G. Landers.
p. cm.
Includes bibliographical references and index.
ISBN 978-0-674-03591-1 (alk. paper)
1. Blacks—Caribbean Area—History—18th century. 2. Blacks —Caribbean
Area—History—19th century. 3. Creoles—Caribbean Area—History—
18th century. 4. Creoles—Caribbean Area—History—19th century.
5. Revolutions—Caribbean Area—History—18th century. 6. Revolutions—
Caribbean Area—History—19th century. 7. Caribbean Area—History—
To 1810. 8. Caribbean Area—History—1810–1945. I. Title.
F2191.B55L36 2010
305.8960729—dc22 2009026421

Acknowledgments

MY DEBTS are many, but this book owes its obvious inspiration to Ira Berlin, whose scholarship and professional generosity set a wonderful example for me and many others. Ira supported my work in many ways before I ever knew him, and I am happy to be able to acknowledge him here and to express my deepest gratitude.

Many other fine scholars and friends have also given me encouragement and assistance. Bud Bailyn and Karen Kupperman encouraged me when the project first took shape as a biography of Big Prince Whitten. James Walvin later suggested pulling my diverse Atlantic interests together in a single work. As the project took on a more complex and wide-ranging form, I drew on the deeper expertise of historians whose work I have long admired. Sylvia Frey, Philip Morgan, and Vernon Burton answered my queries about Revolutionary South Carolina, and Peter Wood was my original guide to that colony's rich history. David Geggus, Madison Smartt Bell, Laurent Dubois, and Julius Scott generously shared research notes and insights on

Saint Domingue. For information on the multiracial history of the Gulf Coast, I am indebted to the scholarship of Gwendolyn Midlo Hall, Ginger Gould, Andrew McMichael, Daniel Usner, and my sorely missed friend, Kimberly Hanger. Matt Childs, Manuel Barcia Paz, and Oscar Grandío Moráguez pointed me to valuable references in the Cuban archives, and I gained much from our lively discussions on the African history of colonial Cuba. Sherry Johnson was typically generous in sharing archival materials on Cuba and Florida that she had microfilmed in Spain, and Frank Marotti generously shared copies of Patriot War Claims he had collected. My colleague William Luis loaned me an important book published in Cuba that I would not have had access to otherwise. I have also learned much from the wonderful scholars of precolonial African history I have been fortunate to meet and query over the years, including Toyin Falola, Robin Law, Paul Lovejoy, Joseph Miller, James Sweet, John Thornton, and Donald Wright, as well as the graduate students now following their paths at York University and Vanderbilt University. I am indebted to Paul Lovejoy and Joseph Miller for their professional support over the years. The work of my longtime colleague Mariza de Carvalho Soares and that of other scholars working on the history of Africans in Brazil, such as Alberto da Costa e Silva, Silvia Lara, João Reis, Stuart Schwartz, Manolo Florentino, and Robert Slenes, have also been a source of inspiration.

My graduate study at the University of Florida provided me with the skills I needed to pursue these varied historical trails. Equally if not more important were my wonderful friends and colleagues in Florida, on whom I have relied ever since for feedback and help on my various books: I gratefully acknowledge James Cusick, Kathleen Deagan, Michael Gannon, Eugene Lyon, Susan Parker, and Daniel Schafer. I cannot thank them enough.

My colleagues at Vanderbilt University have also provided scholarly support and friendship that carried me through some rough times; I would like to thank Michael Bess, Richard Blackett, Marshall Eakin, Celso Castilho, Joel Harrington, J. León Helguera, Frank Robinson, and Eddie Wright-Rios in particular. A special debt is owed to my friend Paula Covington, Vanderbilt's Latin American bibliographer. Paula helped me track difficult sources, read my work, and became a valued member of my Ecclesiastical Sources for Slave Societies team in Cuba. I would also like to acknowledge the friendship and support I have received from Mona Frederick, Executive Director of Vanderbilt's Robert Penn Warren Center for the Humanities, who has generously funded the interdisciplinary Circum-Atlantic Studies Working Group that I direct, as well as our annual Black Atlantic History Lecture Series. I also thank Sean Goudie, with whom I launched these programs, the colleagues who have formed part of this group over the years, and our stimulating guest speakers, all of whose interesting work has enriched my own.

I have been fortunate to train some excellent graduate students at Vanderbilt, and three of them in particular helped me with this book. Barry Robinson, David Wheat, and Pablo Gómez provided valuable research assistance, technical expertise, and critical editorial feedback when I needed it. I learned from them all and am very proud of the scholars they have become.

This book rests on extensive work in assorted archives in Spain, Cuba, and the United States. In Spain I extend my gratitude to the staffs of the Archivo General de Indias in Seville and the Archivo Histórico Nacional in Madrid. I also thank my mentor and friend, Jim Amelang, for his hospitality in Madrid. In Cuba I would like to thank Coralia Alonso, who since my first days as a graduate researcher in the Archivo Nacional de la República de Cuba has treated me with great warmth and hospitality. Monseñor Ramón Suárez Polcari, Chancellor of the Archdiocese of Havana and a historian of the church in Cuba, has also welcomed me and my research teams to work in his wonderful archive. The staff at the Archivo Histórico Provincial and at the Cathedral of San Carlos de Borromeo in Matanzas have been equally welcoming over the years. I am grateful for the efficient and friendly assistance I received at the National Archives and Records Administration and at the Library of Congress Manuscript Division on various research trips. In Florida, the staffs of the Special and Area Studies Collections of the George A. Smathers Libraries at the University of Florida welcomed me each summer, and I give special thanks to Jim Cusick, Bruce Chappell, Carl Van Ness, Richard Phillips, Paul Losch, and Keith Manuel. The staff at the St. Augustine Historical Society Research Library, and in particular Charles Tingley, have been most helpful. I received additional research help at the State Archives of Florida in Tallahassee, the Amelia Island Museum of History, the Bryan-Lang Historical Library in Woodbine, Georgia, and from Deborah Hase, mayor of St. Marys, Georgia.

I also owe thanks to many who helped me locate and reproduce the illustrations in the book. Of particular note is Jerome Handler, Senior Scholar at the Virginia Foundation for the Humanities, who provided images from The Atlantic Slave Trade and Slave Life in the Americas website. I would also like to thank Neal Adam Watson of the State Archives of Florida, Darcie MacMahon of the Florida Museum of Natural History, Nicole Joniec of the Library Company of Philadelphia, Esperanza B. de Varona, Lesbia O. Varona, and Annie Sansone Martínez of the Cuban Heritage Collection at the University of Miami Libraries. Jim Cusick of the P. K. Yonge Library of Florida History not only provided important archival help but also pointed me to the image that became this book's cover portrait. My talented husband, Jim Landers, created the maps in the book. I am grateful each day for the support of the wonderful administrative staff of my history department, Brenda Hummel, Jane Anderson, and Heidi Welch.

Some material from this book appeared in an earlier version in my first book, *Black Society in Spanish Florida*. Since then I have welcomed the chance to present my developing project at various international conferences and at invited seminars at Johns Hopkins University, Harvard University, New York University, the Wilberforce Institute for the Study of Slavery and Emancipation, University of Hull, the Harriet Tubman Institute for Research on the Global Migrations of African Peoples, York University, The Huntington Library, the Centro de Estudos Afro-Orientais, the Universidade Federal Fluminense, the Juan March Foundation, and the McNeil Center for Early American Studies, among others.

This book would not have been possible without the generous financial support I received from Vanderbilt University, the National Endowment for the Humanities, the Conference on Latin American History, the Center for Latin American Studies, University of Florida, and the Historic St. Augustine Research Institute.

I would like to express my deepest appreciation to Joyce Seltzer of Harvard University Press for her guidance and encouragement in shaping this book, to the outside reviewers who gave me such important feedback, and to my wonderful copy editor, Mary Ellen Geer, who was always supportive and understanding.

Finally, my thanks to the family and friends who hosted and cheered me in Gainesville, in particular my sister Sissy Brennan and her family, Mike, Heather, and Tristen, and Kathy Deagan, Susan Parker, and Bonnie McEwan, who did the same in St. Augustine and Tallahassee. My own family, Jimmy and Vance, have endured my extended absences without complaint, and I deeply appreciate their love and support.

Contents

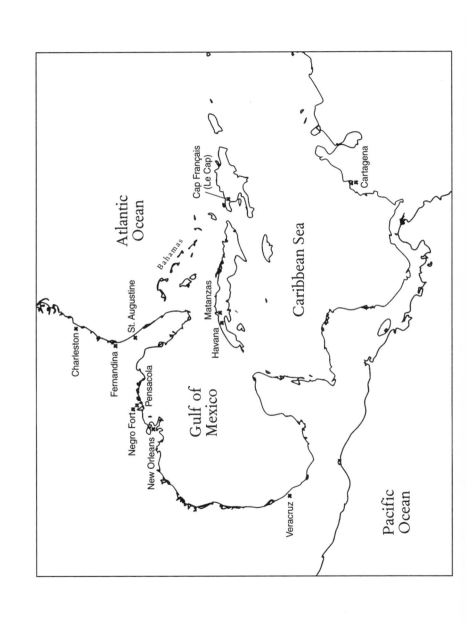

Atlantic Ocean

Charleston

Fernandina

St. Augustine

Bahamas

Cap Français
(Le Cap)

Cartagena

Caribbean Sea

Negro Fort

Pensacola

New Orleans

Gulf of Mexico

Havana

Matanzas

Veracruz

Pacific Ocean

Introduction

There is a tide in the affairs of men
Which, taken at the flood, leads on to fortune;
Omitted, all the voyage of their life
Is bound in shallows and in miseries.
On such a full sea are we now afloat,
And we must take the current when it serves,
Or lose our ventures.

Shakespeare, *Julius Caesar*, Act 4, Scene 3

SOMETIME NEAR THE END of the seventeenth century, British traders purchased a young Mandinga man in West Africa and transported him to Barbados. From there the youth was shipped on to South Carolina, where he joined other Africans and still more numerous indigenous captives to form the "charter generation" of slaves on that colonial frontier.[1] The Mandinga were a people famed for their animal husbandry, and the young man may have become one of the enslaved "Cattle Hunters" who tracked rapidly growing herds through the dense Carolina forests.[2] When the local Yamasee Indians rose against their British oppressors in 1715, the Mandinga man and other enslaved Africans recognized the chance for their own liberation.

Mandinga war tunic, decorated with leather-covered Koranic scriptures and charms. William Arnett Collection; courtesy of the Florida Museum of Natural History, University of Florida.

Joining in common cause with the Yamasee against their mutual enemy, the slaves fought for three years with Chief George's forces, all the while gaining valuable military skills and cultural, political, and geographic knowledge. After the war went badly for the rebels, Carolina's Yamasee and African allies escaped together to Spanish Florida, where they claimed the religious sanctuary promised in 1693 by the Catholic monarch.[3]

Upon his conversion to Catholicism, the young Mandinga slave and former Muslim transformed himself from a "chattel" of the British into Francisco Menéndez, a free subject of the

Spanish King. The polyglot and literate Menéndez personified the cosmopolitan Atlantic Creole as described by Ira Berlin— someone with "linguistic dexterity, cultural plasticity, and social agility."[4] It is quite likely that he had already demonstrated these characteristics on the West African coast; in the Americas, he simply added to his repertoire. Menéndez's military experience earned him a commission as captain of the black militia of St. Augustine, and in 1738 he became the leader of the free black town of Gracia Real de Santa Teresa de Mose. Menéndez may have been accustomed to leadership. The English traveler Richard Jobson, who visited Upper Guinea a century earlier, wrote that the Mandingas "are Lords, and Commaunders of this country" whose tributaries included the Wolofs and Fulas.[5] Africans of distinct cultural and political backgrounds made up the community of Gracia Real de Santa Teresa de Mose, including those designated in Spanish records as Congos, Carabalíes, Minas, and Mandingas, and some men had indigenous wives. Spanish officials, however, referred to all of them as Menéndez's subjects.[6]

Over the next quarter-century, Menéndez and his militia defended their adopted homeland against both British and Indian attacks. Menéndez wrote several eloquent letters to the King of Spain, detailing his military services and requesting a proprietary captainship. When the monarch failed to respond, Menéndez took to the seas as a Spanish corsair, seeking to make his way to "Old Spain" so he could discuss the matter with the king in person.[7] In 1763, the British acquired Florida by treaty and Menéndez led his freed "subjects" into exile in Cuba, where they remade their lives on a new Spanish frontier.[8] The arc of

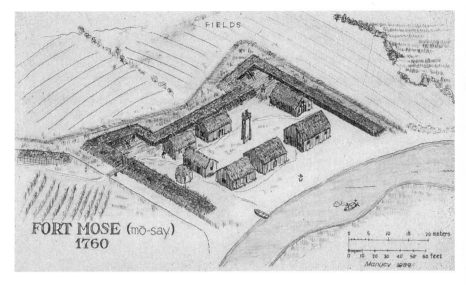

FIELDS

FORT MOSE (mō-say)
1760

Manucy 1989

Gracia Real de Santa Teresa de Mose, 1760. Illustration by Albert Manucy; courtesy of the Florida Museum of Natural History, University of Florida.

Menéndez's fascinating life, during which he reshaped his identity and circumstances multiple times, demonstrates how enslaved persons learned about and acted on possibilities to regain their lost liberty. His is an amazing story, and yet it was only one of many.

In this book I employ the histories of a diverse but connected cohort of Atlantic Creoles like Menéndez as a prism through which to examine the active participation of Africans and their descendants in the age of Atlantic revolutions. Olaudah Equiano, whose lone voice once spoke for millions, has been joined by others like Baquaqua, Little Ephraim Robin John, and Anacona Robin Robin John.[9] With the use of previously unstudied

Spanish-language sources, new voices may now be added to this still limited narrative. The time span covered by this book is roughly 1760 to 1850, a period of radical economic, social, and political change across the Atlantic world.[10] The geographic focus, however, shifts from the better studied areas of northern Europe and northern North America to the southern mainland of North America and the Caribbean. In this multicultural arena, many peoples and powers competed—Africans of various distinct ethnicities, a wide array of indigenous nations, European powers such as Great Britain, France, and Spain, and, eventually, the new government of the United States. Conflicts were frequent, and there were many opportunities for Atlantic Creoles to "take the tide" and alter a life's course.

Because Atlantic Creoles were so often on the front lines of these contests—European and American revolutions, Indian wars, slave revolts, and the international efforts to abolish slavery—they were keenly attuned to shifting political currents. These African and African-descended actors had access to a wide range of political information, both printed and oral, and they made reasoned and informed choices in their attempt to win and maintain liberty. They were often critical to the balance of power and soon became adept at interpreting political events and manipulating them, when possible, to achieve freedom. Their initiative and agency—their acts of resistance, flight, and marronage (the formation of fugitive slave communities in the wild), and their shifting relationships to various European, American, and Native American powers—shaped the course of international events, as well as local responses to them.

The Black Loyalists who followed the British standard in the

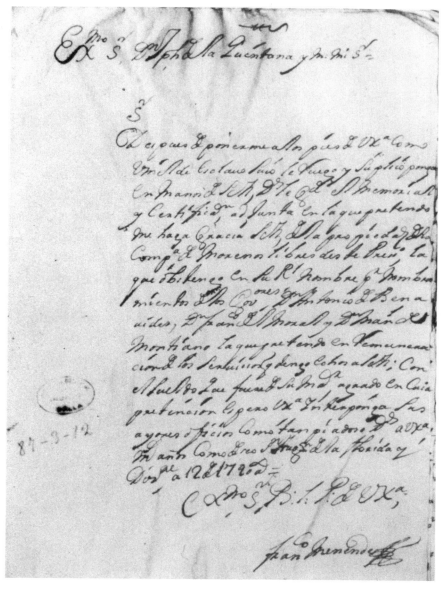

Petition of Francisco Menéndez to King Philip V of Spain, asking for a reward for his services during the invasion of General James Oglethorpe in 1740. Courtesy of the P. K. Yonge Library of Florida History and the Florida Museum of Natural History, University of Florida.

American Revolution and the slave rebels who followed Toussaint in Saint Domingue have become the subject of important historical scholarship.[11] But some individuals, both free and enslaved, who were involved in those events chose alternate paths that are equally interesting and less well known. The Atlantic Creoles about whom I write fought variously for the King of Kongo, the King of England, the King of France, the French Jacobins, Muskogee and Seminole chiefs, the King of Spain, and sometimes for themselves. Each shift of allegiance required a reevaluation of political platforms and programs, with the possibilities for freedom that each offered. As they changed allegiances and identities, Atlantic Creoles also helped to shape the course of history. Their stories make possible a more complex understanding of the traditional narratives and popular views of the Age of Revolutions, and demonstrate their active political and philosophical engagement in the most important events of their day.

Although the English and French sources for these events are rich, it was the Spanish juridical and archival traditions that recognized loyal Africans and Indians as imperial subjects with a legal personality, and therefore a voice, in Spanish records. Materials actually produced by persons of African and native descent are common: they include loyalty oaths; petitions to Spanish officials and to the King, such as that written by Menéndez; legal suits; interrogatories; civil, religious, and criminal records; and more. Through these varied sources it is possible to gain access to verbatim statements of the Atlantic Creoles, as well as insights into their thinking.

Africans and Spaniards shared many understandings of the

proper relationship between ruler and subject. Loyal subjects generated reciprocal obligations from those they served, and both groups organized their societies as sets of interlocking corporate and family structures. These cultural similarities allowed even those Africans newly admitted into the Spanish polity to quickly learn Spanish legal and cultural norms. Once considered movable property, these newly "human" and free individuals were quick to pursue the rights and privileges accorded them through membership in centuries-old Spanish legal, religious, and military corporations. As they exercised their freedom, Atlantic Creoles repeatedly stressed their loyalty, their service, and their devotion to the Spanish King and to the "True Faith" in written documents. They also enacted these values in public ceremonies. When they felt aggrieved—and some had reason to—they remonstrated, usually blaming any failure to honor promises and obligations on local officials. The distant Spanish King, dependent as he often was on their services to hold his far-flung and threatened frontiers, almost always supported the Atlantic Creoles.

The enslaved African whom the English called Big Prince Whitten lived through the misery of the Atlantic slave trade, the American, French, Haitian, and Latin American revolutions, Indian wars, and, in Cuba, slave revolts and the fight for abolition. Whitten and others like him learned what it was to be a slave in an English colony. They gradually became acculturated to the norms of Anglo slavery—learning plantation regimes, learning English, forming relationships with other Africans and with "country-born" slaves, and eventually starting families. The 1770s were the peak years of the Carolina slave trade, and as more and more Africans poured into flourishing Carolina plantations, freedom must have seemed an ever more remote possibility for Whitten and his fellow slaves.

But then came the American Revolution. Its stirring rhetoric moved many who were actually enslaved to claim their own inalienable right to liberty and to fight for it. South Carolina experienced some of the bloodiest fighting in the American Revolution, and enslaved families embroiled in that violence made political choices that might save or ruin them. As battles raged around them, they gained first-hand knowledge of the politics and racial dispositions of both Patriots and Loyalists. Rejecting both, the Whittens and hundreds like them risked everything to escape across the international border and, as Menéndez and others had before them, to claim religious sanctuary in Spanish territory. There they acquired legal personalities and rights, shedding the dishonor of enslavement. Unable to tolerate such a threat to the chattel slave system, the new U.S. government pressured Spain to renounce the sanctuary policy in 1790; thereafter, freedom seekers would have to find alternate routes.

In the following year, slaves in Saint Domingue initiated the largest and most successful slave revolt in the western hemisphere. They, too, had to decide how to reshape their lives as free persons. They might have established an African-style kingdom, as other slave rebels had done in Spanish and Portuguese America. Courted by Republican France, Spain, and Great Britain, they had offers of freedom and alliance from each. Toussaint Louverture is the best-known figure of the revolt, but he did not launch it. Lesser-known individuals took that risk, and, ultimately, different political paths than Toussaint. Georges

(Jorge) Biassou styled himself the leader of the Counter-Revolution, allying himself first with the King of France and then with that of Spain. This decision cost him what might have been a more significant place in history, and in retrospect looks reactionary, but Biassou's correspondence shows that he made his decision to ally with Spain on an informed and pragmatic basis. At the war's conclusion Biassou and the rest of Spain's black auxiliaries, like those who had earlier fought for the British King, were ungratefully dispersed across the Atlantic.

Biassou and his followers found themselves transported to the Spanish borderlands of Florida. The British, French, and Americans all had designs on the region, and the weakened Spanish government, attacked by Napoleon at home and by revolutionaries across its empire, could do little but protest an escalating series of military interventions. In the chaos, escaped slaves joined indigenous allies in creating a series of maroon communities in the still unsettled hinterlands. They also participated in assorted Loyalist plots to reestablish British commercial and territorial hegemony in the Lower South. One was the ephemeral indigenous State of Muskogee, which in 1800 waged an ill-fated war against Spain. The War of 1812 also involved Atlantic Creoles throughout the Spanish borderlands in still-simmering imperial contests. That year the U.S. government's covert attempt to seize Spanish East Florida was thwarted by black veterans of the American and Saint Domingue revolutions as well as black troops from Cuba.

In Spanish West Florida, meanwhile, slaves escaped from both Spanish and American masters and linked their freedom to British interests instead. But the British eventually abandoned their Negro Colonial Marines as they had many of Lord Dunmore's Ethiopian troops during the American Revolution. When U.S. forces destroyed their fort on the Apalachicola River, survivors like Abraham and Nero slipped away to the Seminole nation to fight another day. Their political awareness and engagement mirrored those of Spain's black auxiliaries: each group recognized that their common interest ultimately lay in defending Spain against the territorial ambitions of the new United States government. With the U.S. acquisition of Louisiana, West Florida, and finally East Florida, Atlantic Creoles were left with few possibilities for freedom on the North American mainland. They could leave, or they could fight. A large group evacuated to Cuba. Others retreated southward down the Florida peninsula to the swamps of the Withlacoochee.

When Atlantic Creoles from the North American mainland arrived in Havana, the city was already home to an important and sizeable free black population with a long tradition of rights and privileges in Cuban society. The wealthy and educated Gabriel Dorotea Barba and his fellow militiamen were involved either directly or ideologically in the most significant political revolutions of their day, including the American and French Revolutions, the slave revolt in Saint Domingue, the independence movements in Latin America, and ultimately the revolution represented by abolition. They avidly followed the news as Spanish liberals waged a fierce war of resistance against Napoleonic troops, and in 1812 they joined other Spanish subjects across the empire in celebrating Spain's new Liberal Constitution and the expanded rights it guaranteed. Like Menéndez,

Whitten, and Biassou, Barba and his fellow militiamen generated a generous paper trail for historians to follow. Their petitions speak to their sense of entitlement as Spanish subjects. But the involvement of one of their own in the Aponte slave conspiracy of 1812 cast suspicion on all of them.

As Atlantic Creoles struggled to maintain their traditional rights in Cuba, Black Seminoles like Abraham and Nero and Spain's African-born militiamen like Prince Whitten joined forces to try to prevent the U.S. advance into Florida. They helped undo the so-called Patriot Rebellion of 1812 but could not prevent Andrew Jackson from destroying the Seminole heartland six years later. By this time the Spanish empire was disintegrating, and U.S. expansionism could not be stopped. In 1821 Spain ceded East Florida to the United States, and Prince Whitten led his black troops into exile in Cuba, retracing the exodus of Francisco Menéndez and the people of Mose more than half a century earlier. The Black Seminoles fought on through another long war against the forces of the United States before Abraham also led his people into exile in Arkansas.

Cuba's Atlantic Creoles enjoyed a brief resurgence in the 1820s, but it was short-lived. The return of absolutism in Spain, the rising power of Cuba's sugar plantocracy, and the Africanization of the population spelled the doom of the island's once-flourishing free black class. Atlantic Creoles like Jorge Davison struggled to maintain traditional privileges, but their legal and social position deteriorated as the nineteenth century progressed. Free blacks formed one-fifth of the population of the city of Matanzas in the early nineteenth century; though not as wealthy and privileged as their counterparts in Havana, they served in militias, joined religious confraternities, and formed theater and literary groups, in part to distinguish themselves from the new Africans who were pouring into Cuba. After major slave revolts rocked the province in the 1830s and 1840s and officials launched the gruesome repression known as La Escalera, many of Cuba's Atlantic Creoles scattered in yet another tragic diaspora, with some sailing off to an unknown African continent.

As all their histories show, Atlantic Creoles were extraordinarily mobile, both geographically and socially, and their horizons had few limits. These were not people who felt constrained by place or defined by slavery. Nor was race their primary identification; that imposition came later. In this revolutionary era, political exigencies demanded more fluid identities. The great instability of the age and of the spaces they traversed created tremendous danger for these Creoles, but also opportunity. The Atlantic Creoles who surface in this narrative are those who repeatedly risked danger, found an opening, seized the moment, and freed themselves. Some lived apart—under their own governance while they could, or with indigenous people with whom they found common cause. Others assessed the strengths and weaknesses of various European powers and supported the one that might best secure them liberty. These alliances were rarely stable, and Atlantic Creoles always had to be ready to adjust quickly to changing conditions. Their mutability and adaptability were survival tools that enabled them to build their lives anew when necessary. And it almost always was. The wars and political transitions they experienced led to repeated dislocations and exile, yet they found ways to begin again.

These Atlantic Creoles were a diverse group, born in West Africa, in Haut du Cap, in Jamaica, in Havana, or in the Indian nations of Florida. Some were born enslaved; others were always free. Some were literate, urban, and propertied, while others rose out of more degraded circumstances. What united them was not only their time and place, but a determined quest for freedom. Refusing to be "bound in shallows and in miseries," they took the tide, and while few went on to gain fortunes, many achieved liberty. It has been a privilege to write about their little remarked, but fascinating, lives.

I

African Choices in the Revolutionary South

For twenty-six years and seven months I have served with the most constant zeal and love in Your Majesty's Urban Company of Color and on all occasions I have pursued the rebels who have risen in this province.

Juan Bautista Whitten, St. Augustine, July 31, 1819[1]

JUAN BAUTISTA WHITTEN, as he came to be known in Spanish records, was one of the millions of Africans who were swept into the Atlantic slave trade in the eighteenth century. Born somewhere on the "coast of Guinea" in about 1758, according to his own best estimates, Whitten was virtually the Forrest Gump of his day—present at almost all the major turning points in the history of his time. Whitten spent the first fifteen years of his life in Upper Guinea, the next ten in South Carolina, another thirty-five in Spanish Florida, and the final years of his long life in Cuba. His successive and successful refashionings made Whitten a model Atlantic Creole.[2] His remarkable career, which spanned the course of the American, French, Haitian, and Latin American revolutions as well as the eventual abolition of the

Atlantic slave trade, helps us understand how Africans in the Americas actually experienced and interpreted the age of revolutions and the failed promises of that era.

We do not know what his African name was, or how he came to be enslaved, but in the 1770s Whitten survived the horrors of the Middle Passage to disembark at Charleston, South Carolina. The physician charged with visiting the incoming ships and reporting on the health of the enslaved on board claimed that while crossing the Atlantic, some of the traders threw overboard as many as two-thirds of their captives. He described the "Filth, Putrid Air, Putrid Dysantries" on the ship and added, "it is a wonder any escape with Life." Whitten was one of the strong, or lucky, who did.[3] Unlike Olaudah Equiano or Quobna Ottobah Cugoano, Mahommah Gardo Baquaqua, or the Calabar princes Little Ephraim Robin John and Ancona Robin Robin John, Whitten left us no record of his terrible experience on the Middle Passage, nor, in fact, much information at all about his life as a slave.[4] His was an atypical experience, perhaps, because he spent less than a decade enslaved on a plantation. In any case, Whitten did not let slavery define him.

Even before the young African descended the gangplank to the required quarantine at the "pest house" at Sullivan's Island in the Charleston harbor, he would have realized that many of his countrymen had preceded him across the Atlantic.[5] Many of their bodies littered the marshes opposite Charleston, and Whitten might have seen them as his ship approached the harbor. He might have heard "plaintive African songs, in cadence with the oars" as black canoe men rowed passengers and goods from ocean-going vessels to shore or seen the many "negro-boats" from which black fishermen hauled in blackfish and trout for sale in the city.[6] No other city in British North America imported more enslaved Africans than Charleston, which led a Swiss visitor in 1737 to remark that South Carolina was "like a negro country."[7] By 1770 the colony was home to 80,000 persons of African descent who formed roughly 60 percent of the population; a majority of these were from the Upper Guinea region.[8]

Although Carolina planters worried about their minority numbers and the ever-present risk of insurrection by "Domestick enemies," they continued to clamor for slaves. As a correspondent to the *South Carolina Gazette* sardonically commented only a year before the slave revolt at Stono in 1739, "Negroes may be said to be the Bait proper for catching a Carolina planter, as certain as Beef to catch a Shark."[9] Carolina only briefly supported a non-importation resolution to protest British taxation on slaves, but once Charleston traders heard that Rhode Island, New York, and Pennsylvania had reneged on the agreement, they followed suit. Once again the floodgates of the slave trade opened. Pent-up planter demand coupled with fears of the coming war meant that slave imports and prices rose sharply in 1772 and 1773. Charleston's leading slave trader, Henry Laurens, predicted in March of that year that "the Province will be overstocked by the present Years importation." Laurens estimated that slave imports in 1773 would reach 8,000 to 10,000, and these figures are confirmed by reports from the *South Carolina Gazette*.[10] By 1774, however, the "Rage to buy Negroes" had passed, and on October 20, 1774, the Philadelphia delegates to the first Continental Congress declared, "We will neither im-

Slave ad by Henry Laurens and partners in the *South Carolina Gazette*, April 26, 1760. Courtesy of "The Atlantic Slave Trade and Slave Life in the Americas: A Visual Record" website, *http://hitchcock.itc.virginia.edu/Slavery*, Virginia Foundation for the Humanities and the University of Virginia Library.

port nor purchase, any slave imported after the first day of December next; after which time, we will wholly discontinue the slave trade." Two ships that arrived in Charleston in March of 1775 with large numbers of Angolan slaves were sent on to the West Indies, allegedly with their whole cargoes.[11] Whitten may well have been among the last Africans to arrive in Carolina before the outbreak of the American Revolution.

At the house of one of the many slave trading firms in the city, Whitten would have stood among other African men, women, and children to be examined by prospective buyers. Peter Whitten, a Justice of the Peace for Charles Town District and Collector of the Poor-Tax for St. John's Parish, Berkeley County, purchased our protagonist to work on his inland plantation about forty miles from Charleston.[12] His new slave could not have been much more than fifteen years old at the time, a "Man boy" in the parlance of the trade, but Peter Whitten named him "Big Prince." Even at that young age, he must have been an imposing figure; ten years later he was described as "6′ and brawny."[13]

There are no documents that describe Prince's ethnicity, but the Trans-Atlantic Slave Trade Database shows that in the years 1751–1775, 58.2 percent of all slaves imported into South Carolina and Georgia (35,774) came from the Upper Guinea region.[14] Henry Laurens wrote of the Charleston planters' overwhelming preference for "large, strong People like the Gambians," adding that "tall, robust people best sute our business." Laurens and his contemporaries used the generic term "Gambians" to refer to diverse peoples who lived along the Gambia River and in southern Senegal, among whom the Mandinga, Wolof, and Fula were most numerous. Spanish records, uncharacteristically, fail to specify Prince's precise ethnicity, but he might have belonged to any of those groups.[15] A slave ship captain from Charleston complained that he was short of space because the "Gambians" were "as large as one & a half in any [other] part of Guinea." They were also reputed to be among the healthiest slaves on arrival in South Carolina because the voyage to

Charleston was shorter than from other African locales. The Africans living along the Gambia River were noted for their fierce shore-based attacks on the slave ships that plied their rivers, as well as for suicidal rebellions at James Fort in the Gambia River and on shipboard. When slaves took control of his ship in the Gambia River, Captain Thomas Davis blew up the *New Britannia*. He took his own life as well as those of 236 slaves, 96 free blacks, and all his crew, except for one man who had gotten into a boat moments before to try to "take up some slaves who had thrown themselves overboard." Such dramatic events were surely reported up and down the river, just as they were among trader networks. In 1769 a large African force almost overran Fort James itself. Incidents such as these caused some captains to refuse to trade in the Gambia, and Charleston planters must have been willing to pay a high price to make the risk worthwhile.[16]

As Prince walked through the streets of Charleston with the man who had just bought him, the African character of the place would have been as obvious to him as to the city's European visitors. An anonymous "English Traveller" reported that in 1774 "Charles Town" was home to 30,000 "black Negro slaves" and only "9 or 10,000 white inhabitants."[17] The young African would have noticed black stevedores and sailors, coachmen, workmen, and artisans of every kind, as well as black women with foodstuffs and crafts arrayed around them for sale at Charleston's Lower Market. The chants of street hucksters selling oysters, shrimp, fruits, vegetables, baked goods, and other edibles from woven grass baskets balanced on their heads might also have reminded him of his home. As runaway advertisements noted, many of these black artisans and entrepreneurs would have borne familiar scarification patterns. Some may have displayed filed teeth.[18]

Heading down Bay Street, Prince and his new owner would have boarded one of the river boats that carried passengers and supplies up the Cooper River toward Whitten's inland plantation. Slave crews dominated the river and coastal traffic of South Carolina, and many of the patroons or pilots of these vessels were also black. One Camden merchant who traveled from Charleston up the Cooper River found "only negroes on board." Slaves from the upriver plantations also traveled the Cooper in canoes and pettiaugars, stopping to trade or visit with friends and relatives on neighboring plantations where it was not uncommon for them to share food, drink, and sometimes musical entertainment. The mobility, independence, and geopolitical awareness of the area's black boatmen benefited other members of the enslaved community, and as Prince traveled inland, he was probably already acquiring information about his future destination and the politics of the new country.[19]

Prince's river journey up the Cooper River ended at Monck's Corner, an old trading post about twenty-six miles from Charleston that boasted several taverns and stores where area planters socialized and exchanged information.[20] From the way station at Monck's Corner, a road ran northward to the ferry on the Santee River and on to the nearest town of Camden. The Whitten plantation lay along this important corridor, as did the Cantey plantation, where Prince would find a wife.[21]

The region Prince was entering was still a frontier. Catawba Indians allied to the British and Cherokees whose land the British would eventually take still formed part of the turbulent multiracial environment. The nearest town of Camden had only been established in 1768; five years later, jurors complained of the settlement's continuing isolation and of the danger from "Wolves and Tygers, Bears" and from "idle and disorderly vagrants constantly hunting in the woods and destroying Deer for their hides."[22]

But Charleston's elites saw profits to be made and sent large numbers of newly arrived Africans into the wilderness to make them. Africans soon outnumbered whites in St. John's Parish. In the wake of the Stono Rebellion of 1739, locals mounted nightly patrols of the parish that rounded up a number of suspected slave conspirators and transported them to Charleston for trial. There, fifty of the captured slaves were executed at the rate of ten a day in a grisly display of uncertain power.[23] Nine years later, planters discovered another nascent rebellion: 16 whites and 104 slaves from St. John's and surrounding parishes allegedly planned to set Charleston ablaze and escape to Spanish St. Augustine.[24] These rebels, like others before and later, headed to St. Augustine after hearing of Spain's offer to free escaped slaves who would convert to Catholicism. The nearby refuge proved so provocative that Britain launched an expensive military and naval effort to seize St. Augustine in 1740.[25] That expedition proved a failure, and runaway ads from South Carolina newspapers document continuing attempts by runaways to flee to St. Augustine. In 1754 a group of multilingual Havana-born slaves even tried to sail from Charleston to Cuba in search of freedom.[26] Despite constant worries about escape and rebellion, planters continued to import slaves, and by the 1770s Africans formed at least 90 percent of the population of St. John's Parish.[27] Prince was thus entering a region that was largely African and famed for insurrection. Local slaves could tell tales of flight and resistance, of great imperial conflicts, and of alternate forms of government and freedom to the south.

The dense pine forests and swamps of St. John's Parish offered slaves another possible refuge, but early settlers had established critical timber and naval stores industries in the same forests. The British offered bounties on tar, pitch, rosin, and turpentine to encourage production, and by 1713 the planter William Cantey, Jr., and a crew of thirteen slaves were producing 200 barrels of pitch a year.[28] Area slaves also cut and sawed timber that planters shipped to Charleston and on to other parts of the British Caribbean. Harvesting the forests proved profitable to Cantey and others like him. By 1779, one-fourth of the region's estates had more than fifty slaves living on them.[29] Producing naval stores and cutting timber required crews of skilled men working communally, and under the tutelage of such experienced slaves, Prince learned the forest industry and became a carpenter on the Whitten plantation.[30] The valuable occupational skills he acquired in the Carolina forests would serve Prince well in later life.[31]

Even as Prince was adjusting to life on the Whitten plantation, Atlantic politics were shaping his destiny. In the summer of 1775, Charleston's leading figures expressed indignation over the closing of Boston's port, created a Council of Safety with slave trader Henry Laurens as president, and elected delegates to attend the First Continental Congress in Philadelphia to be held the following September. At the same time the Grand

Jury of Camden, on which several members of the numerous Cantey family sat, issued a proclamation protesting taxation without representation and remarking on their "Birthrights as Freemen." "And whereas we rather choose to die freemen than live Slaves, bound by Laws in the formation of which we have no participation," they "resolved to maintain our Constitutional Rights at the Hazard of our Lives and Fortunes."[32] The irony of the refusal to "live Slaves" seems to have escaped the authors of this proclamation, but such fiery rhetoric would have resonated with attentive slaves throughout the region. As one historian noted, the Southern slaveholder's dilemma was "to prevent their slaves from imbibing the heady notions of liberty and equality, which had become their own rallying cry against Britain."[33]

It was a losing proposition. Charleston merchant Josiah Smith, Jr., wrote that "our Province at present is in a ticklish Situation, on account of our numerous Domesticks, who have been deluded by some villainous Persons into the notion of being all set free" on the imminent arrival of the new royal governor, Lord William Campbell. Smith added that the rumor of British emancipation "is the common Talk throughout the Province, and has occasioned impertinent behaviour" in many slaves.[34] Contemporaries throughout the colonies were well aware that the slave telegraph communicated such important political news rapidly. After a report that "twenty thousand negroes" from South Carolina and Georgia would surely desert to the British to become free, John Adams wrote in his diary, "The negroes have a wonderful art of communicating intelligence among themselves; it will run several hundreds of miles in a week or fortnight."[35] Worried whites in Charleston hastily raised three companies of militias to patrol the streets and "keep those mistaken creatures in awe."[36]

Adding to the paranoia about slave revolt were persistent rumors that the British also planned to arm and deploy Cherokee Indians against protesting colonists to curb their insubordination. So, in July of 1775, when King Prow and a delegation of friendly Catawba Indians visited Camden and Charleston to inquire about the confusing political developments of the day, the newly created Council of Safety promptly enlisted them to patrol outside of Charleston.[37]

But even the presence of armed mounted patrols did not calm the panic in Charleston. In August 1775, jurors charged the free black harbor pilot Thomas Jeremiah with conspiring with the British to incite slave insurrection. Governor Campbell objected to the lack of evidence against Jeremiah and described him as "a free Negro of considerable property, one of the most valuable, & useful men in his way, in the Province." Despite the governor's protests, however, jurors sentenced the black pilot to death, and he was hanged and "burned to ashes" in the public square. Jeremiah died protesting his innocence. An assembled crowd that included many people of color heard the doomed man warn that "God's judgment would one day overtake them for shedding his innocent blood."[38]

Violence against Carolina slaves had by this time become almost commonplace; the *South Carolina Gazette* reported frequent acts of public terror including castration, gibbeting, burning alive, cropping ears, and decapitation. Without shame, slave owners advertised for the heads of their runaways, and occasionally the newspaper also reported the slaves' revenge for their mistreatment.[39]

By that fall a short-lived treaty of neutrality between Loyalists (Tories) and Patriots (Whigs) broke down, and violence erupted throughout the countryside. Patriot forces began arresting Loyalists in the interior, including "Captain Jones," a "Colored Powderman," and the mulatto William Hunt.[40] In these encounters, Patriots like the Canteys found themselves confronting Loyalist relatives like the McGirtts.[41] The December battles of 1775 known as the Snow Campaign ended in Patriot victory and the dispersal of many of the back country's most ardent Loyalists southward to Florida, where British Governor Patrick Tonyn commissioned them as officers in the East Florida Rangers. Emboldened Patriots demanded more than neutrality from their remaining Loyalist neighbors, and after harassment, intimidation, and sometimes acts of outright brutality, more Tories joined the southward exodus.[42]

Many departing Loyalists took their slaves with them to Florida, and little is known about how this outmigration disrupted slave families in the region. But slaves also moved on their own. Perhaps as many as 500 slaves flocked to Sullivan's Island in the Charleston harbor, waiting to be picked up by departing British ships. To staunch the flow of runaway slaves, fifty-four Patriot Rangers "dressed as Indians" staged an early morning attack on the runaways' camp, killing a disputed number of them. Henry Laurens wrote that he hoped the raid would "serve to humble our Negroes in general."[43] Apparently, it did not. Three months later Laurens authorized the murder of another group of "Rebellious Negroes" gathered on Tybee Island off the coast of Georgia. This time seventy Patriots "painted and dressed as Indians" and thirty unidentified Native Americans carried out the slaughter. The disguised Patriots reportedly acted with the "most savage barbarity" and "exceeded the ferocity of the Indians." That the Patriots felt the need to disguise themselves suggests they may have felt at least some shame about their actions, but they were also trying to pit indigenous and African groups against each other.[44]

The planters' fears of South Carolina's slave majority eventually trumped their loyalty to Britain. In December 1775, South Carolina's reluctant revolutionaries became the first colonists to declare their independence. On July 4, 1776, the Second Continental Congress followed suit, and war began in the north.[45]

During this tumultuous period Prince met a woman named Judy, who was a slave on the nearby Cantey plantation, and by 1777 the couple had formed what would be a lifelong bond. Judy, later described in a runaway ad as "a smart, active wench," was country-born, and her language skills and knowledge of local customs must have assisted Prince's rapid cultural adaptation. In 1778 Judy and Prince had their first son, whom they named Glasgow, and the following year their daughter, Polly, was born.[46] When the children were still infants, the chaos of the American Revolution engulfed Carolina and this new family.

The British launched their southern campaign in Georgia in late 1778, and from Georgia they moved northward to South Carolina. Sir Henry Clinton, commander of Britain's southern campaign, repeated Lord Dunmore's earlier offer to free slaves who would serve the British military. The overwhelming response led Loyalists to enact strict measures to control the "Bandittis of Negroes who flock to the conquerors," but when Clinton's large fleet sailed into the Charleston harbor with 14,000 troops the following year, black observers must have thought liberation was at hand. Most would be disappointed. A hard siege ensued before Patriot defenders finally surrendered Charleston to British occupation on May 12, 1780.[47]

With that victory, the British began to establish garrisons throughout the interior. General Charles Cornwallis marched a large force of 2500 troops through St. John's Parish, past the Whitten and Cantey plantations, to establish his headquarters at Camden. Cornwallis and Lt. Colonel Banastre "Bloody" Tarleton, infamous for killing surrendered Patriots, held Camden for almost a year. In response, local "men of substance" such as Francis Marion, from nearby Monck's Corner, became Patriot guerrillas. The locals' deep knowledge of the swampy and wooded terrain made them formidable opponents of even the best-trained British regulars, and Marion became known as the "Swamp Fox." Soon the Loyalist and Patriot forces were fighting "bloody war without quarter" all around the Whitten and Cantey plantations, in what one scholar called South Carolina's "Uncivil War."[48] In August 1780, Cornwallis and Tarleton routed General Gates and the Patriot forces at the Battle of Camden and then exacted gruesome retaliation on the locals for the "Error of Insurrection." Loyalist Rangers Daniel McGirtt, Thomas "Burnt-Foot" Brown, and William "Bloody Bill" Cunningham also returned from their exile in Florida to take vengeance on their former neighbors for their earlier mistreatment. For her refusal to divulge the location of Marion's forces, Mary

Cantey Richardson was flogged by "Bloody" Tarleton, who then dug up the body of her deceased husband and burned their plantation. In another act of terror, "Bloody Bill" Cunningham hanged or chopped to death fourteen surrendered prisoners.[49]

Carolinian Patriot Eliza Wilkinson recorded the terror when a group of Loyalist Rangers raided her plantation, noting that "what augmented it was, they had several armed negroes with them, who threatened and abused us greatly." McGirtt's multiracial band behaved better when they, too, visited Wilkinson's plantation. Some were later captured, and Wilkinson pleaded for leniency for the "four whites and three blacks."[50] Francis Marion's forces also included some men of color. The force Marion first presented to the American army in 1780 included "twenty men and boys, some white, some black and all mounted." The famed image of Marion inviting a British officer to dine on yams at his Snow Island camp also depicts several black men in Marion's camp.[51]

Commanders on both sides seemed horrified by the level of barbarity that grew out of this internecine warfare. Patriot General Nathanael Greene wrote that "the Whigs and Tories pursue one another with the most relentless fury, killing and destroying each other wherever they meet. . . . The great bodies of militia that have been in service this year employed against the enemy, and in quelling the Tories have almost laid waste the country."[52] Greene's aide wrote, "I envy everything I see, except the poor unhappy blacks who, to the disgrace of human nature are subject to every species of oppression while we are contending for the rights and liberties of mankind." Some of the British officers were equally dismayed. British General

Charles O'Hara wrote that the region near Camden was "beyond description wretched, every Misery which the bloodest cruel War ever produced we have constantly before us."[53] Before leaving the area, the Loyalist Rangers pursued a scorched-earth policy, burning the towns of Camden and Ninety-Six and leaving smoldering ruins where once stores, mills, and plantations had been.[54]

Prince Whitten and his family lived through the worst of these cruelties. During the Loyalist occupation of the Carolina interior, Colonel John Watson camped at Mount Hope, one of the Cantey plantations north of the Santee River. After many months of hard fighting, Patriot forces retook Monck's Corner in August 1781, and Francis Marion succeeded in expelling Colonel Watson from the Cantey plantation. It remained the Swamp Fox's headquarters until the war's end. Correspondence of the opposing commanders, written from the Cantey plantation, describes the violence in St. John's Parish; Watson and Marion each charged the other with "violating the law of nations." Both were probably correct.[55] The eighteen months of terrible fighting in St. John's Parish disrupted agriculture as armies on both sides commandeered slaves and precious food supplies. People went hungry, and slaves got the least to eat.[56]

Refugees from the violence flooded into Charleston, where they obtained a modicum of safety but had to endure miserable living conditions in squalid camps. As if the fighting and famine had not done enough damage, smallpox arrived in Carolina in the fall of 1779. British forces spread the virus on their marches through the interior in 1780, and it hit the Whitten household. Little Polly Whitten was later described as "gently pitted with the pox," but at least she survived. Many slaves who had taken advantage of the chaos to desert their plantations and run for British camps were not so lucky. Great numbers of infected slaves died in makeshift British camps or were left to die in agony along the roadsides as they attempted to flee southward with the British.[57]

The British did, however, recruit, arm, and uniform approximately 700 ex-slaves during their occupation of Charleston from 1781 to 1782. General Alexander Leslie organized some of the black recruits into a cavalry of Black Dragoons that patrolled the area north of Charleston and down the Cooper River. Patriots were dismayed by the sight, but still-enslaved blacks could have seen the possibility of freedom in these armed and uniformed blacks. Some Loyalists such as Lord Dunmore and John Cruden pressed for an even larger force of 10,000 "hardy, intrepid and determined blacks," but other British officials demurred, fearing the long-term consequences.[58]

Two men of color who fought in the Carolina campaigns knew St. John's Parish well and may even have known Prince and Judy. Thomas Johnston was born in Charles Town "in the Family of John Izard Esqr. of Free Parents." Johnston served Izard as "his first Servant of Confidence in all Respects," and in appreciation, Izard gave Johnston ten acres of land to farm. But as war escalated, in October 1780, Johnston was "Pressed into his Majesty's Service" like other men of color. Thereafter, he served as a guide to the British legion commanded by "Bloody" Banastre Tarleton, and he was present during Tarleton's surprise attack on Patriot forces at Monck's Corner. Johnston managed to escape to London at the war's end, where he petitioned the British government for some reward for his service.[59]

Another black man who served the Loyalists in the campaign in St. John's Parish did not survive to experience poverty in London. Harry, once the slave of Mr. Gaillard, was employed as a Loyalist spy, first by Lt. Colonel Francis Rawdon and then by Lt. Colonel Balfour. One day Harry set out from Monck's Corner to scout the Greenland Swamp, where he was captured and beheaded by the local Patriot forces commanded by the famed Swamp Fox. Obeying Governor John Rutledge's orders to execute any blacks giving intelligence or provisions to the British, the Patriots placed Harry's head on a stake at the edge of the swamp as a warning to other slaves who might be tempted to aid the Loyalists.[60]

The Whittens and many other area slaves thus had first-hand knowledge of the political positions and racial dispositions of both Patriots and Loyalists, and most scholars agree that blacks served the Loyalists in larger numbers.[61] Not all of them went willingly. The British commissioner John Cruden sequestered many slaves and put them back to work on plantations and in lumbering operations, attempting to maintain what was left of the region's economy. Both Patriots and Loyalists also resorted to plundering slaves as war booty; it is estimated that South Carolina lost between 20,000 and 30,000 slaves before the British and their Loyalist allies finally departed the ruined colony in 1783.[62] The many years of bloody fighting and raiding had reduced the slave population in St. John's Berkeley Parish by half.[63]

Loyalist cavalry forces led by Colonels William Young and "Bloody Bill" Cunningham captured several hundred slaves from St. John's Parish, and both men incorporated blacks into their forces. Marion described fighting some of Young's "Coloured Dragoons."[64] Perhaps Prince was among them. If so, he would have acquired important military training in one of the bloodiest of wars, and this might explain his later military successes for the Spanish. One Patriot account stated that the Whittens were "plundered as the spoils of war" by Colonel William Young's cavalry troop.[65] But it is also possible that Prince and his family knew Young and had decided to follow him voluntarily. After all, Patriots had a habit of decapitating or burning Loyalist sympathizers at the stake, while Loyalists offered at least a chance at freedom.

Leaving South Carolina, Colonel Young and the Whittens traveled southward toward Florida, Britain's last Loyalist stronghold.[66] Florida had been under British control for less than twenty years, but in that brief period Loyalist planters from Carolina and Georgia had transformed the province, establishing prosperous new plantations on the lowcountry model where thick jungles had been. This back-breaking labor was accomplished by more than 9,000 slaves the Loyalists transplanted to what would be their last colony on the Atlantic seaboard, and by the thousands of "new" Africans they imported from slave factories on Bance Island in the Sierra Leone River, or along the Rio Pongo.[67]

The slaves sweated and died for nothing. In 1783, the Treaty of Paris ended the American Revolution and returned Florida to Spain. As dejected Loyalist planters packed their belongings to evacuate to the Bahamas, Nova Scotia, and other still-English locales, hundreds of their slaves seized the moment and ran away rather than face unknown places and climates, or forced separation from loved ones. Some ran to the Seminole hinterlands, while others decided to remain in Spanish Florida.[68]

And what of the Whittens? Somehow, in the summer of 1785, Prince, Judy, Polly, and Glasgow had become the slaves of Jacob Weed, a Lt. Colonel in Georgia's Patriot forces. Whether Weed seized or purchased the family from Young is unknown, but as a skilled carpenter and lumberman, Prince would have proved very valuable to Weed's newly established lumbering and sawmill operations along the St. Marys River.[69]

But just across the St. Marys River, a body of water only several miles wide at some places, was another country and the chance for a different life for the Whittens and others like them. Prince may have learned about Florida's religious sanctuary policy from stories told in St. John's Parish or from one of the Spanish traders, sailors, or officials who frequented the taverns and stores of St. Marys. One cold Sunday morning, in December of 1786, a year and a half after being enslaved by Jacob Weed and after at least three failed attempts, the Whittens made their way across the dark water of the St. Marys into Spanish Florida. Attempting to recover them, Weed placed runaway ads which described Prince as "6 feet high, strong built and brawny, a carpenter by trade, 30 years of age . . . talkative"; his wife, Judy, as "a smart, active wench . . . also about 30 or upward and country-born 5′ 7 or 8″ high"; and their children, Glasgow, "about 8 years of age, a well looking boy of open countenance and obliging disposition," and Polly, "6 years old, lively eyes and gently pitted with the pox." Weed's notice stated that he believed Prince had "carried them off with him to Florida to avoid a separation from his family to which he is much attached"—which is exactly what Whitten did.[70]

In crossing the newly established international border of the St. Marys River, the Whittens finally found freedom, but they did not escape danger. Because Spanish Florida had the misfortune to be the southern desire of the new United States of America, a nation "as ambitious as it is industrious," and because it had an important Atlantic port in St. Augustine—on the northern rim of the Caribbean and the southern fringe of the Anglo world—the Whitten family would continue to be swept up in the dramatic political and military events that swirled around them.[71]

The Whittens found a multicultural world in Florida—it was Spanish only officially. A Spanish report of 1790 estimated that natural Spaniards, including troops and dependents, accounted for only about one-sixth of the total population of 3500, making Florida among Spain's most heterogeneous possessions in the Americas.[72] The largest group of non-Spaniards in the colony consisted of approximately 460 Italians, Greeks, and Minorcans, remnants of Dr. Andrew Turnbull's ill-fated attempt to establish an indigo plantation at New Smyrna in 1768. They were, in the main, Roman Catholics, and although they spoke a variety of languages—Catalán, Italian, Greek, and assorted dialects—they were Mediterranean people and could easily assimilate into the Spanish culture. In St. Augustine they became fishermen and merchants or raised produce on rented lands to sell at the public market; these were all occupations which free persons of African descent in Spanish communities commonly held.[73]

A number of "British" also remained in Florida—a designation the Spaniards used loosely to identify English-speaking people of many ethnic backgrounds, including English, Irish, Scotch, even Swiss.[74] In general, they were welcomed by the Spanish administrators, since they operated large plantations that helped supply the colony and were a source of credit to the often impoverished government. This group also included people with useful skills and connections to the American state and national governments, which led some of its members later to become involved in assorted plots to wrest control of the colony from their Spanish hosts.[75]

Many "new" Africans also inhabited Florida. Expecting to transform Florida into something resembling South Carolina, influential planters such as Richard Oswald, James Grant, and John Moultrie had imported large numbers of slaves during the British rule, chiefly from Bance Island in the Sierra Leone River and the Rio Pongo. When the Patriots drove Loyalist planters from South Carolina and Georgia southward to Florida, they brought almost 9,000 more slaves into the province.[76]

During the eighteen-month transition from British to Spanish rule, many of those slaves approached Spanish government officials to request the religious sanctuary that Francisco Menéndez and other runaways had earlier claimed. Although Florida's incoming governor, Manuel de Zéspedes, doubted their religious motivation—he charged that "not one of them has manifested once here the least inclination to be instructed in and converted to our Holy Faith"—he was forced to honor his Crown's century-old offer to shelter any slaves of the Protestants who sought the "True Faith." It was the governor's belief that the fugitives were simply seeking liberty or escape from a cruel master, and although he may well have been correct, he was obligated to receive all who sought religious sanctuary.[77]

To protect potential converts, the governor required all non-Spaniards to present themselves and declare their intentions to remain or to depart the province. Anyone wishing to remove a slave from the province also had to obtain a license bearing the governor's signature. Any of the English settlers who planned to remain also had to register any blacks or mulattoes, either free or slave, "in their control." Finally, "every vagrant Negro without a known owner or else a document that attests to his freedom" had to report to the authorities within twenty days to clarify his or her status and obtain a work contract. Those failing to report would forfeit their freedom and be enslaved by the Spanish King.[78] British Florida's outgoing governor, Patrick Tonyn, protested that these requirements violated the provisions of the Treaty of Paris that allowed any who wished to leave the province, and he observed that many slaves were held without title and that many free blacks did not have legal documents to prove this status. Despite Tonyn's objections, Zéspedes enforced his decree, and more than 250 blacks hoping to legitimate their free status came forward to be registered.[79]

Among these 250 former slaves was Prince Whitten. In the fall of 1788 Prince presented himself at the governor's office on the town square and dictated a statement to the Spanish notary about how he had come to Florida, initiating what would be a

View from the governor's window of the counting house and the royal treasury, St. Augustine, Florida, November 1764. Original watercolor sketch, British Library, London. Courtesy of the St. Augustine Historical Society.

long paper trail in the Spanish records.[80] As previous governors of Florida and Cuba had done, Governor Zéspedes set an example by taking some of the black refugees into his own home. The rest he parceled out among townspeople and plantation owners who were able to shelter them, at least temporarily.[81] This was the beginning of many subsequent connections between the townspeople and the former slaves. Because the black freedmen and women lived and worked among the townspeople daily, it was almost inevitable in this Spanish community that other social relations would follow. African and Spanish views of family and society were highly compatible, and each group surely recognized the value the other placed on kinship.[82] A central feature of Mandinga culture along the Gambia River was the adoption or assimilation of children or other strangers through relationships of trust, protection, patronage, and reciprocity.[83]

Aided by their early contacts and patrons, their rapid adoption of Catholicism, their "respectable" behavior, and their valuable military and occupational skills, refugees from Anglo slavery like the Whittens became important members of the free black community in Spanish Florida. They worked hard, defended their community when called upon, and made free lives for themselves, acquiring property and intermarrying with other successful runaways. The Whittens and their fellow freedmen proved to be a valuable source of skilled labor and military reserves for the Spanish community, and despite attempts by some of their former owners to recover their chattel through legal channels, the once skeptical Governor Zéspedes consistently supported these blacks' right to liberty.[84]

Legally protected and free at last, Prince Whitten began to establish himself in Spanish Florida. Over the course of the next thirty-five years, Prince and Judy and Glasgow and Polly transformed themselves from fugitive slaves into loyal Spanish subjects. The instant Prince and his family had crossed the St. Marys River—that Spanish Jordan—and reached the other shore, they were "born again." They were made human, acquiring personhood and autonomy. They took on new names, new legal personalities, and new corporate identities and began to enjoy precious liberties long denied them. One was simple geographic mobility: they could go where they wanted. Choice was another. They could choose what work they would do, where they would live, and whom they would marry. They could control their persons, their property, and even others. They gained access and voice, learning quickly how to make claims on a legal system that recognized and protected them. They also learned how to work the social and religious systems that incorporated them.

Religious transformation was the key to the Whittens' new liberties, for it was upon their claim to want conversion that all other rights rested. It is difficult to overestimate the significance of the Roman Catholic Church as a vehicle for African assimilation in terms of social acceptance and advancement in Spanish communities. In a sense it was the one true equalizer, for within the church all were "brothers in Christ." The Catholic Church had incorporated Africans centuries before Spain's expansion into the Americas, and although the Catholic evangelization effort among Africans in the Americas may have appeared minimal compared to that among the Native Americans, the Catholic Church did welcome and encourage black converts.[85]

It is not surprising that newly freed men and women conditioned to a chattel slave system that limited their access to Protestant church membership would seize the opportunity to have themselves and their children baptized in St. Augustine's Catholic Church. The corporate structure of the Catholic Church had important cultural implications for both free and enslaved Africans, offering them affiliation, brotherhood, protection, and status. Prince and Judy Whitten joined other refugees in seeking church membership for their children even before officially registering with government authorities. At about age

Christian baptism of an African in thirteenth-century Spain. Courtesy
of the Florida Museum of Natural History, University of Florida.

nine, Glasgow became Francisco Domingo Mariano Witten,
and seven-year-old Polly became María Rafaela Witten.[86] Done
properly, it took more time and effort to convert adults, and
Prince and Judy could not be baptized until they had successfully passed the priest's examination on the basic tenets of the
Church.[87] Language impediments must surely have slowed the
process, but four years after the baptisms of their children
Prince and Judy also entered the Catholic Church, taking the
baptismal names Juan Bautista Whitten and María Rafaela
Quenty [*sic*].[88]

Baptism into the Catholic faith served several important
functions for black converts. Most important in the view of the

priests was the religious function of removing the stigma of original sin and bringing the baptized into the brotherhood of the church. Perhaps equally important for black converts, however, was the social function of establishing an extended kin network between the baptized and his or her godparents, and between the parents and godparents, who thus became *compadres*. A prominent Spaniard, don Manuel Fernández Bendicho, who was also by then their next-door neighbor, served as Prince and Judy's godfather at their baptism.[89] With Fernández Bendicho standing beside the couple in the church in a public act of patronage, the family's social ascent had begun. The new Catholics Prince and Judy Whitten soon became among the most popular godparents in the black community of St. Augustine: Prince sponsored twenty-three individuals, while Judy served as godmother for thirty-one persons.[90] Acquiring so many "dependents" enhanced the Whittens' status in the Catholic community and reinforced their respectability.

The Catholic Church also offered another avenue for advancement for the Whittens and others like them. Remarking on the special need to educate children in Catholic precepts in a colony populated by so many foreigners, Governor Zéspedes established a school for boys in St. Augustine in 1786. He ordered Father Thomas Hassett (who had earlier established a school for children of color in Philadelphia) to enumerate all the boys living in town and to visit their parents and explain the importance of educating their children in reading, writing, arithmetic, and Christian doctrine. Black youths were welcome at the new school, but in theory they were to sit in a separate section of the classroom. Despite this attempt at segregation, the governor required that black pupils receive the same spiritual and temporal instruction as white students. The teachers were not to permit students to call each other names or "remind them of the faults of their fathers"; rather, all were to be treated alike as faithful Christians with "love and impartial charity."

It may not have been easy for the Whittens to take advantage of this educational opportunity. Although the government assumed the costs of the school, the regulations required the children to be clean and well-groomed, and to have shined shoes. Father Hassett described the colony in 1788 as "miserable" and "dying" for lack of money, trade, and population, and even poor white parents may not have been able to afford the luxury of withdrawing children from work to attend school.[91] Nevertheless, Prince and Judy understood the value of an education, having fled from a system which largely prohibited the education of blacks. They enrolled Glasgow in the school, and his subsequent literacy was an asset to the family in later years.[92]

Among the students of African descent who attended school with Glasgow were Antonio and Mateo Sánchez, the quadroon sons of the most important planter in the province, don Francisco Xavier Sánchez, and his mulatta consort from South Carolina, María Beatrice de Piedra. The boys joined their half-brothers, Román and Domingo Sánchez, sons of don Francisco and his white wife, doña María del Carmen Hill, also of South Carolina. Attending school with these half-brothers was their former slave, who had spent time in both households—Mariano Ambara (Edimboro), the son of Prince's Congo compadres, Felipe and Filis Edimboro. Whatever Glasgow remembered of the two-caste slave system he left in South Carolina was immediately challenged when he walked into this classroom. School rules and Spanish medieval traditions fostered a corporate identity among the students, requiring group attendance at such functions as Sunday Mass, religious processions, and the funerals of classmates. Thus, as in many other corporate institutions in the Spanish world (such as the military, church brotherhoods, and guilds), racial difference was, at least within its confines, neutralized.[93]

Prince Whitten may have entered Florida with little in the way of material goods, but the valuable occupational skills he had acquired in Carolina allowed him to support his family. The Spanish work requirement for the freed newcomers could be considered a form of social control, and it clearly was designed to make useful subjects out of potentially disruptive foreign and unassimilated elements. Still, from the perspective of a former slave who had for so long been unable to control his own destiny or that of his family, the ability to select an employer and be paid for labor must have seemed a considerable improvement over his former condition.

Prince's first known employment was on the plantation of Ambrose Nelson, north of St. Augustine and on the southern bank of the St. Marys River over which the Whittens had crossed to freedom. Other planters in the region were threatened by the example that the newly freed slaves provided to their still enslaved chattel. William Pengree complained that "the negro Prince and his family, who in reality belong to Colonel Weed, have behaved with such shamelessness and presumption since they have moved to the River, that two of my negroes have fled with the idea of becoming free; I have been able to catch one and have sent to Georgia in search for the other." Pengree asked that Prince be forbidden from further association with his slaves, which suggests that Prince was spreading the word about freedom.[94] Not long afterward, Prince learned that "the American Major Weed had vowed to recover them by force, if it costs him his life," and Nelson petitioned the governor to allow the Whittens to move into St. Augustine. The governor agreed. We can only wonder what might have provoked such a vehement declaration from Weed, but his honor and possible profit may have been at stake—Weed had accepted a commission to return Prince and Judy and the children to their former owners in Carolina.[95]

As soon as the danger of recapture had passed, Prince and his family returned to the countryside, this time taking up residence at the North River plantation of James McGirtt with whom Prince signed another year-long work contract. How and why Prince and Judy went to work for a planter linked by marriage to Judy's former owner in South Carolina is unknown, but the contract stipulated that Prince would labor as a carpenter and Judy would wash or cook for McGirtt in exchange for room and board and twenty-five pesos a year.[96] Nine months later Judy gave birth to the first of her children to be born free, but the family's joy turned to grief when, eight days later, the baby boy died. The church sacristan baptized Juan Fatio *in extremis* "in a private home," and the next day Father Miguel O'Reilly officiated as the family buried the child in the Catholic cemetery in St. Augustine.[97]

Sometime after the death of the Whittens' infant son, McGirtt began to demand that Judy do field work. Prince promptly went to court to protest that he could not "permit" it. The use of that word alone speaks volumes. It was Prince who controlled his family, not McGirtt. "With the utmost respect," Whitten asked for the return of his work license and the amount he was owed for the labor performed in the nine and a half months he had worked for McGirtt.[98] It had not taken Whitten long to learn to exercise the rights available to him under Spanish law, and the man who had once been considered chattel property now challenged a white employer's violation of his contract.[99]

With her son's help, Judy later filed a suit against members of the influential Sánchez family for alleged insults and physical mistreatment. Judy asked the court to admonish her abusers and identified herself in the complaint as a *vecina* or property-holding member of the community, making no mention of her race. She had, in essence, placed herself on equal legal footing with the Spaniards she was suing. Spanish law permitted women, slaves, and even children a voice in the courts, but it did not consider all testimony equal, and class was the single most important determinant of veracity. Although the court gave her no satisfaction, Judy's legal and social challenge would have been inconceivable, and dangerous, in South Carolina.[100]

Their move into town helped integrate the Whittens into Spanish corporate culture. In 1789 St. Augustine celebrated the accession of Carlos IV to the Spanish throne. To mark the occasion, the government house where Prince had claimed his freedom was richly decorated. On the upper balcony, on an altar draped with wine-red and white cloths, were displayed portraits of the King and Queen. Uniformed soldiers of the Third

Battalion of Cuba stood guard. The governor, accompanied by all the government officials and men of note in the community, began the celebration by parading on horseback around the Plaza, acknowledging the troops posted at every corner. The vicar and other ecclesiastics received the procession at the Catholic Church, and then everyone proceeded to a stage set in the middle of the Plaza. There the governor and other functionaries gave a round of speeches interrupted by many "Vivas," the ringing of bells, and a triple salvo from the artillery at the Castillo de San Marcos and offshore war ships. At the conclusion of the speeches, Governor Zéspedes threw out to the assembled crowds silver coins minted at his own expense which bore the bust of King Carlos IV on one side and on the other three images: a jasmine flower—the symbol of Florida—a castle, and a lion, representing the Kingdoms of Castile and León. As might be expected, Zéspedes's name also appeared on the coins. The governor and his cortege then remounted their horses to parade through town to the military barracks and the great stone fortress, the Castillo de San Marcos, where the celebratory acts were repeated to much public acclaim.

That evening and for the next two nights, the streets and houses of St. Augustine were illuminated by lanterns and blazing bonfires, and people danced through the night as music played. The elites danced and ate refreshments at the governor's house, but the plebeians danced on the Plaza. On any of the three nights the Whittens might have been among the crowds applauding as the men of the Third Battalion performed Pedro Calderón de la Barca's comedy *Amigo, amante y leal* ("Loving and Loyal Friend"). On the third day the townspeople attended a solemn mass where they heard singing, more salvos, and prayers for divine favor for the "just and beneficent" new monarchs. As a closing act the guild of carpenters, wearing red insignia on their hats and carrying burning torches, paraded through the streets in a "triumphal carriage pulled by six horses." At each corner the carpenters, too, shouted their "Vivas" for King Carlos IV and Queen María Luisa.[101] Theirs was the only guild to mount such a display. Because no list of the guild members survives, we cannot say with certainty that Prince was among them, but the corporate pride exhibited in their procession and their salute to the monarchs must have been noted by the black carpenter.[102]

The lavish public theater and the symbols and rituals of the accession ceremonies that Prince witnessed were specifically designed to impress the assembled crowds and to reinforce devotion to the Spanish monarchy. If any of the freed refugees from Carolina and Georgia had any lingering doubts about having chosen the Spanish monarchy over the British, and over the newly established government of the United States, after 1790 there was no turning back. In May of that year, Spain yielded to strong diplomatic pressure by U.S. Secretary of State Thomas Jefferson and abrogated the sanctuary policy that Spain had first established in 1693. The Spanish governor posted notices in Southern newspapers announcing that thereafter fugitive slaves could no longer expect to be received and freed in St. Augustine. Responding to a request for clarification from Florida's governor, the Captain General of Cuba declared that "there was absolutely no doubt" that runaways who had already been freed, like the Whittens, retained their freedom and their rights as Spanish subjects.[103]

Having gained freedom, the Whittens worked to expand their economic opportunities. In St. Augustine they had more access to information and patronage networks, as well as more diverse employment. Prince began to supplement his earnings from carpentry by securing stone-quarrying and timbering contracts from the Spanish government. In an informal apprenticeship, the Whittens also took in an *agregada* or dependent, a free black girl named Margarita about the same age as Glasgow and Polly, whom Judy began training to be a domestic. The 1793 census shows the Whitten family living in a rented house on San Carlos Street, where some of the community's most influential citizens lived. Several doors down from the Whittens, the planter don Francisco Xavier Sánchez had established a home for his eight free quadroon children and their five slaves.[104] By the following year the Whittens had acquired a slave of their own, Isabel Plouden, for whose child Glasgow and Polly (now Francisco and María) served as godparents.[105] Living on one side of the Whittens was don Manuel Fernández Bendicho, their patron and godfather.[106] On the other side lived the Scotsman don Juan Leslie, head of the Panton Leslie & Co. Indian trading house. Leslie had fourteen slaves living in his household as well as an eighteen-year-old apprentice, Jorge J. F. Clarke. Like Sánchez, both Leslie and Clarke established mixed-race families (Clarke with Leslie's slave, Flora). Both of these influential men also became patrons of Prince Whitten and his family through Prince's enlistment in the free black militia of Florida.[107]

Spain had depended upon informal black military service in the Caribbean since the sixteenth century, and black interpreters and soldiers had helped establish Florida. The colony's first black militia was established in 1683 and helped to defend Florida from pirates and Indians. In the eighteenth century Spain's new Bourbon rulers formalized "disciplined" militias of *pardos* (mulattoes) and *morenos* (blacks) and encouraged enlistment by exempting recruits from certain municipal taxes or levies. Two other changes were also socially significant. The Bourbon reforms allowed black militiamen to elect their own officers (a practice already observed in the provincial militias), and most important, the crown extended the *fuero militar* to *pardo* and *moreno* units. The *fuero* was a corporate charter with important implications. By its provisions, black militiamen were exempt from prosecution in civilian courts and gained equal juridical status with white militiamen. The *fuero* also granted other rights to blacks who served in the military—hospitalization, retirement and death benefits, as well as the right to wear uniforms and bear arms.[108] Officials in the Viceroyalty of New Spain resisted the social advancement of black militiamen and sought to abridge the benefits of their *fuero*, generally limiting its enjoyment to officers in active service.[109] But Spanish military officials in Florida and other areas around the Caribbean sorely needed all the help they could get and depended heavily on black recruits. Africans and their descendants clearly appreciated the juridical and social benefits of militia membership, and despite the dangers such service involved, they developed traditions of long-term family service.[110] Prince, and later Glasgow, would become part of that tradition.

Whitten and the other freedmen and women who had survived the dangers of the American Revolution, and had chosen Spanish monarchy over British, had hardly settled into their new identities when they were once again embroiled in revolutionary turmoil—this time by the aftershocks of the French Revolution. In 1791 the slaves of Saint Domingue rose in bloody rebellion against the brutality of their oppression. Quoting the rhetoric of "natural rights," they killed their "masters" and destroyed the once-flourishing sugar plantations of the island. News of this world-changing event spread as rapidly as the fires that burned through Saint Domingue's cane fields, and planters everywhere feared their own slaves would also rise.[111] Alarmed by the rapid circulation of republican ideology throughout the greater Caribbean, Spanish governors attempted to quarantine their colonies from the "contagion" by forbidding the introduction of French ideas, books, citizens, and slaves originating from French territories.[112]

But revolutionary ideas were hard to contain. In 1793 Diego Morphy, Spain's vice-consul in Charleston, reported the alarming news that Citizen Edmond Genêt, French Minister Plenipotentiary to the United States, and Citizen Mangourit, French consul to South Carolina, were raising an army of backwoodsmen from Mississippi, Georgia, and Tennessee to invade and "liberate" Florida.[113] The Revolutionary Legion of the Floridas intended to make East Florida "a Part of the French Republic" until the conclusion of their invasion, after which "said country is to become independent . . . with the Proviso of adopting a strictly democratical Republican Government. The Rights of Man to form the Basis of their Constitution."[114] The plotters made an alliance with the Creek Indians, prepared several armed vessels, two transports, food and arms, and declared: "We wait only for the fleet and Florida is ours and the tree of liberty will grow everywhere."[115]

Hearing this news, Florida's governor hastily wrote to Governor George Matthews of Georgia to report that an invasion was being organized from his state. Fearing larger repercussions for the United States, Matthews issued orders to seize anyone found violating U.S. neutrality, but he also took the occasion to complain to the Spanish governor about his failure to return runaway slaves belonging to Georgia's citizens.[116]

Florida's governor promised more cooperation and began preparing for the expected invasion. Late in June an advance force from Georgia burned the frontier post of Fort Juana, and a hastily convened Council of War in St. Augustine voted to "arm all the free black and mulattoes in the province, for being fugitives from the State of Georgia, they will be loyal and will defend themselves to the death in order not to return to their former slavery."[117] Whitten's next-door neighbor, Juan Leslie, was named to command the newly formed free black militia, in which Prince enlisted and performed his first military service for Spain. Most of the free blacks who reported for duty were also freed slaves from the former British colonies, and they elected Whitten as their Sergeant.[118]

In July the Revolutionary Legion under the command of General Elijah Clarke launched a full invasion from Georgia and took the fort of San Nicolás (present-day Jacksonville) on the St. Johns River. The invaders also briefly occupied Amelia Island, and the Spaniards withdrew from two smaller forts. The following month, however, Whitten and forty-one members of the free black militia joined forty Cuban infantrymen, thirteen white militiamen, and some Seminole allies in a naval assault that dislodged the invaders. For the rest of the summer Sergeant Prince Whitten led a small party of free black cavalry in frontier patrols.[119]

The relative independence and mobility of Whitten and the free black troops, who functioned as mounted guerrillas on the Florida frontier, seems remarkable in light of the widespread paranoia regarding slave revolts. The "planters' darkest hour in the Caribbean" was 1795, notable for the Second Maroon War in Jamaica, slave revolts in Demerara (Guyana) and Coro (Venezuela), and the Pointe Coupee slave conspiracy in Louisiana, to name only a few of the best-known examples of black revolt.[120]

On one of their scouting expeditions the free black militiamen found a call to revolution posted on a tree that read:

Attention, Slaves of the Spanish Tyrants. All persons of whatever denomination can now participate in the great blessings of liberty and escape from the yoke of Spanish tyranny by coming to the glorious Republican standard which flies triumphantly on the northern shore of the St. Marys where you will be welcomed with friendship and protected in your person and property so that you can once again enjoy the blessings of liberty and equality.[121]

Whitten and his compatriots were not enticed by this offer to cross back into the American territory they had struggled so hard to escape. Through such revolutionary broadsides and the alarms raised in St. Augustine, as well as the sight of the French republican flag briefly raised over Amelia Island, former slaves were fully familiar with the ideology of the French Republic. They knew they had political options, but they still supported the Spanish monarchy, even in the face of unofficial racial discrimination.

Governor Juan Nepomuceno de Quesada, who had earlier denied land grants to free blacks in terms that suggested at least some personal racism, found that Whitten and his men had proved their loyalty in difficult times. In his report to the Captain General of Cuba, Quesada commended the service of his "excellent company of free blacks."[122] The free black militia of Florida had proved itself in its first armed conflict and acquired at least some honor in a culture which valued military valor so highly.

Whitten would have many opportunities to display his valor. Over the course of his twenty-six-year military career, he defended his family, their hard-won liberty, and his adopted monarchy against Jacobins, Mikosuki Indians, U.S. Marines, pirates, and assorted insurrectionists from South America. Through it all, and despite great hardships, much danger, and little reward, Whitten remained loyal to the Spanish Crown that had freed him and his family.

2

The Counter-Revolution
in Saint Domingue

I am the chief of the Counter-Revolution . . . I began the war,
almost without arms, without munitions, without supplies, and
almost without resources on August 23, 1791, a time that will
always be remembered among the most magnificent of the
Universe.

Jorge Biassou, General of the Conquered Territories of the North of
Santo Domingo, July 15, 1793[1]

LIKE PRINCE WHITTEN, the Saint Domingue–born Georges
Biassou "took the current" of revolution sweeping the Atlantic,
hoping it would lead "on to fortune." Instead, and against all
his expectations, he ended his days in relative obscurity on the
Spanish Florida frontier. Biassou grew up a slave on the sugar
plantations of Haut du Cap, on the hillsides that overlooked the
harbor of Cap Français (Le Cap). From those plantations it was
only a forty-minute walk to Le Cap, "the Paris of the Antilles,"
and it was common for slaves to make that pilgrimage on weekends to attend the market, visit the taverns, and see the sights.
Saint Domingue's cosmopolitan commercial center boasted a
printing press, a weekly newspaper (the *Avis Divers & Petites*

Affiches Américaines), impressive religious edifices that included the two-block-long Notre Dame church with its bell tower and clock, libraries, a theater, the Royal Society for the Sciences and Arts, and a Masonic Lodge, among other amenities. Members of that order included free blacks and *gens de couleur* (men of color), several of whom were apparently associates of Toussaint Louverture. The city's wealthier inhabitants built multi-storied masonry houses, some with gardens and aviaries filled with colorful birds from Senegal, Guyana, Mississippi, and other tropical locales. Lower-class residents lived in modest shacks on muddy streets lined with numerous taverns selling the cheap rum called *tafia*, as well as billiard parlors where gambling and other vices ran rampant. Ships from many nations docked in the harbor, bringing goods, passengers, sailors, and news from around the Atlantic.[2]

Despite Biassou's certainty in 1793 that "all of Europe" and "the Universe" recognized him as the leader of the only successful slave revolt in the hemisphere, and that his place in history was secure forever, he has been supplanted in public memory by his former aide, Toussaint Louverture. Biassou freely admitted that it was Toussaint who had first proposed the uprising, but Biassou alleged that "when it came time to begin, he did not dare. . . . I am the supreme leader, I was the first who took up arms, and it was I who received the other chiefs who followed me. . . . No one will doubt that only I was always in charge of everything."[3] In the early days of the uprising, Toussaint wrote to Biassou, addressing him as "Brigadier of the King's Army at Grand Boucan" and "my very dear friend." He begged Biassou to delay a military operation until they could

The slave ship *La Marie-Séraphique* on its arrival in Le Cap from Angola, 1773. Watercolor by unknown artist, Musée du Chateau des Ducs de Bretagne, Nantes, France. Courtesy of "The Atlantic Slave Trade and Slave Life in the Americas: A Visual Record" website, *http://hitchcock.itc.virginia.edu/Slavery*, Virginia Foundation for the Humanities and the University of Virginia Library.

make better defensive preparations at Haut du Cap. He asked for crowbars to tumble rocks down on advancing enemy forces, and news from Biassou's spy on the exact location of some powder works. Toussaint also expressed annoyance that Jean-François was enjoying himself "with his ladies, but he hasn't done me the honor of writing to me for several days." Toussaint suggested that if Biassou thought he had done well with the preparations, he might tell "Bouqueman." He added, "I ask you to assure your mother and sister of my humble respect," and closed in the polite language of the day, "I have the honor, my dear friend, of being your very humble, obedient servant."[4]

Biassou and the more famous Toussaint had known each other since their younger days and always addressed each other as friends.[5] Their friendship may have been formed through their connections to the Fathers of Charity in Le Cap. Biassou's mother, Diana, worked in one of the two hospitals owned by the Jesuits prior to their expulsion from the colony in 1763, and scholars believe Biassou was probably a slave driver on the Fathers' sugar plantation near Haut du Cap.[6] Toussaint was a horse doctor/coachman/slave driver on the Bréda plantation, also in Haut du Cap, but he had acquired freedom sometime in the 1770s. The hospitals of Le Cap commonly employed free people of color as nurses and, given Toussaint's skill at herbal healing, it is at least possible that he worked at the hospital where Biassou would have visited his mother. Biassou described Toussaint as "one of my confederates . . . in whom I have total confidence" and as a "man who knows well his God and his religion and a man of the Church living on the Breda plantation above Guarico [the Spanish name for Le Cap]."[7] The later correspondence of both men was conducted through secretary-scribes, but the interesting political and literary allusions as well as the references to Catholic devotion found in their letters and proclamations suggest that Biassou and Toussaint may have benefited from at least some rudimentary education through the church.[8]

The relatively privileged positions of Biassou and Toussaint and their proximity to Le Cap meant that both would have been aware of the revolutionary fervor that was sweeping the Atlantic world in the wake of the American and French Revolutions.[9] It was from Le Cap that more than 500 black troops of the Chasseurs-Voluntaires de Saint-Domingue, dressed in the King's Blue Coats, embarked in 1779 to support American Revolutionaries fighting in Savannah.[10] It was from the nearby mountain town of Dondon that Vincent Ogé launched his abortive rebellion in 1790, and it was in the Parade Ground of Le Cap where he and his ally Jean-Baptiste Chavannes, who had served proudly in his blue coat in Savannah, were broken on the wheel and dismembered, as two regiments of free black militia and many slaves watched. Several days later, twenty-one more of Ogé's followers, including a white priest, were hanged in the same square. The leaders' heads rotted on pikes in the square for some time thereafter in a mute and horrific warning to other potential rebels.[11]

The rebels of Saint Domingue had had access to French political pamphlets from the earliest days of the rebellion and were fully versed in the revolutionary rhetoric of the day.[12] They followed the political events in France with great interest and knew that revolutionaries had arrested King Louis XVI and Marie Antoinette and proclaimed France a republic.[13] Rumors of a suppressed emancipation decree had circulated widely since word of the French Revolution, with its radical republican motto "Liberty, Equality, and Fraternity or Death," first reached the Caribbean. These rumors took on added force in the summer of 1791 when news came to Saint Domingue of the French

National Assembly's May 15th decree granting suffrage and rights to free people of color born of free parents. In the south, soldiers mutinied in the garrison at Port-au-Prince, and slave revolts broke out on several plantations. In Le Cap, white colonists hung in effigy the French priest Henri Baptiste Grégoire, president of the French abolition society, Société des Amis des Noirs, who had proposed the admission of free men of color to the Assembly.[14] Each day seemed to bring new and inflammatory reports from France. In August the colonists heard the shocking news that Louis XVI and his family had been captured while trying to flee the country. Of course, white colonists and black slaves processed this information quite differently.

On August 14, 1791, Georges Biassou was among the 200 *commandeurs* from 100 nearby estates who met at the Lenormand de Mézy plantation. The planters did not find this unusual; they customarily permitted gatherings of trusted slaves on Sunday for feasts and drumming. This time, however, the men met not to dine together, but to plan an uprising that would change history. Presiding at that gathering was Boukman Dutty, the colossal slave driver/coachman for the Clément estate who was alleged also to be a vodou priest.[15] Fragmentary accounts of the meeting state that a "mulatto or quadroon" read an announcement of amelioration legislation passed by the King and the National Assembly in Paris, after which the assembled slave leaders debated whether to wait for expected French troops or to take independent action.[16] This was not the first or the last political debate the rebels would have among themselves, and positions shifted frequently with the tides of revolution and war.

On August 22, at a place called Bois Caïman on the Choiseul plantation in Petite-Anse, the plotters met again. After sacrificing a black pig and drinking its blood, the participants took swatches of its hair to insert in protective amulets, swore a sacred oath, and then Boukman launched the full-blown revolt. Among the other slave leaders would be Georges Biassou, Jeannot Bullet, and Jean-François Papillon. The freedman Toussaint waited at the Bréda plantation to see how events would unfold.[17] Within hours several thousand slaves attacked the surprised and outnumbered whites, set fire to the great houses and the cane fields, and smashed the sugar refining equipment and tools associated with their brutal labor regime. Soon, more than a thousand plantations across the northern plain were reduced to ash.[18]

The earliest phase of the slave revolt was, by all accounts, the bloodiest: confusion and terror reigned as various rebel bands fought for territory, supplies, and supremacy. The insurgents established a series of camps in Grande-Rivière, southeast of Le Cap, and a week after the fires started, 10,000 slaves were said to have formed into "three armies, of whom seven or eight hundred are on horseback and tolerably well-armed." The rest were said to be "almost without arms," confirming Biassou's opening claim.[19]

Though poorly armed, many slaves seemed animated by the belief that pig hairs and other charms would protect them. Only weeks after the revolt began, a captured rebel was executed after jeering at and mocking his captors. One soldier reported that the man "gave the signal himself and met death without fear or complaint." Hidden in the dead man's clothing were "pamphlets printed in France, filled with commonplaces about the Rights of Man and the Sacred Revolution." Around his neck he wore a "sack full of hair, herbs, and bits of bone."[20] Both might have been considered protective amulets. This syncretism of French political ideology and African gris-gris (a protective amulet) was emblematic of the mixed messages and shifting positions of the insurgents in the following years.[21]

The rebellion's most notorious leader, Jeannot Bullet, had led many fearless cavalry charges in the early days of the revolt, but he gained infamy for the gruesome tortures he enacted on his prisoners, some allegedly instigated by his consort, Manette Berard.[22] He roasted captives alive, blew up others with gunpowder, and hung one poor soul by a hook through his chin until the man expired thirty-six hours later. Despite his apparent thirst for blood, Jeannot kept alive valuable white captives such as parish priests and others who might serve in later negotiations. One captive, the French lawyer Gros, survived to write a first-hand account of some of the inhumane scenes he witnessed at Jeannot's camp. Horrified by the barbarity, he was also struck by the common belief of the rebels that the imprisoned French king, Louis XVI, "had issued them orders to arm themselves, and to restore him to Liberty." Gros continued, "the Revolt of the Slaves, is but a Counter-Revolution."[23]

Jeannot's former ally, Jean-François, finally tried and executed the "monster" on November 1, 1791, but he was probably acting on Biassou's orders. The dapper Jean-François was a runaway slave whom Biassou described as a man "of grand projects, many words, and few deeds."[24] Although contemporary and later accounts ridiculed Jean-François for the fanciful titles and colorful uniforms he adopted and the Cross of Saint Louis with which he decorated himself, they also state that it was Jean-François who assumed general command of the rebellion on Boukman's death.[25] It seems clear, however, from the correspondence of Biassou (which is admittedly self-serving), as well as that of Toussaint, and even Jean-François's own statements to Gros, that initially, at least, Jean-François answered to Biassou. Biassou described Jean-François as "excessively devoted to Pleasure, which caused him to neglect Affairs of the highest Importance." Toussaint dismissively wrote to Biassou: "As for Jean-François he can always keep going on carriage rides with the ladies."[26] The rescued lawyer, Gros, understandably described his savior somewhat more favorably, but even his attempts at compliments reflect the inveterate racism of the day. Gros described Jean-François as having "a Degree of good Sense, a Fund of Humanity, and a Ray of Genious, far superior to any Sentiment than might have been expected from his Kind."[27]

Judgments such as these helped shape the generally negative perceptions of Biassou by modern scholars. Historians often repeat one lurid description of Biassou's war tent, "filled with kittens of all shades, with snakes, with dead men's bones and other African fetishes. At night huge campfires were lit with naked women dancing horrible dances around them, chanting words understood only on the coast of Africa. When the excitement reached its climax, Biassou would appear with his *boccors* (religious specialists) to proclaim in the name of God that every slave killed in battle would re-awaken in his homeland of Africa."[28] That such a scene took place is doubtful, given Biassou's repeated claims for Christianity. Rather, it seems, later writers adopted the contemporary belief that all participants in Saint Domingue's slave revolt were primitive and dangerous because of their war conduct as well as their "pagan" practices.[29]

In fact, Gros found himself pleasantly surprised by the good order that prevailed in Biassou's camp. Without any previous known military training, Biassou had become the leader of an untrained and polyglot army that most agree he controlled with "iron discipline." Against the odds, he held on for almost four years as General of the Conquered Territories of the North. His fearful reputation, therefore, may have been a useful tool. Gros wrote, "The well known Character of Biassou filled me with Dread; though I was agreeably surprised at seeing him extremely disposed to Peace." Biassou told Gros that among his reasons for desiring peace, "that of his Family's Welfare was predominant."[30] Biassou had reason to fear for them in the escalating carnage. One witness wrote, "The country is filled with dead bodies, which lie unburied. The negroes have left the whites, with stakes, &c. drove through them into the ground; and the white troops, who now take no prisoners, but kill everything black or yellow, leave the negroes dead upon the field."[31]

Only three months after the start of the rebellion, not long after the execution of Jeannot, Boukman was killed in battle. The rebels at Dondon did not hear of Boukman's death until a month later, and then Gros wrote that "it was impossible to describe the Effect it had upon the Negroes," who believed he had been "killed in one of the justest of all Causes: the Defence of his King."[32] Biassou and the other chiefs in the camp went into mourning for Boukman and ordered "a solemn Service to be performed." Since Boukman was said to be a vodou priest, but there were also Catholic priests in the camps, the nature of this service is unclear.[33] Meanwhile, white colonists in Le Cap marked Boukman's death by placing the slave leader's head on a stake in the main square, as they had done earlier with Ogé and Chavannes.[34]

Although the rebellion had lost two powerful leaders, another was emerging. Sometime during this period Toussaint allied himself to his old friend Biassou, becoming his aide and camp physician, or Médecin Général. Despite his lesser title and customary modesty (or, some might argue, his secrecy and guile), Toussaint shaped subsequent negotiations with colonial authorities. In late September, 1791, the French National Assembly declared amnesty for all free persons for "acts of revolution" and sent three revolutionary commissioners to try to establish some order in Saint Domingue. When a copy of the amnesty proclamation reached Biassou's camp, he had it read aloud to his troops (to whom, actually, this decree would not have applied because they were slaves). Apparently the slaves understood this and declared their determination to continue the war, but Toussaint had the proclamation read a second time and then gave a speech which allegedly so moved the masses that they seemed willing to go back to their plantations.[35]

Recognizing their material limitations, the rebel leaders began negotiations to try to secure amnesty for themselves, at least. They had to hide their plans from the black masses they had mobilized but now feared they could not control, and "who shrewdly suspected" that they might be sold out.[36] On December 4, 1791, in a move that C. L. R. James described as "Judas work," Biassou, Jean-François, and Toussaint sued for peace and offered to return the rebellious slaves to their plantations in exchange for their own freedom and political rights and those of their families and officers.[37] Jean-François bluntly told Gros, who was acting as his secretary, "In taking up Arms, I never pretended to fight for the General Liberty of the country." Gros credited Toussaint with persuading Biassou to accept a reduced number of pardons in the offer.[38]

Biassou and Jean-François sent two letters to the newly arrived French commissioners. In the first letter, on which Jean-François's name appears first, they explained their own fear of "a multitude of *nègres* from Africa, most of whom can barely say two words in French, but who at the same time were accustomed to fight wars in their own countries." In the second, on which Biassou's name is given first, they wrote the commissioners that "in our role as chiefs we have a great deal of power over them" (the *nègre* slaves), but they also warned that it was difficult to end the rebellion when most of the slaves feared receiving the same treatment as Ogé. "You would not believe, sirs, how they are struck by what they call this treason."[39]

Nonetheless, the reactionary planters of the Colonial Assembly of Saint Domingue rudely and unwisely rejected the rebels' offer. In response, Biassou angrily ordered the execution of all his white prisoners, vowing that they would pay "for the insolence of the Assembly which has dared to write to me with so little respect." Toussaint stayed his superior's order, but the war raged on.[40] The following month, in January 1792, Biassou led several spectacular raids on Le Cap. In the first his forces raided the Providence Hospital of the Fathers of Charity to rescue Biassou's mother, Diana, who was still enslaved there. Historians have repeated allegations that Biassou slayed the other patients on his way out, but the earliest and most reliable sources make no report of this massacre. Only one source reports the deaths of two white patients, so most of the ill apparently escaped. Moreover, since Toussaint had sent his regards to Biassou's mother and sister three months earlier, Biassou must have already secured their liberty.[41] Meanwhile, Jean-François also had success in capturing Ouanaminthe on the Spanish border (known in Spanish sources as Juana Méndez).

In France, influenced by Abbé Grégoire and the Amis des Noirs, the French National Assembly in April 1792 voted for suffrage for free people of color. Once again, the obdurate Colonial Assembly stood firm and ruled slavery perpetual.[42] At this impasse, the French National Assembly dispatched 6,000 troops and a second set of commissioners to Saint Domingue. Hoping for a better result this time, in July of 1792 the "Chiefs of the Revolt" wrote another lengthy statement to the Colonial Assembly and the new French commissioners. Proclaiming the justice of their rebellion and their equality with the "avaricious" whites who had oppressed them, they demanded general liberty and a general amnesty, this time not for only a few, but for the "four hundred and eighty thousand individuals who allow you to enjoy all you possess." Flipping racial stereotypes on their head, they stated that the white planters of the island exercised dominion not by any other right "except that you are stronger and more barbaric than we." They continued that "all being children of the same father created in the same image . . . We are your equals, then, by natural right. . . . Have you not sworn to uphold the French Constitution . . . have you forgotten that you formally vowed the declaration of the rights of man?" The statement closed with the words, "Here, Gentlemen, is the request of men who are like you, and here is their final resolution: they are resolved to live free or die." This ringing declaration that reminded its recipients of the failed promises of the French Revolution was signed Biassou, Jean-François, and Belair (Toussaint's young nephew). Believing that the declarations of the distant French Assembly would never be enforced in reactionary Saint Domingue, Biassou apparently planned to write his own constitution, and for that purpose he sought the help of the abolitionist priest of Dondon, the Abbé Guillaume Sylvestre Delahaye.[43]

In August 1792 the National Assembly deposed Louis XVI and declared France a republic, although that news did not reach Saint Domingue until October. Meanwhile, although half of the French troops had quickly died of disease, the remaining men under Etienne Laveaux energetically pursued the rebel forces, engaging in a series of battles on the northern plains outside Le Cap. In January 1793, Biassou was credited with a courageous defense of the fort at Milot, where he made a show of marching atop the ramparts in full view of the French troops.[44]

As Biassou was defying the French troops, Louis XVI went to the guillotine and the rebels of Saint Domingue were left without a king to defend.[45] Biassou claimed that he wept daily for the loss of the "best King on the earth" and lamented that he had not been able to transport himself and his armies to Paris, that "theater of horrors" created by "1200 evildoers, who call themselves philosophes" but who were actually "cannibals."[46] This may have been nothing more than rhetoric, but one wonders if Biassou's seemingly personal sense of connection was kindled by seeing the six-foot-high painting of Louis XVI that graced the Government Hall in the former Jesuit headquarters, just opposite the painting of Christ.[47]

The following month, in February 1793, England and Spain declared war on France, and both powers began courting Biassou and the black rebels of the north. The French Commissioner Léger-Félicité Sonthonax took the initiative to also offer the northern rebels freedom and alliance in the name of the French Republic, but he did so independently and Saint Domingue's Colonial Assembly would have none of it. In June of 1793 fierce fighting broke out between the French governor of Saint Domingue, a native who sided with the planters, and the forces of the radical French commissioners who had declared the slaves free. Le Cap was soon in flames, and panicked whites fled the city for ships bound for Philadelphia and Charleston.[48]

Biassou, Jean-François, and Toussaint rejected the overtures of the French commissioners who had regained Le Cap, although they were by that time almost in a state of starvation. Some of the rebels considered the commissioners' offer a trick and believed that only a king could make and keep such a promise. Biassou and Jean-François allegedly responded, "Since the beginning of the world we have obeyed the will of a king. We have lost the king of France but we are dear to him of Spain who constantly shows us reward and assistance. We therefore cannot recognize you until you have enthroned a king."[49]

"Incendie du Cap" (Burning of Le Cap). Anonymous illustration from *Saint-Domingue, ou histoire de ses revolutions* (Paris, 1815). Courtesy of The Library Company of Philadelphia.

They even convinced the commissioners' Kongo-born envoy, Macaya, to join them. Macaya later proclaimed: "I am the subject of three kings: of the king of Congo, master of all blacks; of the King of France, who represents my father; of the King of Spain, who represents my mother."[50]

Opting for monarchy, and with no French king to claim their loyalty, Biassou, Jean-François, and Toussaint accepted the Spanish offer of alliance, declaring in a rhetorical flourish that they would "rather be slaves of the Spaniards than free with the French."[51] In fact, they never intended to return to slavery under any regime and were determined to cut the best deal possible for themselves, their kin, and their troops. Scholars have ever since contrasted the "counterrevolutionary stance" of Biassou and Jean-François with the more truly revolutionary ideologies of Toussaint.[52] Toussaint would eventually switch his allegiance to the French Republic, but Biassou and Jean-François remained committed to Spain. This decision cost them a more significant place in history and in retrospect appears reactionary and ill-advised, but considered in the context of their times, their difficult choice is more understandable.

Information about the French revolution circulated with lightning speed across the Caribbean and triggered powerful reactions, but accurate information about the dramatic events engulfing them was difficult for any of the participants, black or white, to come by.[53] It is hard to say what the rebels knew of the British system and what it could offer, but the French colonial devil they did know. Those who frequented Le Cap, like Biassou, Jean-François, and Toussaint, would have had frequent contact with merchants and sailors, some of whom were free blacks, from Spanish ports such as St. Augustine and Havana.[54] Presumably the rebels of Saint Domingue would have known of the opportunities the Spanish king made available to freed slaves in the Caribbean, including land and salaries for military service. Thus there was an informed and pragmatic basis for their decision.

Although Spanish officers frequently disparaged blacks, faced with a chronic shortage of worthy regular troops and inadequate financial and material resources, they had long relied on black militias to help them maintain a tenuous sovereignty in the region.[55] Persistent prejudice and ranking inequalities did not dissuade men of African descent from enlisting, and by 1770 more than three thousand men had joined Cuba's black militia, making up one-fourth of Spain's largest army in the Caribbean.[56]

The institutional precedents that permitted Spain to enlist former slaves in military service and to incorporate them into a Spanish polity had long been in place, and one may presume that the leaders of the slave revolt would have had some knowledge of them. None of Spain's previous military recruits or pioneers, however, had been leaders of a slave revolt of such proportions. For this reason the alliance that Spain struck with the revolutionary leaders Biassou, Jean-François, and Toussaint Louverture was an uneasy one, marked by distrust on both sides. Spanish officials did feel compelled in general to honor the promises of freedom, relocation, and support made in the name of their king, but they also watched the former slaves with fear and suspicion and tried to isolate them and the dangerous ideas they represented. It is clear that Spain's black allies were embittered by the graceless way some Spanish officials treated them and never anticipated the diaspora they would experience at the end of the war, but Biassou and Jean-François at least lived out their lives as free men in the service of Spain.

Spain designated its new armies of risen slaves the Black Auxiliaries of Charles IV, a much more formal title and affiliation than earlier or later black militias ever received. At the border town of San Rafael, the Spanish Captain General and Governor of Santo Domingo, Joaquín García, ceremoniously decorated Biassou, Jean-François, and Toussaint with gold medals bearing the likeness of the king, and presented them with documents expressing the gratitude and confidence of the Spanish government.[57] From Dondon some of Toussaint's followers allegedly (and prophetically) warned, "You have received commissions and you have guarantees. Guard your liveries and your parchments. One day they will serve you as the fastidious titles of our former aristocrats served them."[58]

Newly supplied and under a Spanish flag, the forces of Biassou, Jean-François, and Toussaint fought many bloody battles against the French. One of the rebels' primary supporters, Father Josef Vásquez, himself a mulatto, wrote from Dajabón that "if divine Providence had not favored us with the blacks [allies], we would have been victims of the fury of the savage masses." He added that although the Spaniards did not fully trust the new allies who fought against the slaves, "it is they who have taken prisoners, they who have given the King 200 slaves, and they who have fought the campaign."[59]

Over the course of the late summer and fall of 1793, both Jean-François and Toussaint began to challenge Biassou's nom-

Rea Gra.

BIASOU

Primer Gefe delos Negros de Santo Domingo.

Portrait of Georges Biassou. From Juan López Cancelada Dubroca and Mariano José de Zúñiga y Ontiveros, *Vida de J. J. Dessalines, gefe de los negros de Santo Domingo* (Mexico City, 1806). Courtesy of Rare Books Collection, Special and Area Studies Collections, George A. Smathers Library, University of Florida.

inal command. Biassou, however, produced a statement that Toussaint had sent to the Spanish King from Dondon on July 15, 1793, acknowledging Biassou as "our true General . . . who we have always recognized as such," and recommending that the title of Generalissimo be conferred on him: "to do otherwise would be unjust since it is his by right."[60]

On August 29, 1793, the same day when Commissioner Sonthonax proclaimed the abolition of slavery in the north, Toussaint issued a call for unity, liberty, and equality and for the first time signed himself "Toussaint Louverture, General of the armies of the king [of Spain]."[61] Meanwhile, from his camp at San Miguel, Biassou continued to pepper the Spanish governor with proofs of his leadership and demands that he recognize it. Biassou repeatedly attacked Jean-François as "vain" and his presumptions to leadership as "absurd." He pointed out that his rival only held the town of Juana Méndez, whereas thousands had surrendered to Biassou. He added, "There is not an obligation that he [Jean-François] does not owe me."[62] The disputes among the leaders become so worrisome that King Carlos IV of Spain and his Council of State met to determine how they should be reconciled.[63] Another rebel leader, Commandant Jean Guiambois, also hoped to mediate differences between the two squabbling rebels and wrote Biassou from his camp on the Artibonite Plain. Addressing Biassou as "dear brother" and "dear General," he argued that if he and Biassou and Jean-François united their forces and hearts, they would save lives. "We are three chiefs, but one heart." He went on to say that there was more glory in peace than in further bloodshed, and that past evils should be forgotten and vengeance forsworn. Guiambois included a letter sent to him by Jean-Pierre Lambert, a veteran of the American Revolution, that also deplored the bloodshed and destruction. It urged him to end the horror of war and bring peace, schools, and manufacturing to their beautiful island. In doing so, Lambert wrote, he would be known as "Major Guiambois, Savior of the New World" rather than "Avenger of the New World."[64]

Despite these efforts at reconciliation, Toussaint broke with the Spaniards in May of 1794 and offered his services and loyalty to the French Republic, in what Biassou charged was a "Faustian bargain." Historians theorize that Toussaint's defection from the Spaniards was in part motivated by his own ambition and that he felt his advancement within the Spanish camp was blocked by Biassou and Jean-François, who remained loyal to Spain.[65] Before long the Black Auxiliaries of Carlos IV were losing battles against Toussaint, who surprised and defeated Spanish forces at San Raphael on May 6, 1794. Two months later at Bayajá, rebel forces massacred more than one thousand French men, women, and children who had accepted Spanish offers of protection and returned from the United States, where they had fled at the outset of the rebellion. Biassou and Jean-François each blamed the other for the carnage, but Spanish sources generally place the responsibility on Jean-François.[66] Although Spaniards were also involved in the killings, the Spanish governor of Bayajá, the Marqués of Casa Calvo, later referred to the incident as a "cruel crime" which "inspired in the sanguinary hearts and entrails [of the blacks] the reckless belief that they had reconquered the town and saved the Spanish garrison from a plot against them by the French émigrés." If the black troops actually believed that the returning French planters who had rejected their freedom were plotting to overturn the Spaniards who had accepted it, then their actions become more explicable, if no less bloody. C. L. R. James wrote that Jean-François had spent that morning in the confessional with Father Vásquez and that it was the priest, in fact, who gave the sign to commence the slaughter. If this is true, the actions of Biassou and Jean-François on that horrible day may have been sanctioned by their own beloved priest and counselor.[67]

Spain and the Directory of the French Republic finally concluded a peace treaty in 1795, by which Spain ceded western Hispaniola to the French and agreed to disband the Black Auxiliaries of Carlos IV. Governor Casa Calvo recommended that the Crown abolish black military employment and titles immediately. Bothered by the auxiliaries' "pretensions to superiority," he argued that he had seen evidence of their fury at Bayajá, and "although they paint themselves with other colors, they are the same who murdered their owners, violated their wives, and destroyed all those with property." He also warned that while some of the black auxiliaries thought the abandonment of their property would excuse their crimes and be proof of fidelity, their sacrifices were only "illusions" and were made in their own self-interest.[68] Governor Casa Calvo told Biassou, Jean-François, and the other military leaders that they would have to evacuate Hispaniola because the French Republic did not find their presence "compatible," but he urged the "simple soldiers" to remain, as they had been offered freedom by both the French Republic and Spain. The Republic would need laborers to restore the burned plantations.

The black armies wanted, instead, to maintain their units, ranks, salaries, and rations and to embark together for some designated place where they would be given lands to cultivate and be permitted to form a town. They had not given everything only to return to their former states. They argued that they would then constitute a ready force, able to fight for the king of Spain wherever he should care to send them. There was, in fact, royal precedent for this: only decades before, the militia of the town of Gracia Real de Santa Teresa de Mose in Florida, also composed of former slaves, was evacuated en masse to Cuba in 1763, granted homesteads together, and allowed to retain their militia titles and perquisites.[69]

Over Casa Calvo's supposed opposition, "a considerable number" of soldiers embarked with their leaders for Havana, where he predicted they would expect "the same distinctions, prerogatives, luxury, and excessive tolerance" they had in Bayajá. He assured the captain general of Cuba that he had never promised the "venomous vipers" they would be allowed to remain in Havana.[70]

The governor and captain general of Santo Domingo, Joaquín García, had once written glowing reports about the exploits of the "valiant warriors" whom he decorated in the king's name, but as soon as the fighting ceased he, too, advocated that they be shipped to Havana. He wrote Cuba's governor that the blacks were "capable of being domesticated" and that any misdeeds of theirs (presumably a reference to Bayajá) were attributable to the bad governance they had experienced (under the French). García was already under serious pressure from angry Spanish citizens who were also being forced to evacuate the island and were urging Spanish troops to mutiny and renounce the treaty with France. In such a volatile situation, García did not even allow the black troops time to dispose of their property or settle family affairs before leaving.[71] In the rapid evacuation families were separated and Biassou was forced to leave behind his own mother, whom he had allegedly rescued from slavery in the early years of the revolt.[72] The embittered black general lodged a formal complaint against Governor García and urged his dismissal.[73]

On the last day of December, 1795, Spanish officials carefully recorded the exodus of the Black Auxiliaries of Carlos IV from Bayajá. Jean-François led the largest group, which consisted of 70 military officials, 282 soldiers, 334 women, and 94 children. The exiles sailed away for Havana in a small flotilla of four ships.[74]

Wherever the dispersed black veterans traveled, they spread conflicting images and messages. They were successful slave rebels who had fought a bloody war and had freed themselves and large numbers of their families and troops by force of arms. Seasoned by war against the French planters, French and British troops, and their own countrymen, and well acquainted with "dangerous notions" of liberty, equality, and fraternity, despite their monarchical rhetoric, these men became objects of fear throughout the Atlantic world. Some were, in fact, involved in later revolutionary actions and slave conspiracies.[75] But the veterans also wore the uniforms and medals of Spain, and they bore titles and documents testifying to the King's gratitude and detailing the privileges he granted his black allies.

Havana's blacks gathered at the docks to celebrate the arrival of the black troops. Cuba's captain general, Luis de Las Casas, however, was no more anxious than the governors of Bayajá and Santo Domingo were to have a large number of unemployed, armed, and experienced "wolves," as they were now referred to, on his hands. Las Casas hastily convoked a war council which decided to deport the black armies, using as its authority the royal order forbidding the introduction of blacks from French areas.[76]

Jean-François did not accept this decision without protest. He immediately responded with a formal statement in which he reminded the Cuban officials of the "offices, decorations, and military appointments" given the blacks by the Spanish Court, which should have been "sufficient proof of their loyalty and submission." He also reminded them of the "personal sacrifices each auxiliary made leaving hearth and home . . . in blind obedience" to the King's orders. He added the implied threat that the situation in which the Black Auxiliaries found themselves (floating on board crowded ships in Havana harbor) made them question whether they should reconsider the "advantageous treaties proposed by agents of the British Crown." In closing, Jean-François said his troops felt betrayed, and he made three demands of the Spaniards: that they vouch for the safety of Father Vásquez, who had not yet arrived in Havana; that his troops be allowed to return to Bayajá if they would not be permitted to disembark in Havana; and that Las Casas tell them if they were "prisoners of the state or vassals of the King of Spain."[77]

Las Casas answered that he could not permit the blacks to await the arrival of Father Vásquez but that he would allow the priest to join them later should he so choose. The governor had no objections to their returning to Bayajá (or anywhere but Havana), but he bristled at Jean-François's last demand, denouncing it as "petulant"; he said that the prisoners of state, "of which there are many in this city," were kept in tight and secure jail cells, whereas the blacks had been received and treated well, given all that they asked, and allowed to freely choose their destinations.[78]

In fact, however, both Governors García and Las Casas apparently envisioned the Isle of Pines off Cuba's southern coast as an ideal repository where the numerous blacks could be contained, monitored, and "civilized" for some time. Governor García proposed that once they had proved themselves capable of some useful occupation, the "good blacks" could slowly be released into the general population. Meanwhile, children born on the island and raised under Spanish laws would not bear "such a horrific aspect."[79] In the end, Jean-François and twelve of his military subordinates, along with their extended families, totaling 136 persons, sailed away from Havana for Cádiz, Spain. Although his life there was not without conflict, Jean-François continued his military service to Spain until his death.[80] The remainder of Jean-François's group was dispersed as follows: 115 persons to Campeche, on the coast of the Yucatan; 148 to Trinidad de Barlovento; 307 to Truxillo, Honduras; and 74 to Portobelo, Panama. Borrowing García's tactic, Las Casas planned to forward the unwanted blacks to a new locale without any advance notice and hope that the next governor would receive them. Trinidad was in need of homesteaders, and Las Casas hoped its governor might give the discarded allies lands in keeping with the policy of *repoblación*, whereby Spain granted vacant lands to settlers who then defended its vast frontiers. The Viceroy of New Spain had allocated 124,451 pesos of Cuba's government payroll for the expenses of the Black Auxiliaries—a considerable sum, given that the Spanish governor of Florida earned 4,000 pesos that year. However, with the Viceroy's approval, Governor Las Casas kept 100,000 pesos to cover the expenses of the exodus and sent only 6,000 pesos each with the groups headed for Trinidad and Trujillo, he said "to better assure that they would be admitted there." Presumably he planned to do the same for those of Jean-François's dependents headed to Campeche and Portobelo.[81]

Both García and Las Casas recognized that they had to honor the promises of the Spanish King to support his loyal black allies. Not only was the King's honor at stake, but England had let it be known that should the Spanish blacks be discontent with their new locations, they had only to say the word and transports would relocate them to the British holding of their choice. Brigadier General Jean-Baptiste Villate, the mulatto commander of Guarico and another veteran of the American Revolution, also advised that the French would be glad to receive them if they chose to return.[82]

Biassou's entourage received the same reception in Cuba accorded Jean-François and his men: Governor Las Casas refused the group permission to disembark and gave the general only a day to decide on the Isle of Pines or St. Augustine, Florida, as a destination. After deliberating overnight Biassou chose the latter, and his party sailed northward in January of 1796.[83] Biassou was traveling with his immediate household of five, his slave, and seventeen other dependents. Although he was actually related to only a small core of the group, Biassou referred to all as his "family" because they paid him allegiance and he claimed responsibility for them.[84]

Biassou had enjoyed a position of command for five years before he settled in Florida, and his haughty demeanor immediately alienated Governor Juan Nepomuceno de Quesada, who arranged lodging for Biassou and his immediate family and sent two nights' supper to the house when they arrived, only to have Biassou complain that he had not been invited to dine at the governor's home. Quesada reported this in amazement to his Cuban superior, warning that "I very much fear the proud and vain character he displays . . . it is a great problem to decide how to deal with him."[85]

Biassou's "proud and vain character" was evident in his dress as well as his attitude. The black general strolled through the streets of St. Augustine in fine clothes trimmed in gold, wearing the gold medal of Charles IV, a silver-trimmed saber, and a fancy ivory and silver dagger. This display of his importance and rank was meant to impress the townspeople, unaccustomed to seeing such finery on a black man.[86] The garrison soldiers, attracted by the novelty, took to gathering at Biassou's house to ogle him, and Quesada maintained that they expressed disgust. Biassou must have been equally displeased, because he petitioned that the soldiers be forbidden this pastime.[87] According to Quesada, who may have been projecting his own concerns, "The slaveowners have viewed his arrival with great disgust, for they fear he will set a bad example for the rest of his class."[88] No record exists of the reaction of the "rest of his class" to the arrival of the decorated black military figure and his retinue, but surely free blacks and slaves alike were aware of Biassou's slave origins and the manner in which he rose above them.[89]

From the moment of his arrival, Biassou continued to pepper Florida's officials with complaints.[90] Biassou's annual salary from the Spanish Crown (in Saint Domingue) was 3,840 pesos—not an inconsiderable sum, and only 120 pesos less than the annual salary of Florida's governor. Biassou and his officers had been promised that their salaries would continue and that they would be provided with rations and an annual clothing allowance in Florida. The Crown, however, made no provision to augment St. Augustine's subsidy to cover these costs, and the governors' appeals to the viceroy of New Spain for extra funds were denied. Still suffering from the devastation of the Jacobin invasion of the year before, the Florida treasury could barely support its regular troops, so the additional burden of supporting Biassou and his band was most unwelcome. After much wrangling, the treasury officials of St. Augustine finally agreed to pay Biassou an annual salary of 3,000 pesos, but Quesada noted warily that "since the certificate that he has presented verified the black's claims [to the higher 3,840-peso salary], he is very dissatisfied, and this added to his high temper and taste for drink, although it has not caused any harm to date, I feel will present a problem."[91]

Governor Quesada also complained that although Biassou had been paid his salary in advance, he spent large sums of money and always asked for more. When it was not forthcoming, Biassou demonstrated his lack of deference by writing directly to the governor's superior—Captain General Las Casas of Cuba, who, it should be remembered, had forbidden Biassou to remain in Cuba.

> The many and valuable services which I have received from your Excellency oblige me to disturb you . . . neither I nor my family could ever repay you with more than gratitude, which is constant in us . . . I happily inform you of my arrival at this [port] where I have been paid respects by the governors, the nobles, and the people. I owe this fine reception to the kindness of your Excellency, whom I beg not to fail to forward your desires and orders, which I eagerly look forward to, in order to have the honor of being your most unworthy servant . . . Sir, I hope to deserve your kindness and that you will order that I be advanced money to buy a house. If I am to subsist in this province I would not be able to manage the costs of rent.[92]

This flowery letter is a masterpiece of veiled sarcasm, but it made important points about Biassou's service, the obligation it should have engendered, and his need. Biassou's request was not illogical, because he and his followers had abandoned their property in Saint Domingue and the Spanish Crown customarily provided for evacuated citizens. Biassou understood the value of his critical connection to the Spanish monarch and made the most of it from distant Florida. He knew that Spanish governors and captains general, regardless of their personal sentiments, were required to forward even his most controversial memorials through proper channels to the minister of war in Spain. Biassou's effort was in vain, however, for it failed to stir any sympathy or loose any funds from either official.

The exiled rebels had more luck when they asked for something the governor of Florida actually had to give—vacant land. From the fifteenth century onward free blacks had enjoyed property rights in the Spanish Americas, earning homesteads and other privileges for helping to secure contested frontiers and defending state interests.[93] Spain believed that "to govern is to populate"; drawing on medieval Reconquest patterns, they adopted the policy of *repoblación*. Lands vacated by war, conquest, or epidemic created a dangerous vacuum into which enemies might filter, and the Crown filled these empty places with loyal settlers who, in gratitude, were to defend the royal interest as, indeed, their own.[94] Initially the Crown relocated loyal Indian allies to threatened areas it wished to hold, but Spain also transported Galician and Canary Island populations across the Atlantic to fill critical voids. Free blacks filled the same functions in areas as diverse as Ecuador, Venezuela, Mexico, Colombia, and Spanish Florida.[95] And beginning in the seventeenth century, Spain formulated a policy by which rebellious maroon settlements which could not be militarily defeated might be more usefully "reduced" into legitimate and loyal free black towns.[96]

Biassou and his men petitioned for and received large land grants in Florida as *nuevo pobladores,* or new homesteaders. Although Biassou maintained his town residence, he also began clearing a plantation seven miles north of St. Augustine, lending the place the names of Plantation of the Black General or Bayou Mulatto. Biassou's petition specified that many of his

Petition of Juan Bautista Whitten for land grants for himself and "the other free blacks" in St. Augustine, November 27, 1795. Granted. Spanish Florida Land Records, group 599, series 992, box 12, folder 35. Courtesy of the State Archives of Florida.

countrymen would soon be establishing themselves nearby, which indicated that he and his men were trying to remain a unit and that they were willing to put down roots where free land was theirs.[97] This settlement served Spanish interests as well, because it helped fill the thinly populated northern frontier through which any enemy would have to cross to attack St. Augustine, but it heightened the fears and antipathy of Anglo residents living across the St. Marys River border.

The governor had implied that Biassou was a wastrel, but much of the latter's salary actually went to pay the "salary" of dependents for whom he was responsible, such as his brother-in-law and military heir, Juan Jorge Jacobo. Jacobo had been Biassou's sergeant and adjutant in Saint Domingue, and they fought for the Spaniards at Prus, Plegarias, San Rafael, Plaza Chica de San Miguel, and Barica. Biassou supported Jacobo as long as he could, but eventually Jacobo asked the governor to assume that responsibility, arguing that the single ration he was allowed was insufficient to support his own large family.[98]

Biassou struggled to maintain his position in St. Augustine by public displays of patronage and beneficence, borrowing money from creditors to underwrite a celebration of the Day of Kings (Epiphany) on January 6.[99] In Havana this was a day of role reversal and ethnic and cultural expression, but whether the same sort of costuming, drumming, and African song and dance took place with Biassou's support in St. Augustine is unknown.[100] Hosting entertainments and redistributing wealth enhanced one's status, and Biassou's patronage of events like the Day of Kings no doubt reinforced his position as the most important figure in the black community, as did his occasional gifts to needy dependents.

Biassou's patronage powers and control may have been reduced, but he was still able to exercise other forms of influence as the titular head of an ever-expanding "family." Despite major language and cultural differences and at least a few incidents of conflict, marriage and godparental ties soon linked the former Black Auxiliaries of Carlos IV with members of the free black community in St. Augustine, many of whom were former fugitives from the United States and had experienced the American Revolution. Only three months after arriving in Florida, Biassou's brother-in-law and military heir, Sergeant Juan Jorge Jacobo, married Rafaela Whitten in St. Augustine's cathedral.[101] This union had important political implications—the bride was the daughter of Lieutenant Prince Whitten, whose good standing in the community had been further enhanced by his distinguished military service against the Jacobin invaders of 1795. The marriage of Biassou's heir, Jorge, and Whitten's daughter, Rafaela, thus united the leading families of both groups of blacks who had allied with the cause of the Spanish King against the forces of French republicanism. Subsequent marriages and baptisms added new layers of connection, and the refugees continued to use the structures of the Catholic Church to strengthen their blended community. The overlapping relationships and creation of extended family networks among blacks can be traced up to the evacuation of Florida in 1821 and probably continued thereafter in Cuba.[102]

But Biassou had not forgotten his own family and relations in

Saint Domingue. Before the year was out, he petitioned to be allowed to return to Saint Domingue to search for his "beloved mother" and for other members of his "family" still living there. The Spanish authorities on that island had promised Biassou that any of his dependents left behind would soon be sent to join him, but when he asked them to honor that pledge, the bureaucrats stalled, noting that Biassou's petition did not specify how many "troops" he sought to recover or exactly where they might be located.[103]

Some of Biassou's men, in fact, were still fighting the French, despite their abandonment. English envoys continued to court two of the most able of his subordinates, Pablo Alí and Agustín, and their "good conduct" and "utmost fidelity" to the Spanish cause impressed even Governor García. Several years later he wrote to the Duque de Alcudia reporting the misery in which the men lived since losing their Spanish pay and recommending that they be allowed to pass over to Florida to join Biassou, as they were asking to do. But García's superiors were hardly inclined to reconstitute a force that they had gone to such lengths to disperse.[104]

That summer, serendipity did reunite Biassou with another smaller contingent of Black Auxiliaries from Saint Domingue. Commandant Luis Boeff, once a recipient of a silver medal from Captain General Joaquín García at San Rafael, was escorted into town under armed guard, along with eight of his men. Boeff had been a subordinate of Jean-François's in command of the plaza of Margot and fought under Jean-François at bloody Bayajá. Evacuated from Hispaniola in 1795, Boeff and his men drifted for months on the open sea after their small ship's rudder broke. During the harrowing voyage their Spanish captain died, and the ragged survivors finally wrecked on Cumberland Island off the coast of Georgia. Georgia officials jailed and anxiously interrogated the men about the circumstances surrounding their captain's death, but unable to determine anything concrete, they decided to send the suspects on to St. Augustine. Spanish authorities there also investigated the possible murder of the ship's captain, but as the inquiry proceeded, the men were free to move through the city. During that time Boeff paid a visit to Biassou's St. Augustine home and asked for financial assistance for himself and his men, which Biassou gave. Biassou later testified that he felt a sense of obligation to his compatriot. St. Augustine's tribunal finally refused to prosecute the black auxiliaries for lack of evidence, but neither did it want to allow soldiers who had been at Bayajá to stay in the province, which was "loaded with prisoners, blacks, free and enslaved, and refugees from the United States." Following the precedent established by the governors of Saint Domingue and Cuba, they dispersed the men to different Caribbean locales; only one African-born man of the Lachi nation, Roman, was allowed to remain in Florida.[105]

Boeff and his men still paid homage to Biassou, but the general's prestige suffered when he could no longer provide well for his troops. After he ordered the arrest of one of his men for drunkenness and street fighting, the man insolently denied Biassou's authority and appealed to the governor. Juan Bautista argued that he was now a civilian, not a soldier, and since Biassou had told them to apply to the governor for rations, he considered that he was no longer subject to the general's (Biassou's) orders. Biassou felt compelled to address the governor about this challenge, always referring to Juan Bautista as a soldier under his command and reminding the governor that the Catholic monarch had given him "full powers" to punish and reward those in his service, as Juan Bautista knew full well. Biassou added that even though Juan Bautista may have been ignorant of that fact, he would never before have dared argue with Biassou as he had now done twice. Biassou's honor was clearly at stake in this dispute, but the governor's response is unknown.[106]

After having known the relative splendor of Le Cap and experienced the power he once commanded, Biassou chafed at being relegated to such a small stage as Florida. Return to Saint Domingue was not possible, so he looked for other alternatives. Spain and England had been at war since 1796, and in 1799 Biassou asked to be allowed to go to Spain and fight for the king, stating that he had no way to demonstrate his military services in Florida. Perhaps he hoped to reunite with Jean-François and his dependents there. Governor Enrique White's cover letter assured Cuba's captain general of Biassou's good conduct and "total obedience to the government although at times he has been harassed by some Frenchmen, and even by those of his own color, he has endured it without requiring any other justice than that he asked of me."[107] White may have simply been hoping to get the demanding general off his hands, but despite this favorable reference, the Crown denied Biassou's request. Next Biassou asked simply for any destination other than Florida, but that request was also rejected. The governor finally approved Biassou's request to send his ailing wife and four members of her family to Havana, and Biassou asked that they be granted the daily subsidy that other blacks from Saint Domingue received in Cuba. Efforts to ensure that none of the blacks from Saint Domingue set foot in Cuba had obviously failed, and Biassou may have hoped that the refugee community there might be able to be of some assistance to his family.[108] He would not see his wife again.

Two years later, his dreams of grandeur and a return to the global arena unrealized, Biassou died suddenly and almost unnoticed on the Florida frontier. At his death, Biassou had served eight years in the service of the Spanish monarch, much of it in battle. Biassou's bereaved family and followers arranged a wake and buried him the following day with full honors. Despite his bloody past and allegations of heretical religious practices in Saint Domingue, he was given a full Catholic burial in St. Augustine. After an elaborate mass which included songs, tolling bells, candles, and burning incense, Governor Enrique White and other persons of distinction accompanied Biassou's cortege to the graveyard. They were joined by drummers and an honor guard of twenty members of Biassou's black troops, who discharged a volley at the gravesite. The public notary attested that "every effort was made to accord him the decency due an officer Spain had recognized for military heroism."[109] The parish priest entered Biassou in the death register as "the renowned caudillo of the black royalists of Santo Domingo."[110]

Biassou helped launch the bloody slave revolt in Saint Domingue, and like Prince Whitten, he became well versed in the competing ideologies of monarchy and republicanism. Although born into slavery, the turbulent years he spent leading men in a desperate gamble for freedom gave him a powerful sense of his own grand destiny. That he was contemplating a constitution suggests that he briefly hoped to lead an independent state, but he also claimed leadership of the Counter-Revolution. Once Louis XVI was no more, Biassou switched his allegiance to King Carlos IV of Spain, for whom he fought in Saint Domingue and on the Florida frontier. Although his dreams of glory went largely unfulfilled, he remained a free man and a royalist to his death.

3

Maroons, Loyalist Intrigues, and Ephemeral States

The Spaniards and the Americans are the same. They will kill me if I return.

Samson, Prospect Bluff fort, April 11, 1815[1]

FRENCH-INSPIRED EFFORTS to "plant the tree of liberty" and liberate Florida from the "tyranny" of the Spanish monarchy failed, but Atlantic Creoles remained embroiled in continuing imperial contests in the hinterlands of the Lower South—a vast swath of territory stretching from the Atlantic coast of Florida westward through the lower Mississippi Valley to Texas. France, Britain, Spain, and the United States all had interests in the region, which was still home to large and diverse native populations, including Creeks, Seminoles, Choctaws, and Cherokees, to name only the largest groups.

Political instability in the region was fueled by Spain's inability to respond to the many revolutionary challenges across its far-flung empire, the failure of Napoleon Bonaparte's plan to wrest control of Saint Domingue from Toussaint, and Britain's efforts to regain its lost colonies in North America. In the resulting conflicts, European powers depended on black and indigenous allies to do much of their fighting. This dependency gave both Indians and blacks a certain leverage, but persons of African descent moved between worlds more often and more easily than did indigenous peoples. The enslaved, of necessity, became adept at "reading" political events and manipulated them, when possible, to achieve freedom. Some enlisted in European military adventures, serving competing European interests to advance their own, but they faced harsh retaliation if they chose the losing side. Others chose to remain apart, living in remote maroon settlements, but their social banditry also shaped the course of international events.

Late in the American Revolution, Southern Loyalists had offered arms, freedom, and land to slaves who would enlist in the service of King George III. Although many slave recruits died before they could collect on these promises, some survived to fight on in Georgia and finally in Loyalist East Florida's provincial militia and Rangers. Lord Dunmore hoped to use these "Ethiopian" troops to seize Spanish possessions in West Florida and Louisiana, including critical ports such as Pensacola, Mobile, Natchez, and New Orleans, but these plans went unrealized when the Loyalists were defeated. Over the following decades, diehard Loyalists would return to the region to pursue Dunmore's dream, and once again they would recruit blacks and Indians to do their fighting.[2]

At the Revolutionary War's end, approximately three hundred of Dunmore's black forces, calling themselves soldiers of the King of England, had taken refuge in the woods and swamps along the Savannah River. The inhospitable swamps

and marshes along the Apalachicola River, the bayous surrounding New Orleans, and the interior of central Florida were
also home to sizeable maroon communities.[3] Local planters felt
compelled to try to eradicate them, and they expended considerable resources to do so. In 1786 a force of South Carolina and
Georgia militias, accompanied by their old Catawba Indian allies, mounted a joint expedition to try to destroy a maroon settlement near Patton's Swamp on Bear Creek. By chance they
encountered some of the residents passing in canoes, and exchanged fire. The attackers gleefully and erroneously reported
having killed the maroon leader, Sharper. Continuing on
through the swamp, the militias eventually stumbled upon the
maroons' main camp, killed the lookout, and proceeded to attack the stockaded settlement. Six of the unlucky maroons were
killed outright, and more were assumed injured, because of the
"blankets . . . clotted with blood" they left behind. The attackers destroyed some twenty-one houses and took seven "boats"
before heading home with the women and children they had
taken prisoner. The number of houses suggests a resident population of perhaps eighty to a hundred persons, and the well-
constructed stockade and the number of boats seized indicate
that the settlement was flourishing until attacked. The next day
Sharper reappeared, as if from the dead, leading eighteen members of his community toward Indian territory. A second gun-
fight ensued, but again, Sharper and some of his followers were
able to escape. The pursuers managed to capture another nine
women and children in this exchange.[4]

Shortly thereafter, a fugitive named Sharper and his wife,
Nancy, petitioned for sanctuary in St. Augustine. That option

was obviously not Sharper's first choice, but he and Nancy were received and freed as the Whittens and others had been before them. In 1790, however, Spain bowed to U.S. pressure and agreed to shut down the southbound "underground railroad." Secretary of State Thomas Jefferson commended Spain for the policy shift, saying it was "essential to the good relations" between Spain and the United States.[5] Despite diplomatic agreements ending sanctuary, tangled disputes over slave property continued for many years. The United States sought the return of all escaped slaves who entered Florida after 1783, but the Spanish Crown offered up only those who entered after the notice ending sanctuary had been posted in 1790, and in fact not all of those.[6]

Although Sharper's Savannah River community had been broken up, others rose in its place like the proverbial many-headed Hydra, and settlers complained incessantly about alleged maroon banditry. Savannah planter John Morel's runaway slave, Titus, became notorious in the region. Morel first advertised for his return in the summer of 1785. He described Titus as "country-born . . . my waiting man, about the age of 16, of a black complexion, smooth skin, 5 feet 6 inches high, well known about Savannah."[7] Morel must have briefly recovered his slave, but in the summer of 1789 Titus, accompanied by five other men, three women, and their three children, escaped again. This time he also took with him three slaves belonging to Morel's brother, Peter. Peter Morel advertised that Patty, age nineteen, and her baby boy Adam, nine months old, and fifteen-year-old Daniel had been "enticed away from Bewlie [Plantation] by a negro fellow named Titus belonging to John Morrel, Esq. If they are not gone to Florida, it is supposed they are in the neighborhood of Kilkenney, on Great Ogeechee Neck." Morel added, "If they return home of their own accord they will be forgiven."[8]

Titus and his fellow runaways did, indeed, head for Florida, but they arrived after sanctuary had been revoked. Brian Morel followed them to St. Augustine, where he presented proof of ownership on behalf of his brothers and other planters whose slaves had accompanied Titus. After reviewing Morel's documents, Spanish officials were about to return the fugitives to slavery when they ran off again to the Savannah swamps.[9] Some seven years later James Seagrove, the United States Commissioner assigned to negotiate the exchange of escaped slaves with Florida, wrote the Spanish governor that "the notorious fellow, Titus, with some negroes from Florida, made their way along the seacoast until they got into the Savannah River and among the rice plantations where he was well acquainted. There Titus soon formed a party with some other outlaying negroes who became very troublesome to the people by plunder and as a receptacle for runaways."[10] Titus's community survived eight more years in the Savannah swamps before Georgians again sent an armed force against it, with orders to kill "all who should hesitate to surrender." The pursuers discovered and fired upon Titus's band, but most of the maroons escaped, "it being a very thick swamp." This time the Georgians found no dead, although they reported "a quantity of blood found on the ground." Seagrove added that a "negro belonging to Mr. Maxey may still be with his friend and patron, Titus, in the woods but parties are constantly after them and there is little doubt they will be taken or killed."[11] Since Titus had managed to escape at least three times before, Seagrove's confidence seems unfounded.

In his correspondence Seagrove alluded to a "diabolical plan" to involve Spain and the United States in a "contest" and claimed that the "British are still tampering with the restless and worthless part of our country."[12] The U.S. felt threatened by the "restless and worthless" Lower South largely because its multiracial population was still independent. They associated the ongoing maroon "problem" and Indian unrest with political intrigue on the part of the British, and in some cases this was accurate. Although Commissioner Seagrove described Titus's followers as "negroes," in the triracial Southeast fugitive blacks and Indians had a long history of collaboration, despite constant efforts by Anglo colonists to prevent this.[13] In the chaos of the American Revolution and the major population movements it triggered, however, it is not surprising that blacks and Indians formed new maroon settlements together. Some of the amalgamated communities also included whites who had found themselves "outlawed" during the Atlantic revolutions.

The supporters of William Augustus Bowles are a case in point. For almost twenty years this former Loyalist and self-titled Director General of the "State of Muskogee" maneuvered to achieve an independent Indian nation in the Southeast; he negotiated with government officials in the Bahamas, Nova Scotia, Quebec, London, Spain, Sierra Leone, and the United States to try to attain this goal. The quixotic Bowles is often dismissed because of his grandiose schemes, which at one time included plans for the invasion and liberation of Mexico and Peru. But our interest is in the following that Bowles attracted: he gathered support not only from the Creek, Cherokee, and Seminole nations, but from whites and blacks as well. Many contemporary observers, and indeed many later historians, saw Bowles as a self-interested scoundrel, a "king of Liars," but he maintained support among his black and Indian allies for close to two decades, and he must have spoken to their dreams or represented their perceived best hope for a free life in the face of certain Anglo domination of the Southeast.[14]

During the American Revolution Bowles had served with the British forces posted to Pensacola in West Florida, but a youthful misdeed cost him his career. Dismissed from the British navy, he refashioned himself as a frontiersman and became closely associated with some of the most important Indian leaders of the area. He married women from the Cherokee and Creek nations, but was most closely allied with the latter through his father-in-law, Chief William Perryman. From the 1780s onward, Bowles used those family connections, and the backing of British governmental and commercial agents, to agitate against Spanish and U.S. interests in the Southeast.

In 1790 Bowles led a delegation of Creek and Cherokee Indians to Halifax, Quebec, and on to London, where they asked for official recognition of an independent "United Nations of Creeks and Cherokees." The Venezuelan independence leader Francisco Miranda was then in London asking for similar recognition, but whether the two adventurers met is unknown. Neither man received much more than hospitality from London, although Bowles did get permission for vessels of the new "nation" to freely enter British ports. When Bowles traveled to New Orleans to ask the same recognition of the Spaniards,

Governor Carondelet promptly arrested him and shipped him off to jail in Havana. From Havana he was later shipped to Madrid, and from Madrid to Manila. As he was being returned to Madrid, Bowles escaped in Sierra Leone and convinced the British governor of that colony to help him get to England. Before long he found his way back to Florida, where he doggedly renewed his efforts to establish a sovereign Indian state.[15]

By 1800 Bowles had created the State of Muskogee headquartered in Mikasuki, a Seminole village near modern-day Tallahassee. Styling himself "Director," Bowles designed a state flag and a constitution and raised an army of ambitious and land-hungry Anglos, southeastern Indians (primarily Creeks and Seminoles), and blacks—both fugitive slaves from St. Augustine and Pensacola and slaves of the Seminoles. With a small navy he transported men and goods between New Providence, in the Bahamas, and throughout the river networks of West Florida. Bowles also established his own Admiralty Court to judge the prizes his boats captured and thereby helped finance his state. Bowles's Loyalist supporters in the Bahamas included William McGirtt (who became "Commissary of Marine," "Judge of the Court of Admiralty," and "Minister of State") and William "Bloody Bill" Cunningham. Both men had burned their way through much of St. John's, Berkeley Parish during the American Revolution before relocating to the Bahamas. Another supporter was Lord Dunmore, who had become governor of the Bahamas. These men had all employed former slaves in their military efforts to quash American independence, and they saw Bowles and his black and Indian allies as a way to retake the lost Loyalist strongholds of the South, or at least to break Spain's commercial monopoly in the region. It was probably at this time that Bowles began to incorporate more Africans and their descendants into his nascent state. The Spanish offer of sanctuary was off the table after 1790, so fugitive slaves could either become maroons or hope to be accepted into an indigenous nation. Given Bowles's connections with Britain, his navy, and the initial access he had to arms and supplies from the Bahamas, his new state might have seemed the most viable option left to blacks seeking freedom. For the next three years Bowles's multiracial guerrilla army ranged back and forth across East and West Florida and northward into Georgia, raiding plantations for slaves, cattle, horses, and other goods.[16]

The Spaniards reacted quickly to Bowles's pretensions to sovereignty by attacking Achackwheethle, one of his towns in West Florida, and burning it to the ground. Although Bowles escaped, the Spaniards captured one of his wives, a black woman from the Bahamas, as well as his Scottish secretary and French aide-de-camp, both carrying commissions as captains in the British service.[17] In response, on April 5, 1800, Bowles issued a formal declaration of war against Spain, charging "his Catholic Majesty" with evil intentions against their "Nation" and "Citizens" and closing with "God Save Muskogee."[18] Bowles next seized the Spanish fort of San Marcos de Apalachee near present-day Tallahassee, and held it for five weeks before Spanish forces managed to retake it. Newspaper reports of that event referred to Bowles as "the English adventurer and notorious vagabond" and said that "the Spaniards are in hopes of putting out of the world that common enemy of peace [Bowles] by the offer of great presents to the Indians, who shall deliver him, dead or alive, at Pensacola or St. Augustine."[19]

U.S. Commissioner James Seagrove warned the prominent East Florida planter, magistrate, and militia captain John McQueen, "There are several dreadful vagabonds with parties of Indians and Negroes now (following) Bowles for plunder and if opposed no doubt murder. Robert Allen, that noted young villain with three of the free Negroes from Lotchoway [the Seminole heartland in central Florida] made their appearance near Colerain [Georgia] on Saturday last. Allen and two of his Negroes were taken and (were) under the care of the federal officials from that place, but from (thence) Allen made his escape into Florida where is his party of from twenty-five to thirty Indians, Negroes and infamous whites all of them direct from Bowles headquarters . . . with orders to plunder and break up all the settlements in Florida."[20]

Ever the master propagandist, Bowles sent a document to the *Nassau Gazette* in which he reported that "a great number of discharged British Soldiers and Seamen" were "daily flocking to his Standard" and that

the Muskogee Army has marched to plunder, pillage & lay waste Augustine, from whence they have already brought a number of Prime Slaves & some considerable share of very valuable property, & will entirely lay waste & ravage that Country ere they withdraw from thence nor can Spain send any Troops to act against them unless she wishes to sacrifice them which would be the case with any Troops who would enter their Country as they must bush fight it with them, which no Troops are equal to the doing with success.[21]

The only troops apparently "equal to the doing" of a bush fight were Spanish St. Augustine's free black militiamen. Andrew Atkinson, who had commanded Prince Whitten and fifty other free blacks during the Jacobin invasion of Florida in 1795, warned that calling out the free black militia was "the only thing that presents itself to me that could be done to save us all from ruin."[22]

In the summer of 1800, Bowles's Mikasuki allies launched a series of attacks near St. Augustine. In a dawn raid that June, they attacked the homestead of the Congo militia sergeant Felipe Edimboro, stealing his slave, Jack, who was already at work in the fields. Edimboro witnessed the theft and quickly loaded his family and that of his free black neighbor, Juan Moore, into a canoe to take them to the safety of don Francis Fatio's large plantation upriver. The Mikasuki raiders later captured the wife and seven children of the free black militiaman Tony. Fatio's armed slaves subsequently found and rescued Edimboro's slave Jack, who had escaped from his captors, and Edimboro found and assisted Tony's eldest son, who had also managed an escape.[23] The *Pennsylvania Gazette* reported that the Mikasuki "killed a man at work in his field, scalped him, partly burnt him, and mangled him in a horrid manner" and that within two hours, "the black General and his company went in pursuit of the savages."[24]

The black General was Jorge Biassou. Having fought for

years against French troops and finally for Spain against their former ally Toussaint in Saint Domingue, Biassou and the former auxiliaries of King Carlos IV in Santo Domingo were now fighting a new kind of enemy. Prince Whitten and his fellow fugitives from Carolina and Georgia reported for service as they had in 1795, but this time it was under Biassou's command. Biassou's polyglot forces patrolled the Indian hinterland surrounding St. Augustine and performed guard duty at small outlying forts. While twenty-two free black militiamen helped garrison the northern and western frontiers, General Biassou and the rest of St. Augustine's free black troops guarded the southern frontier near the Matanzas River. Biassou had orders to prevent all Indians from entering the city except those, like the Seminoles, who were friendly and who brought hogs and cattle to sell. His war orders stated that he was to treat the Indians with "humanity and kindness" and to use force only when required, but in other matters to employ his own judgment.[25]

While relying on his black militia for frontier defense, Governor Enrique White worked to maintain good relations with the Seminole villages nearest St. Augustine. He met with Seminole Chiefs Pain [sic], Cholockochuly, and Opia to offer friendship and trade and warned them "not to adhere to the tasks of that bad man, Bowles." White asked the Seminoles' help in securing the return of stolen slaves and "a family of free negroes" unless the free family wished to remain among the Seminoles. He also asked them to locate and deliver the black raider suspected as the murderer of the unlucky farmer in his field.[26]

The following month a large number of Mikasukis led by one of Bowles's white followers named Kenney crossed the St.

Johns River in pettiaugers and stole forty-four slaves from the plantation of Francis Fatio. Fatio's son attempted to retrieve the slaves from Bowles, only to be insulted and have his horses taken from him. All the planters along the St. Johns feared they would be hit next. Captain John McQueen wrote the governor that "nothing would quiet their minds so effectively as you establishing a post of free negroes (if regular troops cannot be spared). The American deserters well armed would help us much and all those that I have conversed with seem willing to unite for the defense of the country."[27] The back militia, however, were too few to monitor Florida's expansive Indian frontier, and the Mikasuki raids continued.

In December Bowles's raiders plundered a new settlement at Matanzas, sixty miles south of St. Augustine, sending the homesteaders fleeing for their lives. The violence escalated in January of 1802 when Bowles's Mikasuki raiders abducted a white woman and her five young children from the Dupont plantation near Matanzas, killing the oldest boy and stealing ten slaves. First Sergeant Jorge Jacobo had assumed command of the black militia following the sudden illness and death of his brother-in-law, General Jorge Biassou, in the summer of 1801. After the attack on the Dupont plantation, Jacobo asked for a promotion to the rank of lieutenant and for the full salary he had received in Saint Domingue—equal to that of a sergeant first class in the royal army. Adopting the petitionary tradition of Biassou, he argued that his pay was only equal to that given the most infirm soldier in his command and that he should be remunerated "in accordance with his class, and the charge and responsibility he exercised in command of his troops." Jacobo reminded the governor that in all previous expeditions out of St. Augustine he had been paid the salary of a sergeant, but since there is no record of the response and since Jacobo had declared himself disappointed but "nonetheless . . . willing and ready to serve his king and country," there is a strong probability that he had to settle for the 2 reales and a ration a day.[28] Meanwhile, the governor appealed to the Captain-General of Cuba for more regular troops, but these were not forthcoming.[29]

Jacobo's disappointment was serious enough that Spanish officials began to report his negative attitude. They noted with approval, on the other hand, Prince Whitten's superior behavior. Whitten had directed the construction of a new strong house at Buena Vista and another at San Nicolás, and in June he led the black militia in two expeditions against the Mikasukis. That August, Whitten's unit also rescued Spanish dragoons trapped by the Indians. The Mikasukis proved an elusive enemy who left behind deserted villages as they melted into the surrounding swamps, but when encountered, they were fierce fighters. Tomas Herrera, an escaped slave from Carolina, was badly wounded and had to be hospitalized after one fight. Another black militiaman named Sparkman was granted permission to return home to St. Augustine to care for his mother after the Mikasukis killed his father, Old Sparkman, probably for reporting their movements.[30]

British officials in the Bahamas had by this time begun to reconsider their support of the State of Muskogee, and Judge Kelsall of the Vice-Admiralty Court in Nassau denounced Bowles as a pirate and his state as a "Mockery of European Forms perverted to the worst of purposes."[31] The United States government also wanted to be rid of Bowles, who blocked their acquisition of Indian lands, and Secretary of War Henry Dearborn ordered Indian Commissioner Benjamin Hawkins to make every effort to apprehend Bowles without compromising the peace.[32] Some Creek and Seminole leaders had also had enough of the violence and responded to Spanish peace overtures. John Kinnard, the mixed-race "King" of the Creeks, wrote Governor White:

> Dear Sir, I take your talks and think them good we don't wish any disturbance with us and you we want the path kepe open that frids may pass and repass to se each other we don't want any war at all it is the mackasukey people that is at war we have nothing to do with them nor the Spanyards the floridy people kild one ingan and tha went and kild one white man for it and says tha are don tha are all gon hunting and wants nomore of it all says tha are your frinds I am Dear Sir yours[33]

The Creeks and Seminoles finally signed a peace treaty with Spain in August 1802 by which they agreed not to give Bowles any further aid, not to trade with foreigners, and to return all stolen slaves and livestock.[34] The following May, at an Indian congress in present-day Alabama, Bowles told the assembled Cherokees, Chickasaws, Choctaws, and Creeks that "he came from a Great Prince, King George, to preserve all the red people from having their lands taken from them as the Americans & Spaniards intended to do." He added that he expected to be named "king of the Four Nations." This time his words fell on deaf ears. Tired of the three-year war, his former Creek allies seized Bowles and turned him over to the Spaniards, receiving a reward for their troubles. Once again, the Spaniards shipped Bowles to Havana, and this time was the last. He died in the Morro Castle in 1805.[35] His unnamed black followers melted back into the hinterlands, dropping out of historical view for some time, but surviving.

The death of one man, and the demise of his chimerical State of Muskogee, however, did not signal the end of slave resistance in the Lower South. The United States had already acquired Louisiana by purchase in 1803.[36] Then, in 1810, American settlers seized the Spanish fort at Baton Rouge (in what was then West Florida); this led President James Madison to annex that district, claiming it was part of the Louisiana Purchase.[37] U.S. expansionists next focused on East Florida.[38] As British troops besieged the U.S. capital in 1812, Georgian "Patriots" led by former governor George Mathews seized Amelia Island and declared the "Republic of Florida."[39]

The Georgians planned to deliver East Florida to the United States, as their compatriots had done with Baton Rouge. The operation was secretly sanctioned by President James Madison and his advisers, Secretary of State James Monroe and former president Thomas Jefferson. The Patriots had regaled their leaders with wild charges about imported black troops from Cuba, Jamaica, the Bahamas, and other West Indian sites and drew frequently on the powerful image of the horror of Saint Domingue's race war. Angered by Spain's use of free black troops, the Patriots promised no quarter would be given to any black captured under arms. In a direct allusion to the ferocious slave revolt in Saint Domingue, Patriot leader John McIntosh wrote U.S. Secretary of State James Monroe, "Our slaves are excited to rebel, and we have an army of negroes raked up in this country, and brought from Cuba to be contended with . . . the whole province (Florida) will be the refuge of fugitive slaves; and from thence emissaries . . . will be detached to bring about the revolt of the slave population of the United States." Georgia's governor David Mitchell echoed these sentiments when he warned, "They have armed every able-bodied negro within their power . . . our southern country will soon be in a state of insurrection."[40] Patriot Colonel Lodowick Ashley declared the death penalty for any "who are by vile and infamous deeds arming the barbaric Negro."[41]

One of the embittered Patriots complained that although Spain had officially abrogated its sanctuary policy in 1790, Florida's military commanders continued to admit runaway slaves from Georgia and incorporate them into their forces. He reported that black scouts ranged between the St. Marys and St. Johns Rivers and that "the Negroes Publicly say they will rule the Countrey."[42]

Spanish Florida's new governor, Sebastián Kindelán, poorly supplied and supported, tried frantically to pursue a diplomatic resolution to this new Patriot threat. He maintained Spanish neutrality by keeping his regular forces in St. Augustine, but he deployed black militiamen and Seminole allies to harry the Patriot forces. The Seminole nation was already wary of the Georgians, and the black troops posted among them helped fan their distrust. Cuba's Captain General sent several companies of Pardo and Moreno Militias from Havana to help defend

Florida against the "Patriots." A number of these black militiamen from Cuba, Louisiana, and Florida had already served together in the Gulf Coast campaigns of the American Revolution and against the British in the Bahamas.[43]

Now, on this one Atlantic frontier, men who had fought in
the American Revolution, the Saint Domingue slave revolt,
spin-offs of the French Revolution, the Indian Wars, and Cuban slave uprisings were joined in one polyglot unit. All were
experienced soldiers, but they were also described as "artisans
and field hands." Among the group were several carpenters,
a butcher, bakers, masons, hostlers, and several skilled guides
and navigators.[44] Despite their humble occupations, a number
now wore medals bearing the likeness of the Spanish monarch,
which had been bestowed with pomp and ceremony in Spanish
plazas across the Atlantic.

In addition to their shared service, a number of family and
extended kin relations now united the culturally diverse black
troops. Sergeant Felipe Edimboro led the free black militia
posted among the Seminoles, and his troops now included his
son and his son-in-law and interpreter, Corporal Second Class
Benjamín Wiggins. Wiggins, the son of English planter Job
Wiggins and his free Senegalese wife, Ana Gallum, grew up
among Seminoles who used his father's ferry to cross the St.
Johns River into Spanish territory. As a result, he was at home
in the English, Senegalese, Spanish, and Seminole cultures.[45]
Jorge Jacobo's captains were his "Gambian"-born father-in-
law, Prince Whitten, and Benjamín Seguí, his mulatto compatriot from Saint Domingue, who was also his daughter's godfather.[46]

During the summer of 1812, as the Patriots seized Amelia Island and occupied plantations and forts on Florida's northern border, the governor ordered all subjects living in the countryside to come into town. Free black militiamen went out on patrols to scout the enemy and herd cattle back to St. Augustine to feed the hungry townspeople. The free mulatto militiaman Juan Antonio Florencio later testified that under the command of Sergeant Prince Whilton [*sic*] and Tony Doctor, the men gathered in forty to sixty head of cattle at a time.[47]

In recognition of their critical service, in September 1812 Governor Kindelán nominated the leaders of the Florida black militia for promotion. (Kindelán had once written, "The negro does not have the valor of the white and it is necessary to treat them harshly and direct them to avoid danger.")[48] Jorge Jacobo was promoted to captain, Prince Whitten to lieutenant, and Benjamín Seguí to second lieutenant. The men's pay was also adjusted, bringing it into line with that of Cuba's black militia. Kindelán issued Captain Jacobo war orders that granted him wide latitude, but in an oblique reference to Saint Domingue the orders enjoined Jacobo not to be "excessively sanguinary" or to exceed the limits of "civilized" nations. These cautions were like those issued earlier to Biassou and suggest that Spanish officials still feared the power of their black troops from Saint Domingue. Despite the lingering distrust, the governor's formulaic nominations and the promotions of Jacobo and his lieutenants required the men of the company, as well as the rest of the officers and soldiers of the Plaza, to recognize and respect these men in their new positions and grant them all "honors, favors, exemptions, and preeminences due them."[49] These distinctions may have encouraged recruitment: by January 1813, Jacobo's militia numbered eighty-seven men, including three sergeants and twelve corporals. One corporal (who later rose to sergeant second-class), León Duvigneau, a literate store owner and baker originally from San Marcos, Saint Domingue, declined any pay for his militia service, preferring to make it a "donation in favor of the mother country." Even when other options were present, the black auxiliaries still allied themselves with Spain.[50]

Although Jacobo, Whitten, and Seguí now shared command, claimants later filing damage suits against the United States government usually refer to Florida's black militia as "Prince's Black Company."[51] This may be because Prince had the starring role in the most dramatic event of the war. The turning point of the Patriot siege came in September of 1812, when the newly promoted Lieutenant Prince Whitten led a band of twenty-five black militiamen, thirty-two of Chief Payne's blacks, and a handful of Seminoles in a well-executed ambush of twenty United States Marines and approximately sixty to seventy Georgia Patriots escorting a supply convoy through Twelve Mile Swamp at night. Whitten's forces took down U.S. Marine Captain John Williams, his sergeant, and the wagon horses in the first volley. For the next two hours Spain's black and Indian troops battled the more numerous Patriot forces, killing many but suffering several casualties as well. That night Whitten's men destroyed one wagon and the next morning used the second to transport their wounded back to St. Augustine. This action lifted the Patriot siege and allowed badly needed supplies to reach St. Augustine.[52] The Patriot accounts (and, therefore, most historical treatments based on the English-language sources) reported that the ambush at Twelve Mile Swamp was the work of the Indians, but Governor Kindelán wrote that the "Indians" were actually "our parties of blacks, whom they [the rebels] think are Indians because they wear the same clothing and go painted."[53]

With their supplies exhausted, the demoralized Patriot and United States forces began to pull back. When later that month a force led by Georgia volunteer Colonel Daniel Newnan failed to break up the Seminole towns near La Chua and was mauled by Chief Payne's polyglot warriors, the invasion was spent. Disease, the ferocity of the black and Indian militias, and weakening U.S. enthusiasm for the land grab when war with England raged, eventually ruined the Patriots. In May 1813 all foreign forces were withdrawn from East Florida and the "Florida Republic" collapsed, as had Bowles's State of Muskogee.[54]

The free black militiamen paid dearly for their allegiance to Spain. The Georgian "Patriots," who were determined to expand the territorial boundaries of the United States and with it the chattel form of slavery, had railed against Spain's use of black troops, and by extension, its more liberal race relations. The fact that the Spanish government granted free blacks land and that former slaves were now property owners as well as soldiers challenged all their notions of the proper social order. As if to erase the evidence, they deliberately targeted free blacks' homesteads, burning many to the ground. While leading an expedition against the Patriots, Prince Whitten rode up to find his once flourishing homestead a smoldering ruin.[55] It must have been a devastating blow, but he and his family had lived through even more vicious times during the American Revolution.

A Congressional Act passed on June 26, 1834, enabled individuals who had suffered in the Patriot invasion to file suit against the U.S. government for recovery of losses and damages. Although Prince Whitten was by then living in Cuba, he filed a claim through an executor in Florida. A number of witnesses came forward to support Whitten's claim, and many believed him always to have been a free man. Through his distinguished military service, his leadership of men, and his behavior, Whitten had, in effect, erased the "stigma" of slavery. John Leonardy, from whom Whitten leased farmland, testified in support of his claim:

I knew Prince Whilton [*sic*] deceased in his life-time—he lived in 1812 about 14 miles from St. Augustine. He left Florida at the Session & change of Flags in 1821, do not know when he died—he was a free Black man—He had lived at Sweet Water Branch about 6 or 7 years before the Revolution of 1812—at the commencement of the Patriot War in 1812 he was living there & had a small dwelling home about 20 or 25 feet long by 14 or 15 feet wide—built of sawed lumber—also a kitchen & corn house of logs—his building altogether was worth [close] to 800 dollars—He had about 10 or 11 acres of land which was cleared cultivated and well-fenced in which he [planted] corn potatoes & pease—the land on which he lived belonged to me I own it yet—I had at the same time a small plantation

about a mile from where he lived, on which I resided at
the commencement of the Patriot War of 1812. He had
planted his crops that year before the invasion of the
country, consisting of corn, peas, potatoes & such vegetables as we usually raised. He had almost ten acres of corn.
When the American & Patriots troops first came into the
country that year we were all ordered by the Governor to
come into St. Augustine & take arms for the defence of
the country. We all did quit our plantations accordingly
& came into the city & Prince Whilton [*sic*] came in &
brought his family with the boat. Prince was immediately
put in the military service by Gov Kindelan, he was made
Lieut of a Black or colored company of troops at first &
afterward commanded that company & served during the
whole of the Patriots War. His place was entirely abandoned when he came to town. Within a few days after
he abandoned his place the enemy (American & Patriot
troops) came into the country & overran all that part of
the province.

I did not go out to Sweet Water Branch during the time
the enemy was in the country but soon after the last troops
left the country I went out there & found that Prince's
place was all destroyed, the buildings & fences were all
burned. I cannot say who destroyed but I suppose it must
have been the invading troops, as there was no other person to do it. They had possession of all the country—He
could not have gone out there with safety at anytime after
the invasion of the country & before the U.S. troops left
the country. When Prince left his place to come into the

city he had then at his place 4 or 5 head of milch cows, also five or six horses . . . he and his family came to town in a canoe or boat down the North River—his home was about ½ a mile from the River—I came in the same day that he did, & I am sure that he brought none of his cows or horses with him—The call from the Governor was a sudden one & we had no time to pick up anything—we came off directly.

Prince left behind him his corn mill & plantation tools & c. might have been worth almost 200 p [pesos] He had two timber carts which were worth $150. He was in the habit of getting out cedar and ranging timber & had considerable at the landing at the time he quit. He had three or four hundred feet of ranging timber at the landing & about 5000 or 6000 feet of cedar—ranging timber was worth about two bits per foot & the cedar was worth then at the landing—about three bits a foot. I do not remember whether he had any other lumber on hand—This lumber was burnt—I saw pieces of it afterwards at the landing when I went there. . . . He had on hand sawed lumber at the time he abandoned his place. I expect about 5000 or 6000 feet worth about $25 per—He had a canoe which he left there worth about 30 dollars—he did not come down to town in his own canoe—he came with the pilots in their boats—The Governor sent them for us. He brought nothing at all with him except his family—they all came with him—He had a grindstone—a whip saw & a crop cut saw. The horses were worth from $40 to $50 each. The cows about $16. The fences around his place were rail fences,—

worth about $200. I cannot say whether the American Patriot troops were in that place because I did not see them there, but I expect they must have been there because they had a station about five miles from there & were constantly traveling the road by there—all communication between the city & Prince's place was cut off—& there was no communication with that section of the country either by land or water—The invading forces kept an armed force around the city & the Spanish government kept an armed schooner at the points to prevent all intrusions by water. Prince's crop of corn in 1812 would have been from 14 to 15 bushels of corn to the acre—potatoes were then worth a dollar a bushel & I expect he would have gathered 100 bushels. He did not plant there in 1813, it was too late before the enemy left the country.

(Signed) John X his mark Leonardy

Taken before me

this 25th day of Febry 1845

signed

J. H. Bronson, Judge & Comm[56]

Although Spain's black guerrillas and their Seminole allies undid the half-hearted Patriot Rebellion, the United States remained firmly committed to an expansionist foreign policy in the Southeast. Its interventions were motivated by territorial ambition, as well as by the fear that Britain would displace the weakened Spanish regimes in the Southeast. The Captain General of Cuba and the Floridas sent a flurry of top-secret letters to Spain's Minister of War, begging for troops and arms and money to repair the decaying fortifications for which he was responsible. He warned repeatedly of the hostile intentions of the United States in the Lower South and also wrote that "the large number of slaves in the island of Cuba, its proximity to Santo Domingo, and the fear of aggression by the blacks of that island" were reason enough to hold the region. He added, "Although its ports are small, they are on the Gulf of Mexico and . . . the sale of New Orleans to the United States opens the way for their ambitions to occupy territories bordering New Spain."[57] Britain, in turn, argued that it needed to intervene in the region precisely because the Spanish government could no longer guarantee the sovereignty of the Indian nations against U.S. aggression. Racial politics were also at play. The very success of the Spanish/Indian/black alliance, in effect, ensured further intervention by Americans who could not tolerate such dangerous collaboration on their frontier. The War of 1812 and the simultaneous Creek War of 1813–1814 evolved into a long-term effort by the U.S. government to end British influence in the region, push the Creeks, Seminoles, and blacks out of their settlements in western and central Florida, and eventually to drive out the Spaniards as well.[58]

During the War of 1812, as during the American Revolution, the British borrowed Spanish strategies and deliberately encouraged slaves of the enemy to desert plantations, enlist in royal military service, and be emancipated. The British also promised that after the war's end black recruits would receive land. In April 1814 the British Vice Admiral Alexander Cochrane had issued a proclamation from Bermuda offering to relocate black troops from the Lower South to British possessions, as had been done for some of the Black Loyalists. Enslaved blacks across the lower South responded enthusiastically. Vice Admiral George Cockburn commanded a flotilla of gunboats that sailed southward from the Chesapeake, picking up slave runaways all along the Atlantic coast and barrier islands. Broadsides announcing Cochrane's Proclamation had been posted on Amelia Island in May 1814, and when Cockburn reached Cumberland Island, Georgia, only a short distance from Spanish Florida, Spanish owners also began to lose slaves to the gunboats. The Spanish subject Zephaniah Kingsley, who had a large plantation on Fort George Island, Florida, later wrote, "Who was so unlucky as to see, on Cumberland Island, last war, the magical transformation of his own negroes, whom he left in the field but a few hours before, into regular soldiers, of good discipline and appearance."[59] Despite heated complaints from Florida's governor, Sebastián Kindelán, Cockburn refused to return the runaways, "since British law did not recognize slavery." Denying that slaves were property, Cockburn quoted Blackstone: "The Spirit of Liberty is so deeply implanted in our very Soil that a *Slave or Negro* the Moment he lands in England, falls under the protection of the Laws and so far becomes a *Freeman*."[60] Governor Kindelán wrote his Captain General in Cuba that the slaves had been induced to flee "by the seductive and licentious promise of liberty."[61]

Meanwhile, slaves from Spanish Pensacola were also fleeing toward a British refuge in West Florida. When the Treaty of Ghent ended the War of 1812, British forces prepared to evacuate the Lower South, but before leaving, Colonel Edward Nicolls and his aide, Captain George Woodbine, established a large number of black allies—runaways from Pensacola, Mobile, St. Augustine, and Georgia—as well as beleaguered Red Stick Indian allies, at a small but well-armed fort at Prospect Bluff, on the Apalachicola River. The so-called "Negro Fort" lay within Spanish territory about twenty-five miles north of the Gulf of Mexico. Nicolls and Woodbine gave the escaped slaves red uniforms and arms, drilled them, and formed the men into three companies of Negro Colonial Marines. By the summer of 1815 an estimated force of 1,100 warriors, including several hundred blacks, garrisoned the fort at Prospect Bluff, behind which planted corn fields were said to stretch along the river for more than forty-five miles.[62]

Like William Augustus Bowles before him, Nicolls was a self-appointed British agent to the Creek Nation; he directed fiery letters of remonstrance to the U.S. Indian agent, Benjamin Hawkins, for attacks he said Americans had committed against Creek and Seminole towns. Nicolls charged that Americans attacked Chief Bowlegs' town at La Chua on two separate occasions in March and May of 1815, killing warriors and stealing cattle. Likening Nicolls to Bowles, "that Prince of Liars," Hawkins responded that the Seminoles could appeal for redress to either legitimate Spanish or American officials, but that Nicolls had no authority to speak for the Indians.[63] The charges that Americans (more specifically, Georgians) had burned Seminole villages, stolen cattle, and killed Indians in the process were repeated often by Nicolls, who received some of his information from the Bahamian merchant and Indian trader, Alexander Arbuthnot.[64]

Economic and political interests overlapped in this conflict, as they had in the Bowles years. Forbes & Company, the powerful trading company that had succeeded Panton, Leslie & Company in the Lower South, lost a number of valuable slaves to the "Negro Fort." The runaways not only escaped, they also absconded with valuable supplies, large numbers of cattle and horses, a number of small boats and piraguas, and one large sailboat.[65] The company's agent, Edmund Doyle, believed that the English sponsors of the fort were motivated solely by self-interest, and not by any abolitionist sentiment. He charged that Woodbine seduced away "not more than ten" slaves belonging to the Americans, whose retaliation he feared, but that instead with the "help of their [Nicolls' and Woodbine's] agents and black spies, corrupted the negroes of their friends and Spanish allies."[66] In fact, Nicolls had told black recruits that both the Spaniards and the Americans sought to re-enslave them, and the runaways considered both the enemy.[67]

As commander of the Southern Military Division of the United States, General Andrew Jackson was responsible for protecting Georgian settlers who were pushing westward into Indian territory. For this purpose, he ordered the construction of Fort Scott at the juncture of the Flint and Chattahoochee Rivers, but supply vessels from New Orleans had to pass by the Negro Fort at Prospect Bluff to reach the new fort and settlements. Jackson demanded the "immediate and prompt interference of the Spanish authority to destroy or remove from our frontier this banditti."[68]

Pensacola's new governor, Mauricio de Zúñiga, was in no position to send any troops against the fort, although the Spanish also would have liked to be rid of it. Spanish slaveowners, like the Americans, feared they would continue to lose slaves to Prospect Bluff, and Spanish officials worried that the maroon settlement would become another den of pirates like Galveston, Texas, or Barataria, Louisiana, and would further destabilize the Gulf of Mexico.[69] They also considered the possibility that British aid and protection might encourage slaves from Cuba to escape to similar settlements near Tampa Bay.[70]

The Spaniards demanded that the British themselves destroy the fort, but that would have required lengthy discussions and consent by both governments. In an attempt to resolve the matter locally and more quickly, the Spanish and the British each appointed a commissioner to investigate matters at Prospect Bluff. Captain Vicente Sebastián Pintado represented Spain, and his British counterpart was Captain Robert Spencer. Pintado compiled lists of the missing slaves and the names of their owners in St. Augustine and Pensacola. Pintado's lists detail the age, racial descriptions (black or mulatto), family status, occupations, and estimated values of the runaways, and in some cases the circumstances by which they arrived at Prospect Bluff. The surgeon Don Eugenio Sierra, who was also an agent of Forbes & Company, accompanied Pintado to help identify the runaways. Forbes & Company runaways included Harry, a shipwright, caulker, and navigator, who knew how to read and write and was valued at 2000 pesos; Abraham, a master carpenter valued at 1000 pesos; and Ambrosio, a shoemaker valued at 900 pesos. Garçon, the man identified later as the commander at the Prospect Bluff fort, was a carpenter valued at 700 pesos by his former owner, Don Antonio Montero, who also lost four other men and three women. Others on Pintado's list were sailors, master carpenters, bakers, servants, laundresses, cooks, sawyers, masons, cartwrights, and field hands.[71] Assuming this group is representative, which is likely, the blacks who lived at this settlement were certainly equipped to be self-sufficient. While they may not have been "black Robin Hoods," as one historian called them, neither were they the parasitic "villains" described by the Americans.[72]

Throughout the spring of 1815, slaves continued to flock to the British standard in such numbers that supplies were running short and officials feared the "inconvenience" of "an accumulation of them at Bermuda."[73] Captain Spencer therefore had to rescind Admiral Cochrane's offer to relocate all who would serve the British. He told the assembled crowds of runaways at Prospect Bluff that new orders prevented him from transporting them as promised and warned them (correctly) that after the British departed, they would be preyed upon by the Americans and their Indian allies. In Pintado's presence, Spencer disarmed the Negro Colonial Marines, paid them for their service, and gave each discharge papers. Pintado protested that the discharge papers were, in effect, manumissions, since only free men served in royal armies, and that anyone carrying such papers would be taken for free wherever they went. That is, no doubt, what Spencer intended. Although forced to renege on the earlier promises of sanctuary, the British officer would not allow the Apalachicola runaways to be forcibly returned to slavery. Following the same policy enacted by Admiral Cockburn at Cumberland Island, Spencer only permitted Pintado to interview the runaways to see if any would choose to go with him of their own free will. Of the 128 runaways Pintado was able to interview, only 28 individuals agreed to return to their former owners, and overnight several of those ran away or changed their minds.[74] One of Nicolls's Colonial Marines named Samson proclaimed on being interviewed that the Spaniards and the Americans were the same, and that they would kill him if he returned. In the end, Pintado was only able to persuade ten women with small children to return voluntarily to slavery. He estimated the total number of runaways left at the fort at about 250, and reported that many of the former occupants were leaving for the black Seminole settlements at Tampa Bay.[75]

Convinced that the Spaniards were unable to deal with the "banditti," General Jackson had already ordered General Edmund Pendleton Gaines to destroy the Negro Fort which was "stealing and enticing away our negroes," and which had "been established by some villain for the purpose of murder, rapine, and plunder." Gaines charged Lieutenant Colonel Duncan L. Clinch with the job, and Clinch was reinforced by the Coweta Creeks, led by Chief William McIntosh, the wealthy mixed-race son of a Scots Indian agent. Two gunboats of the United States Navy sailed upriver to join in the attack on the Negro Fort, and on July 17, 1816, Garçon and his men engaged five of the Navy men, killing three and capturing a fourth, whom they later tarred and burned to death. A fifth man escaped to report the event. Garçon informed a Creek delegation sent by the Americans that "he had been left in command of the fort by the British government and that he would sink any American vessels that should attempt to pass it." He also stated (prophetically, as it turns out) that he would blow up the fort rather than surrender. Thanks to the British, Garçon and the Choctaw chief who jointly commanded the fort had at their disposal ten cannon, several thousand muskets and sidearms, ammunition, and military stores that might have sustained a costly siege.[76]

When the battle began on July 27, 1816, the blacks in the fort hoisted the Union Jack and under it a red flag. The defenders hurled insults as well as cannon shots at the Americans and attempted several sorties against McIntosh's warriors, but they were repeatedly driven back into the fort. One of the attacking officers noted with admiration the "spirited opposition" of the blacks.[77] Their red flag made it clear that they would neither ask for nor give quarter, and that they were prepared to fight to the death. Indeed, that was their fate, for a "miraculous" American shot hit the fort's powder magazine and blew it up. The blast allegedly shook Pensacola, sixty miles to the south.[78] Only forty individuals survived the explosion, and few of those lived long. Colonel Clinch wrote, "The explosion was horrible, and the scene beyond description . . . the war yells of the Indians, the cries and lamentations of the wounded, compelled the soldier to pause in the victory to drop a tear for the suffering of his fellow beings." Clinch went on to ascribe the U.S. victory to divine providence and stated that the Americans had been "his instruments in chastising the blood-thirsty and murderous wretches that defended the fort." The Americans, nonetheless, handed Garçon and the Choctaw chief over to their Coweta mercenaries, who promptly executed them.[79]

As Pintado correctly reported, during the summer months of 1815 a number of maroons who had been living at Prospect Bluff had stolen away to find refuge among the Seminole Indian villages in Central Florida and near Tampa Bay. This alliance allowed the fugitives from Prospect Bluff to live to fight another day, but it also guaranteed implacable aggression by the U.S. government, which would eventually control Florida.

That eventuality was hastened by the rapid disintegration of Spain's American empire. The crisis of legitimacy provoked in Spain by the Napoleonic invasion and the abdications of Kings Carlos IV and Ferdinand VII in 1808 led to the creation of a peripatetic Ruling Junta in Spain that some governments refused to recognize. Similar ad hoc juntas sprang up around Latin America, claiming to be representing the "Desired" Ferdinand until he could be freed from Napoleon's grip. After this taste of self-governance, it was only a short leap to full-blown revolution, and in 1810 groups declared independence in Venezuela, New Granada (Colombia), Buenos Aires (Argentina), Chile, and Mexico. Those first efforts to be free of Spanish monarchical rule were unsuccessful, but before long, revolutionaries and mercenaries from the failed independence theaters were traveling back and forth across the Atlantic, looking for financial and political support and for vulnerable footholds from which to attack a weakened Spain.[80] The Lower South was one likely target.

After the U.S. Congressional prohibition against further importation of African slaves took effect in January 1808, many slave traders and planters simply evaded that embargo by moving south across the St. Marys River into Spanish Florida. Zephaniah Kingsley and James Fraser were already successful planters and slave traders based in Charleston before they moved to Florida. Both of these men were married to African women who were crucial to their success. Kingsley's Wolof

wife from Senegal, Ana Madgigine Jai, and his mulatto overseer, Abraham Hannahan, whose daughter was a second wife to
Kingsley, managed his multi-ethnic slaves and his multiple en-
terprises in Florida while he was abroad.[81] Fraser's African wife,
Fenda, was a slave trader herself and the widow of Thomas
Hughes Jackson when she married Fraser in 1799, "according
to the customs of the Rio Pongo."[82] Fenda and her agents on
the Rio Pongo managed Fraser's slave pens at Bangra and did
a brisk business with Florida-bound ships. In 1810 Fraser imported 370 Africans from the Rio Pongo to labor on his new
Greenfield and Roundabout plantations.[83] That same year,
Fraser sent the *Aguila de San Agustin* (formerly known as the
Eagle of Charleston), the *Amanda,* and the *Joana* back to the
Rio Pongo, and they returned to Florida with approximately
300 new Africans who found eager buyers.[84]

The Spanish government welcomed the taxes and industry
that came with the slave trade and made it easy for newcomers
like Kingsley and Fraser to operate in Florida. Fernandina, the
Spanish port city on Amelia Island, lying just south of the U.S.
border, became a free port in 1808, and after that date slave traders registered, had inspected, unloaded, and sold their slave imports at Fernandina rather than St. Augustine.[85] The U.S. government was well aware that the African slave trade had simply
moved south and was determined to try to end it. President
James Madison's 1810 message to Congress noted, "It appears
that American citizens are instrumental in carrying on a traffic
in enslaved Africans, equally in violation of the laws of humanity, and in defiance of those of their own country."[86] President
Madison was correct.

Tax records and ship licenses from Spanish Florida reflect the continued growth of the slaving business at Fernandina. Ships registered to Hibberson & Yonge, Henry Yonge, Fernando Arredondo and his two sons, Fernando Jr. and Joseph Arredondo, Santiago (James) Cashen, Daniel Hurlburt, Zephaniah Kingsley, and John Fraser regularly sailed to and from Africa, other Caribbean ports, and Liverpool.[87] The government surveyor Jorge J. F. Clarke, a leading figure in Fernandina and head of several mixed-race families, later testified before the United States Supreme Court: "The Condition of the country was most prosperous. Every man was making money hand over hand as fast as he could, and in consequence of the restrictive measures of the American government, the trade of the United States with all the world, except Spain, centered in Fernandina."[88]

The prosperity of Fernandina encouraged free black militiamen who had not already established homesteads on the Florida frontier to petition for city lots in Fernandina, on which they built homes, stores, and taverns. Leon Duvigneau and Jorge Jacobo were among those operating stores at Fernandina, and both served in the free back militia that Jacobo commanded. Mixed-race families like those of George J. F. Clarke and his brother Carlos Clarke also made homes in Fernandina.[89]

The fast money, the boisterous boom-town life, and a continuing demand for slaves also attracted a series of paramilitary adventurers or filibusters to Fernandina, some of whom came in the guise of revolutionaries. The first of the "South American" revolutionaries to take up the cause of liberating Florida was actually a Scotsman named Gregor MacGregor. A veteran of the Napoleonic Wars, MacGregor afterwards fought for the independence of Spanish America, serving first with Francisco de Miranda and then with Simón Bolívar, the "George Washington of South America."[90] By 1817 MacGregor was in Philadelphia, where all determined Spanish American revolutionaries gathered to seek support for independence and where he secured a commission to liberate the Floridas from a group of dubious authority called "The Deputies of Free America, Resident in the United States of the North." MacGregor also received support for his invasion of Florida from backers in New York, Philadelphia, Baltimore, Charleston, and Savannah and recruited forces in the latter two cities. Bearing the elaborate title of "Brigadier General of the Armies of the United Provinces of New Granada and Venezuela, and General-in-Chief of the Armies of the Two Floridas," MacGregor arrived at Fernandina in June of 1817 with the stated goal to "take possession of Amelia, and thence to wrest the Floridas from Spain." As the Georgia Patriots also had done, MacGregor planned to "form a constitution on the model of the adjoining States," and "to confederate with the United States."[91]

The residents of Fernandina had followed MacGregor's machinations closely and were well aware of his progress. Many removed themselves, their slaves, and other movable property to the safety of nearby St. Marys, Georgia. The commander of Fernandina, Captain Francisco Morales, undermined by his own largely American militias, surrendered to MacGregor without a fight and was subsequently tried for treason. With a force of less than seventy-five filibusters, MacGregor accepted Morales's capitulation and raised the white flag with green cross of the Republic of the Floridas over Fernandina.[92]

Before long, however, MacGregor's reserves were depleted. Resorting to the same tactic Bowles had employed, MacGregor and his erstwhile "Republicans" set up an admiralty court and began a business in the sale of captured prizes and their cargoes, which often included slaves. One unsuspecting Spanish ship, the *Tentativa*, returned from the African coast carrying 290 enslaved Africans whom the privateers promptly sold to eager American buyers on the docks. The *Niles Weekly Register* charged that "the Negroes will certainly be smuggled into the United States, as many others have been lately." The writer added, "This trade in human flesh is so profitable, that if that island [Amelia] is not taken possession of by the United States, we shall hear of many slave vessels sent as prizes that have very conveniently laid off the port to be captured."[93]

Sensing opportunity, the "Notorious Woodbine" reappeared to assure MacGregor of funds and military support from the Bahamas. Woodbine's plan was to gather a force of recently disbanded British troops and blacks from Nassau and sail for Tampa, where they would join 1500 of Woodbine's Indian allies and march across Florida to seize St. Augustine. MacGregor sailed for Nassau with Woodbine to put the plan in motion, but by December of 1817 he must have realized the futility of the idea and headed for England instead.[94]

As MacGregor and Woodbine left Florida, a second revolutionary sailed into Fernandina on the ship *América Libre*. Although commonly depicted as nothing more than a pirate in

U.S. sources, Luis Aury had served with MacGregor in Bolívar's army in New Granada and rescued over 3000 patriots
when Spanish troops besieged Cartagena in 1815. He became a
privateer in New Orleans, Galveston, and Matagorda, but he
also supported the Spanish liberal Francisco Xavier Mina's unsuccessful attempts to liberate Mexico. Raising the Mexican flag
at Fernandina, Aury proclaimed the Second Republic of the
Floridas in September 1817. Soon after, he was joined by two
leading intellectuals of the revolutionary movement in South
America, Pedro Gual (a supporter of MacGregor who would
become president of Venezuela) and a noted newspaper editor
from Upper Peru (modern Bolivia), Vicente Pazos Kanki. Gual
wrote to a supporter, "The influence of the emancipation of
[the] Floridas on that of Mexico, New Granada, Venezuela,
Buenos Ayres, Chile and Peru, is of more magnitude than it is
generaly imagined." An elected legislature (which in addition
to Gual and Pazos included persons from Charleston, Baltimore, Connecticut, and émigrés from Saint Domingue) wrote
and approved a republican constitution that made no reference
to race or gender and allowed every free inhabitant who had
resided on the island for at least fifteen days to vote after swear-
ing to "truly and faithfully . . . support the cause of the Republic of the Floridas" and "renounce all allegiance to any State
not actually struggling for the emancipation of South America."[95] The constitution also called for a free press, and Pazos
launched a Spanish-language weekly newspaper, *El Telégrafo
de las Floridas,* which promoted the republican rhetoric and
their cause. Aury proclaimed to the residents of Fernandina,
"Citizens, we are Republicans from principle . . . We have come

here to plant the tree of liberty, to foster free institutions, and to wage war against the tyrant of Spain, the oppressor of America, and the enemy of the rights of man." His proclamation was dated "November 5, 1817, and year one of independence."[96]

Florida's Atlantic Creoles would have imbibed this heady rhetoric, but rather than flock to Aury's standard, on September 9, 1817, "about 350 Spanish troops, principally negroes" attacked the "republicans" of Fernandina. Prince Whitten was among them. An unidentified British officer, recently arrived at Fernandina, described the courage of the black troops who "reluctantly obeyed" their Spanish commanders' order to retreat after two battles went badly, although "it is well known [they] may be perfectly relied upon for steadiness and courage."[97]

Rather than celebrating the end of monarchical rule, however, U.S. newspapers focused obsessively on Aury's force of some 130 black Haitians, described by the *Savannah Republican* as "brigands who had participated in the horrors of St. Domingo."[98] The *Baltimore Patriot* decried the general equality that reigned among Aury's troops: "Yes! Seated at the same table, eating the same food, drinking from the same cups and wearing the same insignias."[99] Unfortunately, no rosters exist by which to identify these men, but they may have been viewed as countrymen by Jorge Jacobo and others from Saint Domingue in the Fernandina militia. The failed Patriot John Houston McIntosh called them "a set of desperate bloody dogs" and warned that "if they are not expelled from that place [Fernandina] some unhappy consequence might fall on our country . . . I am told the language of the slaves is already such as to be extremely alarming."[100] Another resident of St. Marys wrote: "We expect daily to see a guillotine erected in Washington Square, Fernandina and some Mexican chief holding up the reeking head of an American citizen, exclaiming 'behold the head of a traitor.'"[101]

Aury was a committed revolutionary, but he, like Bowles and MacGregor before him, resorted to privateering to finance his cash-strapped republic. Belton A. Copp, the U.S. customs agent posted at the port of St. Marys, Georgia, just across the Florida border, estimated that Aury sold more than 1,000 Africans in less than two months, most of whom were "spirited" northward to Georgia or other southern states where importation was forbidden.[102]

After satisfying himself that Aury was acting independently of "any organized government whatever," President Monroe reported to Congress that Fernandina had become "a channel for the illicit introduction of slaves from Africa into the United States, an asylum for fugitive slaves from the neighboring States, and a port for smuggling of every kind." He ordered a small U.S. naval force southward to end the illicit trade.[103] Captain John Elton of the *U.S.S. Saranac* described African rowers ferrying slaves from ship to shore almost continuously and the filthy conditions on the *Jupiter*, which he intercepted and sent to Savannah in November. The captain, Elton wrote, was "an old offender, by the name of Austin."[104] When Elton intercepted the Spanish slaver *Savina*, he was shocked by the suffering on board. The ship had been swept by "coast fever," and only 25 of the 118 Africans who were taken from the Guinea coast remained alive. Elton described the weakened and shivering slaves as "all very young, not exceeding fifteen years of age." He distributed blankets among them, but several people died during the night and Elton estimated that "a number more . . . will, in all probability, terminate their miserable existence before another sun." He added, "It is enough to make the stoutest heart sicken." Elton reported that the Spanish captain was also ill of the "coast fever which in all probability will terminate his mortal career."[105] A decade after the U.S. slave trade embargo was enacted, the *Savannah Republican* reported the *Saranac*'s seizure of a "small schooner of about sixty tons" which held "130 souls . . . packed into a small space." Had the captain managed to evade capture, the paper suggested how he would have disposed of his cargo: "[A] regular chain of posts is established from the head of St. Marys River to the upper country, and through the Indian nation, by means of which, these emaciated wretches are hurried and transferred to every part of the country."[106] Unfortunately, no record survives of what the free black population of Fernandina thought of the ongoing misery they surely witnessed.

In late December American forces arrived to take possession of Amelia Island, by force if necessary, and although Aury and Pazos eloquently protested the illegality of the action, Aury knew better than to resist. On December 23, 1817, the United States flag was hoisted over Fernandina.[107] Commodore Henley reported the peaceful possession of Amelia Island and said he had quarantined Aury's black troops on board one of the ships in the harbor. An editorial in the Venezuelan *Correo del Orinoco* decried the seizure of Amelia, stating that had it been conducted by a despotic monarchy, it would have gone unnoticed, but by "a Republican administration, of virtuous people, enemies of Spanish tyranny and lovers of independence and the liberty of its South American brothers, it is an inexcusable scandal. . . . We share the fate of the oppressed Floridians; we condemn the excesses of the President of the United States; we beg your sympathy for those unfortunates."[108]

In the first decades of the nineteenth century, Atlantic Creoles living in the Lower South experienced multiple political and military upheavals. They followed the progress of the distant Napoleonic Wars and felt the ripple effects. They also lived through a series of armed conflicts including William August Bowles's war against Spain, the War of 1812 and its various aftershocks, and the Creek War. They witnessed at least three nascent states rise and fall: the State of Muskogee, and two Republics of the Floridas. In languages as diverse as Hichiti, French, Spanish, and English, they had been exposed to the rhetoric of monarchy, of natural rights, and of constitutional liberalism, and they had engaged with insurgents from across the Atlantic world who were determined to create new independent republics. They were fully aware of the inexorable expansionism of the United States, and of the commitment of its southern citizenry to doctrines of racial superiority and to chattel slavery, and thus it is no wonder that Atlantic Creoles chose any political option other than that of the American democracy.

4

Black Militiamen and African Rebels in Havana

At the sound of a drum and a trumpet you will find us ready
and fearless to end this empire of tyranny, and in this manner
we will vanquish the arrogance of our enemies.

Anonymous manifesto, Havana, April 1812

WHEN BRITISH TROOPS launched a surprise attack on Havana in 1762, the free black barber Gabriel Dorotea Barba was among the many men of African descent, both free and enslaved, who rushed to the defense of their "homeland." Although he was only a young man at the time, Barba recruited and equipped a battalion of free blacks from his community. That he had the resources and leadership to do so suggests that he was already part of a military tradition. For his act of loyalty, the Spanish Crown rewarded Barba with the rank of captain.[1] The unexpected capture of Havana highlighted the presence of a black bourgeoisie in Cuba. Barba was part of a community of free blacks whose fortunes would rise during the Age of Revolutions as they repeatedly defended the interests of Spain in Havana and abroad. Sadly, their gains would be undone in the following century as the sugar industry transformed race relations on the island and as Cuba took on the contours of a plantation society.

British invaders and elite Cubans alike remarked upon the heroism of the black troops (to whom the British gave no quarter), and even more significantly, black participants themselves maintained proud and public memories of their service.[2] The black militiamen suffered almost one hundred casualties in this invasion, but they also gained honor and a paper trail that proved it. The distinguished service of the *pardo* battalion was recalled and their flag blessed in a special sermon in the church of Espiritu Santo, site of the oldest black confraternity in Cuba. The motto on the flag read "Always Onward to Glory."[3] Documented "Meritos y Servicios" (merits and services) of any kind were a form of social capital on which Spanish subjects could draw for favors, positions, and advancements of various sorts.[4]

Persons of color had been slowly accruing such social capital since battalions of *pardos* (mulattoes) and *morenos* (blacks) were first created in Cuba at the beginning of the seventeenth century. They had long been a mainstay of Cuba's defense, but after the shocking capture of Havana, the "Pearl of the Antilles," Spain depended even more heavily upon these troops. Embarking on a campaign to shore up its military defenses throughout the Americas, the Spanish Crown created "disciplined" militias, including more *pardo* and *moreno* units. In contrast to provincial and urban militias, which were supported by private or corporate sponsors and called up only in emergencies, as was the free black militia in Florida, these were regular units with elected black officers, systematic training, and state-supplied pay, equipment, arms, and uniforms. The men in the disciplined militias received pensions as well as medical and burial benefits. These were all positive inducements for enlistment, but in the status-conscious and hierarchical Spanish world, military service was more than an employment; it was a way to improve one's social standing.

Upon joining these units, men of African descent became part of a—at least theoretically—color-blind military corporation. Officers like Barba were entitled to use the honorific "Don" before their names. The corporate privileges of the new disciplined militias included the important *fuero militar,* an exemption from prosecution in civil courts and from tribute payments that were associated with subjugation and degraded status.[5] Like titles, clothing was an important marker of rank in the Spanish world, and the new black units paid particular attention to the design of their uniforms, informing Spain in detail about their selection of colors, boots, hats, and even buttons.[6] The men wore these impressive outfits as they drilled on Sundays in the central plazas of towns throughout the Atlantic, making an important social statement as they marched. In public ceremonies held in the same plazas, Spanish officials honored black militiamen for exceptional bravery and also upon retirement after twenty-five to fifty years of military service. The *Diario de la Habana* reported the honorific ceremonies and the names of the men who received gold or silver medals bearing the likenesses of the Spanish monarchs or the Escutcheon of Fidelity, such as Prince Whitten requested on his retirement.[7]

By 1770 more than three thousand men of color had joined Cuba's militia, and they constituted more than one-fourth of

Free black militia officer from Veracruz (left) and free black soldier from Havana (right), ca. 1779–1776. From Joseph Hefter, *Artes de México*, no. 102 (Mexico City, 1968). Courtesy of the Florida Museum of Natural History, University
of Florida.

the island's armed forces.[8] An analysis of the 1776 census data for Havana shows that two-thirds of all free men of color between the ages of fifteen and fifty belonged to militias, and in this corporate society, wives, children, and household dependents thereby gained the privileges associated with military service.[9] Expanded military service thus directly contributed to the rise of a free and propertied black elite in Havana and Matanzas and allowed many slaves to achieve emancipation.[10]

Slaves understood this possibility. During the British invasion a group of twenty Cuban slaves, armed only with machetes and acting totally independently, attacked a superior British force at the Morro Castle, capturing seven of the enemy and killing others. The "ladies of Havana" described the slaves' heroism in a letter to the King, who freed them all. He also awarded their leader, Andrés Gutiérrez, the title of Captain. Another slave, Manuel Medina, was similarly rewarded for leading fifty of his fellow slaves to meet the British enemy in Guanabacoa. The compensation claims of owners document other slaves who died fighting the British.[11]

In 1769 Cuba's black militia was sent to help establish Spanish control of New Orleans, and they returned to the region during the American Revolution. In that war Lieutenant José Francisco Sánchez, of the *pardo* battalion, and the *moreno* Manuel Blanco followed Captain Barba's earlier example and raised and uniformed companies of 100 men each. As in Barba's case, the men won captaincies, the right to name their subordinate officers, and the *fuero militar* for all their men.[12]

Cuba's black troops fought for the Spanish monarch, but as they helped liberate British colonials, they gained some acquaintance with the rhetoric of independence. The *pardo* battalion fought under a flag bearing their motto, "Always Onward to Glory," while the motto emblazoned on the flag of Cuba's *moreno* battalions, "Victory or Death," nicely mirrored the sentiment expressed by Patrick Henry. During the American Revolution Captains Gabriel Dorotea Barba, José Antonio Aponte, and other Cuban militiamen fought in the Florida campaigns and in the Bahamas against the British. They also served on Spanish corsairing expeditions throughout the Caribbean, all the while acquiring "geopolitical literacy," that is, knowledge of the politics and socioeconomic systems of places not their own.[13]

Although we are now familiar with the important role that black sailors played in conveying geopolitical information and revolutionary ideology around the Atlantic ports they visited, we know less about the black militiamen who served the same roles.[14] These men were eyewitnesses and participants in many of the most important military contests of their day. They had access to a wide range of political information, both printed and oral, and made rational and informed choices to advance their rights as free men. Some spent as many as twenty years posted abroad before returning to Cuba, forming families and relationships with the free blacks with whom they served in these foreign stations.[15] They acquired intimate knowledge of other places and peoples that expanded their horizons and visions. In addition, as a result of two evacuations of Spanish Florida (the first in 1763, the second in 1821), several generations of former slaves from Florida eventually ended their days as free militiamen in Cuba, reconnecting with black Cuban soldiers and sailors with whom they had previously served.[16]

In joining the Spanish militia, black men across the Atlantic became part of a corporation dating back to the Middle Ages, with special rights and privileges. These included exemptions from taxes and tribute payments and from prosecution in civil courts; the men answered only to military tribunals. Through membership in the militia, black men gained access to Spanish military patrons with whom they served. The men of the Cuban black militia also formed extended family relationships with one another as their children intermarried and as they served as godparents and marriage sponsors for each other. These relationships provided social insurance and group solidarity and also helped to conserve resources that were recycled through dowries and inheritances. When Captain Gabriel Dorotea Barba married María Isabel Aróstegui in 1786, her dowry included 6,000 pesos, jewels, and clothing. When their daughter María Tranquilina married Captain Manuel Salazar, a member of Barba's battalion, María's parents gave her a dowry as well, keeping these resources within the extended family.[17]

The men who joined the *pardo* and *moreno* units came largely from the artisan class, like their fellow militiamen across the Atlantic. Many were carpenters like Prince Whitten; others were masons, barbers, tailors, musicians, and funeral home directors. Some with more education managed to become teachers, artists, poets, and dentists. As social aspirants, they modeled themselves after Spanish professionals, operating successful businesses, buying real estate and slaves, and supporting good works in the community.[18]

One way men like Barba demonstrated their civic values and piety was by creating and supporting officially sanctioned Catholic confraternities or *cofradías*. These brotherhoods provided food, alms, and medicine for the needy, supported the funerals of its members, and participated in important religious observances such as Corpus Christi. Black *cofradías* date to at least the fourteenth century in Spain and to the sixteenth century in the Americas, and like the militias, they were another form of corporate organization that promoted social cohesion, reinforced extended family networks, and recognized leadership generated from within the black community. Public displays of religiosity and of civic organization by the adherents confirmed black claims to Christian brotherhood and membership in the larger Spanish community.[19] Through the civic and religious activity of such *cofradías,* black brothers created an accepted public sphere for themselves that contrasted with the less reputable behavior of newly imported African slaves or *bozales.*[20]

As was true in other Atlantic sites from Rio de Janeiro to Congo Square in New Orleans, enslaved Africans in Havana had developed an alternate form of social organization, gathering in the free time allotted them on Sundays and other feast days for traditional drumming and dance. These *tumbas* or *congadas* worried urban officials, who sought to monitor and control them, and eventually they shaped these informal gatherings into a secularly licensed variant of a religious brotherhood known as *cabildos de nación.*[21] The term "cabildo" originally referred to a town council or a town meeting, and no racial or ethnic meaning was assigned to the term. In areas of heavy African importation such as Cuba, however, the added phrase "de nación" shifted the meaning to refer to groups organized along some form of African ethnicity.[22]

In 1755 Bishop Pedro Agustín Morrell de Santa Cruz recorded the existence of twenty-one *cabildos de nación* in Havana. Responding to complaints about their disturbances, the bishop visited one group's *tumba* and was distressed to note that men and women drank *aguardiente* (rum) until senseless, danced "provocatively, in the custom of their lands," and engaged in all the excesses that followed. The bishop embarked on an outreach campaign, and at one house he prayed the rosary with the gathered Africans and presented them with an image of the Virgin. Encouraged by their response, Morrell de Santa Cruz elaborated a plan to assign a catechist, adept in the appropriate African language, to each house "que es lo mismo que hacen con los indios" (which is the same as is done with the Indians). He recommended against forbidding dances or musical instruments and believed that through peaceful persuasion, the Africans would "open their eyes" and recognize the "abominations" of their former practices. "Houses of the Devil" could be converted into "temples of God" or *hermitas*, thereby producing social order and saving souls at the same time.[23] Although Cuban authorities did not adopt the bishop's plan in full—for instance, there is no evidence that Cuban clerics seriously studied African languages—they did begin to regulate and reshape the disorderly African gatherings described by the bishop.

To be legitimated, the African brothers had to define their devotions as well as rules of conduct in constitutions. Elected officers promised to monitor their own members and expel any miscreants, and they devoted themselves to a patron saint that they honored on its feast day. In hopes that the *cabildos* would promote positive social values and good order, Spanish officials usually approved their requests to organize and granted them licenses. The *cabildos'* well-attended dances and the music and crowds they attracted eventually so disturbed the "honored" citizenry of Havana, however, that a 1792 edict gave them one year to relocate outside the city walls. The same edict ordered the *cabildos* to take the bodies of deceased members to the public mortuary rather than staging celebratory and "disorderly" wakes in their meeting houses. It would seem from the frequency of these pronouncements that early efforts to limit *cabildos* were no more successful than sumptuary and other sorts of restrictive legislation.[24]

The activities and observances of the *cabildos de nación* blended European and African cultural elements. One of their most popular celebrations was the *Día de Reyes*. This was a day of license and role-reversal celebrated on the sixth of January (Epiphany), and possibly chosen for the reason that one of the three Magi (Gaspar, Melchior, or Baltasar) was reputedly black. In these processions, which date to the sixteenth century in Cuba and were modeled after those of fourteenth-century Seville, elected and richly dressed Kings and Queens of various African ethnicities paraded through the streets of Havana to be admired and to receive gifts from onlookers.[25] Given the African respect for kings of all nations testified to by the Kongo rebel Macaya in Saint Domingue, these processions were probably read differently by whites and blacks. Participants performed African songs and dances accompanied by cowbells, drums, scrapers, and hollowed gourd rattles. They wore elaborate costumes of raffia, peacock feathers, animal skins and horns, and beads. Stilt-walkers, lantern-bearers, masked figures, and gymnasts added to the merriment. Throughout the day the Africans paraded under balconies or into courtyards, requesting *aguinaldos* or gratuities for the entertainment they provided onlookers.[26] Guided by an intricate vocabulary of color, artifacts, and symbols, black and white observers read the *cabildo* processions for references to their African deity of choice. For example, Cubans still recognize the patron saint of the Lucumíes, Santa Bárbara, as Shangó, the Virgin of Cobre as Ochún, and San Lázaro as Baba-lú-Ayé.[27]

Cabildos were one corporate religious form that Africans adopted; *cofradías* or confraternities were another. These were quite different institutions, although memberships might overlap. Confraternities more closely approximated accepted Catholic practice and seem to have attracted free blacks like Barba who were upwardly mobile. Rather than dressing in African costumes and parading on stilts through the streets of Havana, the brothers of these *cofradías* would march images of their patron saints through the streets on their special feast days, as Catholics did across the Iberian empires.

By the eighteenth century, in Havana at least, some free blacks belonged to both *cofradías* and *cabildos de nación*. The militiaman José Antonio Aponte, who had served Spain with distinction in the Gulf Coast campaigns of the American Revolution, was reputed to be the *capatáz* (elected leader) of the Lucumí or Yoruba *cabildo*, Shango-Tedum. He may well have been, but Aponte was also a member of a confraternity established in 1800 by the guild of carpenters. The brothers were devoted to St. Joseph, the carpenter, and called themselves the "slaves of our Glorious Patron the Patriarch St. Joseph, and of Jesus, and of his Sainted Mother." They met in the Convent of

El Día de los Reyes (Day of the Kings or Epiphany) by Federico Mialhe, from *Album Pintoresco de la Isla de Cuba*, 1850/1851. Courtesy of "The Atlantic Slave Trade and Slave Life in the Americas: A Visual Record" website, *http:// hitchcock.itc.virginia.edu/Slavery*, Virginia Foundation for the Humanities and the University of Virginia Library.

Saint Francis, near the city wharfs, where another official broth-erhood also gathered.[28]

After the slave revolt in Saint Domingue, Spanish officials across the Atlantic began to worry about the subversive poten-tial of the more African *cabildos*. Cuban slaves were becoming more politicized through the "contagion" of the rebellion in Saint Domingue; in 1795, the slave Romualdo led a small revolt in Puerto Príncipe, Cuba, and the free mulatto Nicolás Morales led an aborted uprising in Bayamo, Cuba. Participants in both alluded to the uprising of the slaves in Saint Domingue.[29] The following year, blacks in Havana flocked to the wharf to try to get a glimpse of Spain's uniformed Black Auxiliaries of Car-los IV, who had sailed into the harbor after being evacuated from Saint Domingue. The once powerful leaders of that is-land's slave revolt, Jorge Biassou and Jean-François, and their followers were not even allowed to set foot on Cuban soil, but nonetheless they made an impact on the large black population of the island. Cuban officials, planters, and free and enslaved blacks all understood what those men represented—the ability of former slaves to free themselves by force of arms. Cuban of-ficials dispersed the Black Auxiliaries across the Atlantic, send-ing Biassou and his followers to Florida and Jean-François with his men and their families to Cádiz. But for years afterward, rumors circulated throughout slave communities in Cuba that Jean-François would return from exile to liberate them.[30]

Jean-François never did return from Cádiz, and it would be many long, hard years before the end of slavery in Cuba. Al-though Britain declared the abolition of the slave trade in 1807 and the United States in 1808, for all intents and purposes the trade in human beings which had been liberalized in Spanish colonies in 1789 went on unabated in Cuba. Spanish and American traders continued to import large shipments of African slaves into Havana and Matanzas. Havana's black militiamen had to escort the miserable Africans being disgorged at the wharfs to the baracoons that would hold them until their purchase. An estimated 300,000 *bozales* entered Cuba between 1789 and 1820.[31] The Cuban trader Fernando de la Maza Arredondo established a branch operation in Fernandina, Florida, to sell some of these "new" Africans to eager planters throughout the Lower South, whose supplies were only inconvenienced by the 1808 embargo.[32]

For Cubans, then, the major news of 1808 was not abolition, but Napoleon's invasion of Spain. Havana prided itself on its urbanity, and black and white readers alike had access to a variety of periodicals that discussed sciences, arts and letters, and international news, including wars and imperial politics. In their pages Cubans followed the progress of the battles in Spain and the fierce resistance of Spanish liberals to Napoleon's troops. They read about the abdication of Carlos IV (whose image decorated the medals of many of the free black militia) in favor of his son, Ferdinand VII. They knew by July that the royals had been captured and were in exile in Bayonne, and that Napoleon's brother, Joseph (known derisively in Spanish America as Pepe Botella for his drinking habits) sat on the throne of Spain.

In September of 1808, loyal Spaniards formed a Central Junta to govern in the place of their deposed monarch, Ferdinand.[33] Many Spanish American colonies also formed local juntas that governed somewhat autonomously, all the while proclaiming loyalty to Ferdinand. Between 1810 and 1825, all the Spanish colonies except Cuba, Puerto Rico, and the Philippines had gained their independence. Cuba, however, never established a provisional junta and prided itself on being the "everfaithful isle." The militarization of Cuba in the late eighteenth century, which included the construction of impressive fortifications and the presence of large numbers of resident peninsular troops, secured and enhanced Cuba's status in the empire. By extension, it also enhanced the status of Cuba's black troops.[34]

Its vulnerable position ensured that Florida would also remain loyal to Spain, and in 1810 a number of the free black troops made donations to Spain's war effort against the French invaders. Sargeant Jorge Jacobo, José Richo, José Brus, and Felipe Embara [sic] each donated 10 pesos, the same amount offered by the Spanish Dons.[35]

Spain's resistance fighters did their best, but they were no match for Napoleon's forces, and by 1810 they were reduced to control of Cádiz, Spain's southern seaport. Spain's Central Junta, by now renamed the Council of Regency, invited American colonies to send delegates to a newly created legislative body called the Cortes, but Spaniards outnumbered Americans by more than two to one.[36]

At least some blacks in Cuba were able to read about these important events because they had been educated. Free black parents like the Whittens and the Barbas understood the importance of education and literacy as a critical marker of status and a route to upward mobility in Spanish America. Free black children with ability and connections were admitted to the Jesuit Colegio de San José de la Habana, where they received excellent classical educations. Ignacio Flores, for instance, a free black child, at the age of nine had already been examined successfully in ten subjects and ranked first in his class. With his teacher's encouragement, Ignacio applied to the Real y Pontificia Universidad de San Gerónimo de la Habana. Following a medieval model, entrance exams (in grammar, philosophy, and theology) were a public event which drew crowds of observers. Ignacio's father was Commandant Antonio Flores, who had served in the *pardo* battalion since 1708 and was a veteran of the British invasion of Havana and of the Pensacola campaign in the American Revolution. Flores proudly issued invitations to his son Ignacio's examination, but at the last moment, two professors of Spanish descent launched a protest campaign. Fearful of the disorder and backlash, the university canceled Ignacio's exams. The senior Flores asked the Council of the Indies in Spain to overrule this decision, arguing that other *pardo* children had been examined "repeatedly in the [Jesuit] convent and other schools of Havana" and that educating *pardos* in the sciences and preparing them as physicians would only redound to the credit of the empire. Flores cited examples where *pardos* had received higher education in Peru and Mexico and quoted a legal treatise and Royal Edict which stated that the children of *pardos* should be regarded as Spaniards. He added that the incident had embarrassed him and his son, as it surely would have in such an honor-conscious environment. Although Flores's articulate challenge failed and the local decision was upheld, his suit demonstrates that a segment of free blacks in Havana were receiving good educations that could benefit their families and community.[37]

Recognizing the need for more access to education, in 1803 Captain Gabriel Dorotea Barba established a school for children of color that operated for at least thirty years. Barba advertised his school in the *Diario de La Habana*. By 1833 it consisted of two school buildings on the Calle de la Luz, one for boys and another for girls. Even more unusual was that Barba held evening classes for slaves whose owners were too busy to teach them the Christian doctrine, as was supposedly required.[38] Several other members of the militia also established schools in Havana in the first decades of the nineteenth century, as did at least four women of color. Poor white children attended these schools as well, although Cuban officials tried to prevent this on the basis that people of African descent should not exercise control over those of Spanish descent. These prohibitions, like so many others, went unheeded, and even the Fathers of Belen admitted students of all origins to their school.[39]

For those not fortunate enough to be educated, public processions and theater offered insights into a larger world. In 1809, in another act of beneficence designed to enhance his social reputation, Captain Barba organized a Christmas production for the entertainment of the public. This may have formed part of the annual Epiphany celebrations. Captain Barba led the cast of characters as the Emperor of China, while other members of the free black militia represented the Emperor of Hindustan, the Emperor and Prince of Germany, the Duke of Bavaria, the King of Prussia, the King of Denmark, a Cardinal, and even the Pontiff. Other men played the King of Chantaje (a sort of Lord of Misrule) and his court, the King of Romans and Chance, and the King of Ariton. One can only wonder about the staging and costuming, but the very exoticism of the characters (all of whom were powerful world figures and none of which had to do with Africa) was designed to impress observers with the erudition and geopolitical knowledge of the performers.[40]

In addition to supporting militia companies, schools, and theater groups, Captain Barba organized a confraternity devoted to Nuestra Señora de Rosario (Our Lady of the Rosary) that met in the chapel of San Nicolás de Bari. The group's charter specified that the brothers' dues would go to help them in their final illnesses and thereafter assist their wives or mothers in the event that they were single. The *cofradía* had installed an image of the Virgin in its chapel and had apparently operated for some time before Barba actually requested the Bishop's authorization in 1811. By that time slave uprisings and abolitionist pressures had exacerbated racial tensions in Havana, and so the Bishop responded that no matter how pious the objective, the brothers would need to secure a license from the Captain General.[41]

While tenuously clinging to a semblance of authority in Cádiz, Spain, the Cortes in 1811 launched a debate on the future of slavery and the slave trade in the Spanish world. Alarmed by the example of slave rebellion in Saint Domingue and by the growing abolitionist sentiment that threatened their way of life, Cuba's powerful sugar planters made every effort to shore up slavery. They sought to create a two-caste racial system like that of the United States, but in order to accomplish that goal they would have to attack the hard-won status and privileges of the free black class. José Arango y Pareño traveled to Cádiz to present the sugar planters' *Representación de la ciudad de la Habana a las cortes españolas,* defending Cuban slavery. But the more liberal members of the Cortes, far removed from the sea of *bozales* the Cuban planters feared would engulf them, had more enlightened views. They knew of Adam Smith's argument that wage labor was superior to slavery and were anxious to modernize Spain and its empire. Much to the dismay of Cuban planters like Arango, the delegate from Mexico proposed abolition throughout the Spanish colonies, noting that "slavery as a violation of natural law, already outlawed by the laws of civilized countries . . . should be abolished forever."[42] Captain General Someruelos understood the danger of allowing Cuba's large black population to have access to such "inflammatory" political rhetoric. The number of African slaves kept growing, and free people of color by this time constituted slightly more than a quarter of Havana's population.[43] Someruelos noted that secret emissaries of Napoleon could be hanged, but "seductive *impresos* [printed materials] circulated in the hands of everyone." Although the Captain General suppressed publication of the sessions of the Cortes in which abolition was discussed, this censorship only fueled the widespread rumors of emancipation.[44]

In the rumor-filled atmosphere of Havana, Captain General Someruelos could not have been pleased by the unexpected arrival of the black brigadier Gil Narciso, a veteran of the slave revolt in Saint Domingue. Narciso had fought with Biassou and Jean-François as a member of the Black Auxiliaries of Carlos

IV, and like them, he was forced into exile when Spain ceded Saint Domingue to the French in 1795. After some fifteen years spent in Guatemala, Narciso was on his way home. His medal and his royal connections required the Captain General to offer at least a grudging reception in Havana, but to contain the black brigadier's potential impact on the population of color, Someruelos housed Narciso and his retinue at the military barracks at Casa Blanca, across the harbor from the city center. He would later question Narciso and his men about their knowledge of the Aponte rebellion and expel them from Cuba.[45]

Despite these "containment" measures, popular rumors about black liberators and abolition once again triggered a series of slave revolts throughout Cuba in 1812. Angry slaves in Bayamo, Holguín, Puerto Principe, and Havana circulated stories that claimed the King of Spain, the Spanish Cortes, the King of England, the King of Haiti (Henri Christophe had crowned himself emperor that year), or the King of Kongo had planned to free them but that local authorities had suppressed their abolition decrees. The authorities reacted swiftly and brutally suppressed these uprisings, executing some of the rebels and sentencing others to hard labor or military service in contested areas of the Caribbean.[46] Ironically, some of the Puerto Principe rebels, like Tiburcio Recio, were deported to Florida where they fought for Spain against Georgian "Patriots" and U.S. Marines.[47]

But not all of the rebels had been detected and exiled. Cuba's authorities were shocked to discover a more serious conspiracy organized right under their noses in Havana. On March 15, slaves and free blacks launched a revolt at the Peñas Altas plantation on the outskirts of town. The leader of the revolt was alleged to be the free black militiaman and sculptor, José Antonio Aponte, of the "slaves of St. Joseph" brotherhood. The authorities arrested Aponte, but other rebels nailed a manifesto to the door of the Captain General's house that read: "At the sound of a drum and a trumpet you will find us ready and fearless to end this empire of tyranny, and in this manner we will vanquish the arrogance of our enemies."[48] Authorities confiscated a *libro de pinturas* at Aponte's house in the barrio Jesús, María y José. It contained drawings of his ancestors, all of whom had also served in Cuba's free black militia, sketches of free black soldiers in uniforms defending whites (perhaps referring to the service in the English invasion of 1762), portraits of King Carlos III and, more ominously, also of Toussaint Louverture, Henri Christophe, and Jean Jacques Dessalines. Cuban officials considered the book a "blueprint for revolution."[49]

Not surprisingly, given the hysteria created by the earlier revolts, many of the men arrested in connection with the Havana uprising were sentenced to die. The horrific spectacle of hangings and decapitations of Aponte and his collaborators went on for more than six months. From the La Cabaña prison where they had been held, tortured, and interrogated for months, the condemned men were marched to the scaffolds that had been constructed at the La Punta fort at the edge of the harbor. There crowds gathered to watch the hangings, and some "applauded the gesticulations" of the victims. Reputed leaders of the uprising were also decapitated and their severed heads placed in steel cages or on pikes for display as a warning to other potential rebels. On April 9, 1812, Aponte and eight other men were hanged, and soon Aponte's head, like Harry's and Boukman's and Ogé's and countless others in this revolutionary age, became an object lesson on the price of rebellion.[50]

One might have thought that in those tense times, when militiamen were being executed for treason, Cuba's black troops would "go to ground." Instead, as these gruesome scenes were played out, officers of Cuba's *pardo* and *moreno* units continued to assert their legal rights through memorials sent to the Cortes in Spain. The distant monarch, and now the distant Cortes, had always been more willing to support the medieval privileges of free people of color than had local Spanish officials. But the black militia officers must have thought they had to take the offensive and challenge the erosion of their hard-won privileges and status or lose them forever. Captain Barba, who by this time had been an acknowledged leader of Cuba's free black community for more than fifty years, led the legal campaign to preserve and advance the rights and privileges of the free black militia, but many other officers also filed complaints. Barba related a series of insults that free black officers had suffered from Spanish Subintendant Inspector Antonio Seydel [*sic*], such as being required to march in the same ranks as ordinary soldiers or to take off their hats in the presence of white officers. He cited violations of specific articles of the 1769 Reglamento that reorganized the black militias. Captain Miguel Porro, who would later fight the Georgia Patriots in Florida, also cited that Reglamento when he refused to doff his hat to a white officer. Cuban officials arrested Porro, and he spent eleven days in jail for his principles before being released.

Undaunted, Barba and his fellow officers continued to press

for equal pay and the status they felt was due them. In one long memorial Barba recounted for the King all the long years of service, the many battles, and the loyalty of the black militia. Using the florid language of the day, he said he hoped to remind the monarch of his obligation to his vassals and trigger the desired response. Barba asked that the sons of black militiamen be given preference in officer appointment over the sons of men who had not served, and that they "never lack the honor, good education, and status that they should inherit from their fathers." Barba closed this request by appealing to "the well-known beneficent heart of Your Majesty," adding that the black militia had no other protection or source of help but "Your Royal majesty whom we consider our only Father."[51]

Cuban officials considered the black militiamen's demands "pretentious," "prideful," and "insubordinate," but they were required to forward them to Spain. When only days after Aponte's execution, the commander of the *moreno* battalion, Ysidro Moreno, demanded that his white superior hand over the unit's service records and stated publicly that if his predecessors did not know how to fulfill their obligations, he did, Cuban officials could hardly contain their anger.[52]

That summer the Cortes in Cádiz finally issued a new Liberal Constitution. By edict it was to be read aloud with great pomp and circumstance in American plazas that were by the same edict to be renamed Plaza of the Constitution. One can still visit the obelisk that was erected in the plaza of St. Augustine on that occasion. A copy of the Constitution reached Cuba in July of 1812, and it must have been galling for the Cuban officials, almost all of whom were monarchists, to have to swear

View of the monument to the Liberal Spanish Constitution, erected in St. Augustine in 1812. Behind the obelisk is the Catholic Church, built in 1790. Courtesy of the St. Augustine Historical Society.

allegiance to the new form of government.[53] Free black Cubans, on the other hand, celebrated the expanded rights it guaranteed. The black militiamen who had risked all to pepper Cádiz with memorials must have rejoiced to see the outcome of their campaign. Among other provisions, the Constitution reversed long-promulgated racial prohibitions and decreed that "Spaniards of African origin" should be helped to study the sciences and have access to an ecclesiastical career, "so as to be ever more useful to the state"—Antonio Flores's argument exactly.[54]

A royal decree of July 24, 1812, also "conceded the honorific distinction of the Royal Effigy" to Captains Ysidro Moreno and Gabriel Dorotea Barba, and on October 19, 1812, both men received their medals in a public ceremony on the plaza.[55] The exultation was short-lived, however. By February of 1814, Napoleon had been defeated with British assistance and Ferdinand was back on the Spanish throne. After prosecuting those of his liberal opponents he could capture, on May 4, 1814, Ferdinand abolished the Liberal Constitution that restrained him, charging that it was modeled after the "revolutionary and democratic French constitution of 1791." Only two years after the Constitution had been launched, it was a dead letter. When news of the return to absolutism reached Havana in July of 1814, Cuba's recently installed Captain General Juan Ruiz de Apodaca did not immediately announce it. He was fearful of the "populations of color" and the many British "sailors with democratic ideas, like all commoners" who were then in Havana. Not until the British ships sailed away from Cuba did Apodaca permit the *Diario de la Habana* to publish news of the restoration of Ferdinand on July 21, 1814.[56]

Although Ferdinand was restored, his empire was slipping away from him. Colonial juntas had become used to self-governance while he was absent, and many were reluctant to give it up. Moreover, the powerful influences of Enlightenment thought and the success of American and Haitian independence movements helped trigger full-blown independence movements in many parts of the Americas. In February of 1815 Ferdinand sent more than 10,000 troops under the command of General Pablo Morillo to suppress independence movements in Tierra Firme (northern South America). This large force passed through Havana on the way to the battlegrounds of Venezuela and New Granada (Colombia). Refugees from those war-torn areas, in turn, scattered throughout the Caribbean. From both groups, people of color in Havana and elsewhere learned about the liberators and the nascent republics of Spanish America. By 1820, Spain's wars were so unpopular that troops bound for the Americas finally mutinied and refused to be shipped out. The Riego Revolt, also known as the Sergeants' Revolt, forced Ferdinand to restore Spain's Liberal Constitution.[57]

Thus, despite the growing power of the Cuban planters, the Liberal Constitution was once again the law of the land in Cuba. This brought new hope to free blacks and public intellectuals, who struggled to liberalize Cuban society and improve the lot of Cuba's large African-born population. On March 28, 1821, Francisco J. de Burgos launched a new periodical dedicated to that purpose. Its title was *El Negrito* (little black man), a diminutive form that may have been intended to minimize backlash from white Cubans threatened by its content. On its front page, a black man with outstretched hand stands below a

EL NEGRITO

MIERCOLES 28 DE MARZO DE 1821.

El mérito y la virtud franquea á los españoles originarios del África las puertas al ciudadanato.

Entre los muchos escritores cuyas luces se han dedicado á la instruccion pública en diferentes ramos, aun no ha habido alguno que llevado de los impulsos de un verdadero patriotismo, y acendrada caridad se haya decidido á analizar á esta porcion de nuestra sociedad el art. 22 de la Constitucion cuyos autores no olvidando la felicidad de éstos lo dictaron para su logro.

Por el art. 5 son españoles todos los hombres libres nácidos y avecindados en los dominios de las españas, y los hijos de éstos; y por el 22 se les habre las puertas del ciudadanato por medio del merecimiento y la virtud á los españoles, que por cualquiera línea son habidos y reputados por originarios de África; manifestándoles á lo que deben aspirar para lograr carta de tales.

Muchos son de opinion que la ilustracion hace las mas veces al hombre desbarrar y cometer excesos; y yo digo, que la ignorancia mas bien lo precipita. El esclavo, no es español por carecer

banner reading "Constitution or Death." The editorial beneath has as its title "Merit and virtue will open the doors of citizenship to Spaniards born in Africa." The newspaper was dedicated to informing populations of color of their rights under the restored Liberal Constitution and encouraging them to become educated. It informed the readers that Article 5 of the Constitution specified that all free people of African descent born in and living in Spanish territories were to be considered Spaniards, as were their children. The same applied to former slaves who achieved their freedom while living in Spanish territories. Article 22 stated that the merit and virtue of those Spaniards, regardless of their African origins, would "open the doors of citizenship to them," and it urged them to aspire to this status. The author noted that while many people believed that enlightenment led to excess, he believed that ignorance was more likely to do so. Slaves were not entitled to citizenship, but the writer argued that if they knew their potential to become citizens through "merit and virtue," they would behave more honorably to achieve this prize. They would also be less likely to behave badly as free citizens because only a former slave could really appreciate the loss of liberty. Article 24 of the restored Constitution also provided a strong incentive for education, because after 1830 any Spaniards (including those free people of African origin) who did not know how to read and write would be excluded from citizenship. The author referred to the duty of Christians to do good works, and said he believed that educating enslaved people as to their rights certainly constituted good works. He argued that he deserved the gratitude of his fellow citizens rather than their opprobrium, and stated that in his next issue he would discuss subsequent articles of the Constitution. Unfortunately, he never had the chance. The authorities found an excuse to shut down his paper, and no subsequent issues appeared.[58]

But in April of 1821 Father Félix Varela, Professor of Philosophy, Chemistry, Physics, and Rhetoric at the noted Seminary College of San Carlos and San Ambrosio, was elected as a delegate to the Spanish Cortes. Varela had created a Department of Constitutional Studies at the seminary, and his students became some of Cuba's most important advocates of independence and of abolition. Varela wrote several memorials on the need to abolish slavery and specified how abolition could be accomplished without harming the interests of the former slaveowners. Varela's plan included freeing slaves who had served at least fifteen consecutive years, and creating public and philanthropic funds to buy the liberty of others.[59]

Only a few months after Varela sailed from Cuba for Spain, a ceremony in St. Augustine marked the end of Spanish sovereignty in Florida. After years of supporting covert plots and military invasions of Spanish territory, the United States had finally acquired Florida legally through the Adams-Onís Treaty of 1819, and by its provisions, the Spanish government was required to evacuate the colony by 1821. Free blacks then faced a hard decision. As in Louisiana, cession treaties required the incoming government of the United States to respect the legal status and property rights of the remaining Spanish citizens, including free blacks. Nevertheless, Cuba's Captain General encouraged Floridians to relocate to other Spanish colonies, including Texas, Mexico, and Cuba. Most Floridians chose the latter, and the last act of social control of Spanish officials in Florida was to supervise Spain's second full-scale evacuation to Cuba. On July 10, 1821, Florida became a territory of the United States.[60]

Some free blacks living in Spanish Florida, like the African-born Sergeant Felipe Edimboro, trusted the cession treaties and remained in the new territory of the United States. Those who stayed must have regretted their decision, because the incoming planters would not tolerate the more relaxed racial system that Spain had installed. Like the Cuban planters, they were determined to install a two-caste racial system and eliminate Florida's intermediate free black class. Over the next years the Anglo newcomers pressured many free blacks in territorial Florida into selling what remained of their property at rock-bottom prices. In the years leading up to the U.S. Civil War, some free blacks joined later exiles going to Cuba, Haiti, and Mexico, where their histories are only beginning to be traced.[61]

After twenty-six years in the military service of Spain, Lieutenant Prince Whitten, anticipating the certain shift in racial politics that would follow U.S. occupation, led more than 130 members of Florida's polyglot free black community into exile in Cuba, where once again they remade their lives. Some of the Black Auxiliaries of Carlos IV from Saint Domingue, like Benjamín Seguí, Pedro Miguel, and Jorge Brus and their families, joined that exodus to Cuba. The first and largest contingent of free black exiles sailed out of St. Augustine on August 22, 1821, with smaller groups following. Some did not leave until as late as 1827, but eventually 40 black militiamen, 27 women, and 78 children were resettled in Cuba at the expense of the royal treasury. The earliest groups arrived in Havana at a moment of fresh possibilities under the restored Constitution, and with some prior contacts among the black militiamen with whom they had served in Florida, but the transition could not have been easy. Prince Witten left behind his family, feeling that his duty lay with his company. Other families were also separated by this change of flags.[62]

A grateful, if impoverished, Spanish Crown gave its loyal black allies from Florida daily subsidies until they could become self-sufficient in Cuba and kept records on the exiled group for some time thereafter, recording deaths and reducing allotments accordingly.[63] Initially the refugees from Florida were maintained in their own military unit; later some of the younger men, like José Bacas, Juan Prayma, and Guillermo and Andrés Sanco, enlisted in Havana's free black battalion. Over the next several years, some of the Florida families left Havana for Matanzas, where Francisco Menéndez had helped relocate Florida's first exiled free black community of Gracia Real de Santa Teresa de Mose.[64]

As Prince Whitten and the black families from Florida were settling into new surroundings and employments, another major conspiracy known as the Soles y Rayos de Bolívar shook Cuba. Authorities discovered and prosecuted a multi-racial group for plotting to overthrow the constitutional monarchy. Inspired by the success of Bolívar, they sought total independence and planned a new republic of Cubanacán.[65]

The reborn hopes of Cuban constitutionalists and abolitionists were dashed when France invaded Spain with the collusion of King Ferdinand in 1823 and abolished the Cortes and the Liberal Constitution. Facing imprisonment, Father Varela and

Cuba's other delegates had to flee Spain, and Ferdinand subsequently sentenced them to death in absentia. Father Varela went first to Philadelphia, where he launched the paper *El Habanero* in 1823, and later he moved to New York, where he continued to publish on the themes of Cuban independence and abolition.[66]

Meanwhile, the wars of independence were winding down. Denied reinforcements from the peninsula by the Sergeants' Revolt, General Tomás Morales, commander of the Spanish armies in the Americas, was forced to concede defeat. After surrendering Maracaibo, Venezuela, to the "Great Liberator," Simón Bolívar, Morales and his troops sailed away for Havana. Black militiamen who had fought in Morales's failed Tierra Firme campaigns returned to Cuba with new medals, at least some exposure to republican ideas, and a wider world view.[67]

The defeat of royal forces in Spanish America led officials in Cuba to feel even more besieged. In 1825 Captain General Someruelos established a series of Military Commissions throughout the poorer and blacker extramural neighborhoods of Havana. The barrios of Guadalupe, San Lázaro, and Jesús, María y José were considered a likely destination for urban maroons, if runaway ads in the *Diario de la Habana* are to be believed.[68] Even if revolution were not so present, the scale of the runaway problem would have worried any slaveowning society. The Real Junta de Fomento, Agricultura y Comercio (Royal Commission for Development, Agriculture, and Commerce) reported more than 2,500 runaways held in its depository in 1829, and almost the same numbers were recorded for 1830, 1831, and 1832.[69]

Records generated by the neighborhood military commissions chart a shift in the types of offenses for which blacks began to be arrested. Although the first year's reports largely focused on "conspiracies" among slaves, by 1826 barrio commissioners seemed to be targeting free black militiamen. Over the course of the following decade, black officers who had enjoyed legal and social elevation under the Bourbon reforms and whose families, like those of Barba, Flores, and Aponte, had proudly served Spain for several generations were now being accused of subversive language, transporting letters from Veracruz, Mexico (where some black militiamen from Cuba had also served), hosting secret reunions of free people of color, and being in possession of stamped paper.[70] Faced with the multiple threats of slave revolts, marronage, British abolitionism, political conspiracies, and independence movements, Cuban planters supported by the reactionary Spanish monarchy launched an eradication campaign against Cuba's historic free black class.

In 1835, suspecting a conspiracy was afoot, soldiers opened fire on ten to twelve blacks leaving the house of Juan Nepomuceno Prieto in the barrio Jesús, María y José. Prieto was a retired Sergeant Second Class of the black battalion and also *capatáz* (elected leader) of the Lucumí *cabildo de nación*. Investigators seized a wide variety of documentation from his house—what amounted to the *cabildo*'s archive. These documents make clear the central role that Prieto and the house played in the lives of the Lucumí community of the neighborhood, where a number of free black militiamen also lived.[71]

Prieto established the *cabildo* in 1819, on his return from a five-year tour of Pensacola, and in 1824 the Captain General granted him a license to host dances and other "diversions" in his home, which also served as the *cabildo*'s meeting place. This detail is significant because it reminds us that *cofradías* or confraternities operated within the physical space of the church, while *cabildos* established connections to nearby churches but maintained their own spaces that were not as easily monitored. This Lucumí *cabildo*'s patroness was Saint Barbara, patroness of the artillery and the counterpart of Shango, the Yoruba deity of war. Members celebrated the saint's feast day by paying for church masses and music and processing with her image from Prieto's house to the auxiliary church in the neighborhood. Prieto's archive shows that he was posting bonds for brothers gone astray of the law, interceding in work agreements, holding money for enslaved brothers, and making *coartación* (graduated self-purchase) payments to their owners to ensure their steady progress toward freedom. He planned the funerals of departed brothers, and paid for their burials and masses for their souls.

Prieto served as godfather for Lucumí *boҙales* who were recently liberated from British-intercepted slave ships such as the *Mexico*, and he even arranged for the delivery, postpartum care, and proper baptism of members' children. One fascinating document provides an account of the exact costs of the midwife's services, a list of the foods provided for the mother with their costs, and the cost of the child's baptismal clothes. Someone, maybe Nepomuceno himself, was producing handwritten indulgences and prayers for the brothers, some of them illustrated in watercolors and featuring blond winged angels. The *cabildo* had also commissioned more formal printed and illustrated prayers dedicated to Nuestra Señora de Montserrat, the black virgin Nuestra Señora de los Remedios, Nuestra Señora del Rosario, and Nuestra Señora del Carmelo. The *cabildo* had even printed an invitation to the Captain General to attend the procession of its patron saint.[72]

Other objects seized from Prieto's house provide evidence that although he was a good Catholic and a loyal and distinguished official of the free black militia, he and his brothers simultaneously observed Christian and African religious practices. Similar patterns of accommodation may be found throughout the Afro-Catholic world. Investigators found several statues of black Africans, which they termed "symbolic of their witchcraft." These were described as being about three feet tall and dressed in charms of some sort. One had a mirror in its belly like the Kongo *nkisi*. In the patio of Prieto's house officials found a bust of another African figure covered by a jar under which some plants were growing, and another container filled with eggs. Also found was one very large elephant tusk and other smaller ones arranged in a sort of display.[73] How the brothers managed to obtain elephant tusks is a fascinating, but unanswered, question. The Spanish officials who interrogated Prieto that day linked him to the rebel Aponte, a former neighbor with whom he shared Lucumí and military connections. As they searched his house, Prieto indignantly told the investigators that whatever was done to him, blacks would do to them, at which point the officials arrested him.[74]

Only four years later, in 1839, officials claimed to have uncovered yet another conspiracy that allegedly involved plotters across the island. Among its participants was León Monzón, the retired captain of Havana's *moreno* battalion. Monzón had been exiled for four years for association with his neighbor and fellow carpenter, José Antonio Aponte, but once his term had been completed, he returned to Cuba and to his military career. By the time he retired in 1829 he had served Spain for thirty-nine years. Despite this long service, Havana authorities were watching Monzón, as they watched so many other free blacks, and on searching his home, they found materials they considered seditious. These included proclamations that the *pardo* and *moreno* units had printed in support of the Liberal Constitution of 1812, as well as pamphlets entitled *Liberty and Tyranny, Republicans in Barcelona*, and *The Political Constitution of the Spanish Monarchy*. The authorities charged Monzón with "having conspired directly by means of reunions and secret societies against the government of His Majesty to whom he owed many favors for having elevated him to the rank and decorations he enjoyed." The leader of this alleged conspiracy, however, was not the free and educated military man, Monzón, but rather an enslaved cook and dock worker named Margarito Blanco, who was said to be the Okongo or leader of a secret society called the Okongo of Ultán. Authorities were shocked that a man of Monzón's "status and circumstances" would be a part of the revolt. Calling his client by his honorific title of Don, Monzón's defense lawyer argued that it was "unimaginable" that Monzón would be involved with "subjects much inferior to him in destiny and interests." He continued, "Furthermore, it is well known by all, that the same line that divides white and black . . . exists between a gifted free man and an African slave." This time Monzón and seven others were sentenced to four years in a prison in Spain and perpetual exile. If even the most loyal and respected of free blacks was suspect, the planter elites who dominated Cuba's political economy could never feel safe, and they determined to be rid of this internecine enemy. In rapid succession, Cuba's Captain General outlawed the popular free black dances and ordered "the most active vigilance of the disciplined and urban militias of color."[75]

Many other cases document the surveillance and repression to which persons of African descent were being subjected in Havana in the 1830s. After centuries of loyal service to a monarchy and hard-won inclusion into a medieval corporate society, the rules of the game had changed for free *pardos* and *morenos* in Cuba. Imperial contests in Europe and revolutions in the Americas had provided opportunities for men like Barba and Flores to demonstrate continued loyalty to their monarchy and win additional perquisites and social prestige. But in the end Spain's distant monarch proved faithless, and so they embraced Enlightenment ideas of equality and the promises of a constitution that would enact it. The return of absolutism and the harsh repression launched by Cuba's plantocracy led some of the island's free blacks to look to other political models and possibilities. Joining cause with the enslaved, men like Aponte attempted a revolution modeled after that of Saint Domingue, but the result was more repression. Over the next decades, as Cuba became more African and as sugar planters bent the government to their will, repression would only get worse. Ironically, as the planter class more severely restricted the black bourgeoisie, more of them would be driven to cast their lot with the *bozales*—this time, to try to eliminate slavery altogether.

5

Black Seminoles: A Nation Besieged

We do not live for ourselves only, but for our wives and children who are as dear to us as those of any other men. When we reach our new home we hope we shall be permitted to remain while the woods remain green and the water runs.

Abraham, Fort Deynaud, Florida, April 30, 1838[1]

AFTER ALMOST A quarter-century of resistance, the Black Seminole named Abraham had yielded. Now he had to prepare his people for the long exodus westward to Indian Territory, where they would have to rebuild their lives. According to most accounts, the former slave who became famous as an interpreter and adviser to the Seminole chief, Micanopy, had once been the property of a Spanish physician in Pensacola. Abraham would thus have been familiar with Spanish law and society, and might have aspired to self-purchase or manumission by his owner or the state, all of which were viable possibilities. Instead, Abraham became a runaway. Sometime during the War of 1812, he made his way up the Apalachicola River to join the maroons gathering at the British fort at Prospect Bluff. There he trained with the British military officer at the fort, Colonel Edward Nicolls, and transformed himself from slave to Colonial Negro Marine.

Abraham probably escaped not from a Spanish physician in Pensacola but from the trading post of Forbes & Company, the Pensacola company that succeeded Panton, Leslie & Company as monopolists for the Indian trade in the Lower South. Forbes & Company inherited an already established commercial network that depended largely upon blacks and Indians. By 1786 Panton, Leslie & Company owned 250 slaves and nineteen separate land grants in Spanish Florida totaling 12,820 acres. Most of the company slaves worked on its various plantations and ranches, but some had specialized functions. For example, the company hired out its slave Langueste to the Spanish government as an interpreter for the Indians and collected his wages. Company slaves traveled to and from the Indian nations regularly, bringing back cattle and trains of pack horses loaded with deerskins. At trading stores like the Almacén de Nuestra Señora de la Concepción, located about six miles south of Palatka on the west bank of the St. Johns River in northern Florida, 50 to 60 slaves worked tending fields of corn and vegetables, herding cattle, and curing and tanning the deerskins their compatriots brought in from the Indian settlements. In the company's St. Augustine warehouse, slaves processed the hides and prepared them for export. As Spain's grip on Florida weakened and assorted plots and invasions wreaked havoc on the outlying ranches, stores, and plantations, Forbes & Company would eventually transfer some of its slaves to Matanzas, Cuba.[2]

Abraham may have been among the five slaves who helped establish Forbes & Company's new trading post at Prospect

"Negro Abraham." From Joshua R. Giddings, *The Exiles of Florida* (Columbus, Ohio, 1858). Courtesy of the Florida State Archives.

Bluff in 1804. By 1808 the post had grown to encompass a store-house, another storage building for deerskins, a granary, a dwelling for the resident agent, several slave houses, and assorted outbuildings. The Forbes & Company slaves had cleared and planted thirty acres around the post, and they also tended a herd of 1,200 cattle.[3] Seminoles and Mikasukis came to the store to trade goods and information, and it was probably in this period that Abraham learned the indigenous languages that would be so critical to him in his "next life."

In 1815 Forbes & Company provided the Spanish official Vicente Sebastián Pintado with a list of 45 slaves they said had been stolen by the British agents Nicholls and Woodbine the year before. The missing slaves were ranked by value, and Abraham's name was second on the list. His occupation was given as master carpenter and the company listed his value at 1,000 pesos. First on the list was Harry, a literate shipwright who was valued by the company at 2,000 pesos, about four times the price of a "prime hand."[4] Pintado interviewed Harry at Prospect Bluff on May 6, 1815, and asked him to return with him, but Harry refused. Abraham did not even present himself for an interview.[5]

By the time Abraham fled from Prospect Bluff to the Seminole heartland in central Florida, he had become a multicultural person, knowledgeable about the Spanish, British, and indigenous worlds and their tumultuous politics. He had information on which to base his decisions, and indeed his life depended on making wise choices. The Spanish system offered him the prospect of freedom sometime in the future, but this may have seemed too far off. The British had promised freedom in return for military service, and he risked his life for them at Prospect Bluff, only to be abandoned when the British Navy sailed away from the Apalachicola River. Life in a remote maroon settlement may have seemed less secure with the advance of armed Americans into the region. In the end, alliance with the still powerful Seminole nation must have offered at least some hope of a free life.

The Seminoles had been incorporating escaped slaves into their society for at least a half-century. The so-called Lower Creeks had accompanied General James Oglethorpe from Georgia southward when he invaded Spanish Florida in 1740, and they returned to claim the lush savannas of central Florida after the Spanish and their Indian allies departed for Cuba in 1763. The Seminoles established a settlement near present-day Gainesville, Florida, which they named La Chua for a nearby sinkhole.[6] Leaders of the Creek nation asked British officials to issue a trade embargo and force the detached groups back into the nation, but Chief Cowkeeper, his brother Long Warrior, and about 130 other Creek families resisted reincorporation and retained their autonomy. Thereafter, the Creek immigrants to Florida were known as Seminoles (a corruption of the Spanish word *cimarrón,* or runaway).[7] The Pennsylvania naturalist William Bartram visited the Seminole capital of Cuscowilla in 1774 and described a prosperous settlement based on agriculture and "innumerable droves of cattle." Bartram noted that the Seminoles had been "tinctured with Spanish civilization." Some wore "little silver crucifixes, affixed to a wampum collar around their necks, or suspended by a small chain upon their breast."[8] Catholic priests had established several small missions in the area and had apparently made some impact on the Seminoles, most of who also spoke and understood Spanish. Despite these earlier affiliations, the Seminoles during Chief Cowkeeper's rule were fiercely loyal to the British government that held Florida from 1763 to 1784. The Seminoles may have felt abandoned by the Spaniards who left, but their loyalty may have also been inspired by the far superior trade goods the English were able to supply.[9] Bartram described the Seminoles as "the most bitter and formidable Indian enemies the Spaniards ever had."[10]

Over the next decades Cowkeeper's successor, Chief Payne, and his nephews and successors, Micanopy and Bowlegs, reshaped Seminole foreign policy and allied with the Spanish government, which had returned to displace the British. This shift had important consequences for individuals of African descent. The Seminoles had earlier made slaves of defeated Yamasee enemies, and if Bartram's assessment is correct, Seminole masters had a low regard for their Yamasee slaves. The Seminoles also owned slaves of African descent, some of whom they had received as "gifts" from the British. Because the British chattel system considered slaves to be property, the Seminoles may have viewed slaves acquired from the British or through purchase in much the same way. There is evidence that Seminoles inherited slaves from family members or made gifts of them on occasion. Generations of slaves of African descent sometimes belonged to the same Seminole family. By the 1790s Chief Payne was reported to "own" some twenty black slaves along with large herds of cattle, horses, sheep, and goats,[11] and the existence of this wealth is attested by archaeological investigations at Payne's Town. Apparently the Seminoles prized En-

glish tea sets. It was the additional labor provided by black ag-
riculturalists that enabled the Seminoles to acquire the surplus
necessary to enter an Atlantic market economy and buy those
tea sets.[12]

The Seminoles, however, seem to have regarded the runaway slaves they accepted into their communities differently
from the slaves they purchased or "owned." One important difference was that the Seminoles had not conquered these people;
instead, these black men came as warriors with critical military
knowledge and useful skills. As a result, they lived more independently than the Seminoles' slaves did, in a sort of feudal
arrangement with the chiefs with whom they affiliated. In
some cases the incoming runaways intermarried with Seminoles, even marrying the widows of chiefs.[13]

Unlike their Anglo neighbors, Spaniards were not threatened
by the blacks living among the Seminoles. Black and Indian militias had operated jointly to protect Spanish frontiers since the
sixteenth century, and Spanish officials regularly posted black
militiamen like Sergeant Felipe Edimboro at Seminole villages.
Viewing the Seminoles as a buffer against Anglo encroachment,
the Spanish government attempted to ensure their friendship
by regularly hosting and gifting them in St. Augustine. The
Crown allotted 6,000 pesos annually for their gifts, which included items such as cloth and clothing, hats, thread and nee-
dles, thimbles, scissors, beads, pipes, knives, axes, razors, mir-
rors, tin pots, spurs, munitions, tobacco, aguardiente (rum), and
food. Seminole women were given gingham and chintz cloth,
and the children received the interesting gift of red paper. Special luxury items such as saddles went to head men like Perry-

man, Long Warrior, Filatuche, and Tupane. On at least four occasions groups identified specifically as *cimarrones* or slave
runaways came to St. Augustine, usually in the company of
Seminoles, and in an act that recognized their autonomy, the
Spaniards gifted them as well.[14]

The Seminoles were linked to the Spanish economy not only
through gifts but through the cattle trade. Free blacks like the
militiaman Juan Bautista Collins were often the intermediar-
ies in that trade. Collins, whose father was French and whose
mother was of African descent from Saint Domingue, operated
a dry goods store in St. Augustine. He kept his account books
in Spanish, English, and French, and he traveled with Spanish
government passports to Havana, Pensacola, and New Orleans
to conduct his business.[15] In 1808 Collins also initiated diplomatic and commercial relations with Chief Bowlegs at La Chua.
His companion and translator on trips to the Seminole villages
was the Anglo/Senegalese militiaman Benjamin Wiggins, who
was also African-born Sergeant Felipe Edimboro's son-in-law.
Wiggins and Collins shared a multiracial, multiethnic, and multilingual background that facilitated their interactions with the
Seminoles. They distributed gifts of cloth, handkerchiefs, belts,
beads, sugar, tobacco, aguardiente, knives, powder, and shot
among their Seminole hosts before getting down to the business
of buying cattle. A roundup might take five months or more as
the men traveled from village to village, buying animals to herd
back to St. Augustine. Collins also herded cattle to Forbes &
Company in Pensacola and could well have known some of the
men like Abraham who later escaped to Prospect Bluff.

On one trip through the Seminole villages, the men bought a

herd of 125 cattle at Chiscochate, 18 of which were sold to them by a black runaway from Georgia named Molly. In the Seminole villages, as in St. Augustine, women who had escaped from chattel slavery could control property and dispose of it as they chose. This was also true for Seminole women. Collins bought cattle from Chief Bowlegs' sister, Simency, and on one occasion she traveled to St. Augustine to testify on his behalf in a lawsuit. Seminole women retained their cattle herds, their traditions of financial independence, and their litigious behavior for some time after the United States acquired Florida. In 1824 the late chief Payne's sister, Bukra Woman, sued the slave trader and merchant Philip R. Yonge for a debt of $1965 he owed her from a cattle sale sixteen years earlier.[16]

The free blacks from St. Augustine who visited the Seminole villages on military, commercial, or diplomatic missions probably recognized some runaway slaves from St. Augustine living among their hosts. One of these, a man named Nero, had been raised as a slave on Francis Fatio's "baronial" estate of New Switzerland, on the St. Johns River. Because the plantation lay at the edge of Seminole lands, there was frequent contact between Fatio's slaves and the Seminoles.[17] Fatio received Seminole hunting parties at his plantation almost as a Spanish governor would, with gifts and food. Sometimes, as during the Bowles years, they came as raiders. It is not surprising that a number of Fatio's slaves learned the Seminole language and culture from these frequent exchanges. One of those slaves was Luis Pacheco, later charged with guiding a U.S. Army unit into a massacre.[18] When Nero was still an adolescent he was either taken by, or joined, Indian raiders (probably Mikasukis) who attacked the

Fatio plantation in 1812. Fatio sent agents out to try to recover the boy, whose family still lived on the plantation, but in vain. Lost temporarily from the historical record, Nero reappears in the aftermath of the destruction of Prospect Bluff.

The year after Nero was taken or ran away, another slave from St. Augustine, named Fernando, made a choice that also led him to Prospect Bluff. Fernando's owner, Catalina Satorios, had planned to take the slave with her when she moved to Charleston in 1812. He was already on the boat when one of Catalina's creditors appeared at the dock, and Fernando was left behind as a security on his mistress's debt. Only days later, the British agent Captain George Woodbine rode into town with an armed escort of blacks from Prospect Bluff, all of whom were former slaves. Although Fernando would have known of the legal routes to freedom available in the Spanish city, Woodbine and his black troops offered the young man an immediate release from bondage. Woodbine denied stealing away any slaves of Spanish owners, but his escort had grown by the time he left town. Catalina learned later from friends that Fernando had ridden out with the "cursed voodbene." Although she paid for "various individuals who went in his pursuit," they did not find Fernando, "nor even his trail." Like Abraham, Harry, Samson, and Nero, Fernando had decided to join the Colonial Negro Marines who were training at Prospect Bluff.[19]

Despite his best efforts, the Spanish agent Vicente Pintado failed to locate all the runaways he had hoped to recover from Prospect Bluff for owners in St. Augustine and Pensacola. He noted that by the time he arrived, many of the maroons had already left Prospect Bluff for Seminole villages near Tampa Bay and along the Suwannee River.[20] Abraham, Harry, Nero, and Fernando may have been among those who saw the terror coming and slipped away before the final battle. If so, it was a momentous decision, for by September 1816, the fort was no more. Many of the men they had trained and fought with, and their families as well, were lost in the terrible explosion that destroyed the fort.[21]

Given the many contacts and long experience the Seminoles already had with persons of African descent, it is not surprising that they offered a refuge to the new wave of black refugees who fled from Prospect Bluff in 1816. Their geopolitical knowledge, military experience, and languages were valuable assets for the Seminoles. The independent "village Negroes," as they were sometimes called in English sources, provided annual tribute and military service to the Seminole chiefs with whom they were associated, but black leaders ruled the black villages.

Reshaping his life once more, Abraham became a trusted interpreter and adviser for Chief Micanopy (Pond Governor).[22] Nero became the adviser and interpreter for the Seminole's principal leader, Chief Bowlegs, and located his village near to that of Bowlegs. Americans who later wrote about the Black Seminoles were unable to conceive of the vassalage relationship between Seminole chiefs and escaped slaves; they thought that all blacks living among the Seminoles were enslaved chattel. Thus they believed that Micanopy "owned" Abraham, and Bowlegs "owned" Nero.[23]

Recognizing that the Americans intended to return them to slavery, Abraham, Nero, Harry, Fernando, and other runaways encouraged a Seminole alliance with the Spaniards, who were also feeling the pressure of American expansionism. The Spaniards stood to lose their colony, the fugitive blacks their freedom, and the Seminoles their rich lands and cattle herds. It may have been a marriage of convenience, but all of them pulled together against the common enemy.[24]

With the Negro Fort at Prospect Bluff destroyed, the Americans were rid of one "problem," but north of the destroyed fort, on the Flint River even closer to advancing American settlements, lay the Mikasuki village that Americans called Fowl Town (in modern Georgia). General Edmund Gaines burned Fowl Town on November 21, 1817, but the surviving residents retaliated in an attack on a party of forty-five American soldiers and settlers who were traveling the Apalachicola River. Almost all the Americans were killed. Several days later, blacks and Indians firing from the banks besieged another river convoy. Travel up that river was deemed "impossible . . . the shore being lined on both sides of the river, with Indians and negroes, who keep up a constant fire."[25] The situation was considered so threatening that in December 1817, Secretary of War John C. Calhoun replaced General Gaines and ordered Andrew Jackson to Fort Scott on the eastern bank of the Flint River. From his new post Jackson promptly launched a series of brutal attacks against the Seminole nation that came to be called the First Seminole War.[26]

Many of the blacks and Indians who had been at Prospect Bluff suspected that the Forbes & Company agents, Edmund Doyle and William Hambly, had betrayed them to the Americans, and the two men became targets of retaliation.[27] In December 1817, Fowl Town warriors seized Doyle and Hambly and took them to Suwannee Old Town for "trial" by King Hei-jah. King Heijah sentenced the men to death, but Nero inter-ceded to save their lives. Nero sent the condemned men to the Spanish garrison at St. Marks for safekeeping, effectively com-muting their sentence. That he was able to deny the warriors their revenge speaks to Nero's influence among the Seminoles. Later, Peter Cook, a witness at Andrew Jackson's trial of the British subjects Alexander Arbuthnot and Robert Ambrister, stated that he, too, had been under Nero's protection and that it was Nero who distributed gunpowder brought in from the Ba-hamas to the black troops. He added that some of the Negro captains would obey none but Nero.[28]

General Gaines wrote to King Heijah, "You harbor a great many of my black people among you, at Sahwahnee. If you give me leave to go by you against them, I shall not hurt anything be-longing to you." King Heijah responded that some blacks might have taken refuge among the English during their war with the Americans (1812), but "it is for you, white people, to settle those things among yourselves. . . . I shall use force to stop any armed Americans from passing my towns or my lands."[29] In March of 1818 General Gaines attacked Mikasuki and killed King Heijah for his impertinent challenge.

Although the British had officially departed the region, blacks and Seminoles were still receiving covert assistance from their allies. Alexander Arbuthnot, a Scottish merchant from the Bahamas, had established a trading post on the Suwannee in 1817 from which to conduct trade with the Seminoles at Bow-legs' Town and with the blacks captained by Nero in his nearby town. Arbuthnot obviously had profits in mind when he arrived, but like Bowles and Nicolls before him, he developed empathy for the Seminoles and became an advocate for the Indian cause. He wrote frequently to the British Minister in Washington and to the Governor of the Bahamas to report "wanton American aggression" against the Seminoles and to forward Chief Bowlegs' and King Heijah's urgent requests for supplies and support from King George. Arbuthnot also appealed to the governors of Havana and St. Augustine for aid for their besieged allies.[30]

The Americans suspected that the British were still inciting and supplying the Indians and blacks in Florida. Their suspicions were confirmed when Arbuthnot sailed back from a trip to the Bahamas with none other than Captain George Woodbine aboard. Also along was Robert Ambrister, and the two men began to train the blacks and Seminoles assembled at Bowlegs' Town. An American, George Perryman, later reported that he saw "negroes on parade [in Suwannee]: he counted about six hundred that bore arms . . . There is said to be about the same number of Indians belonging to their party; and there are both negroes and Indians going daily to their standard." Perryman noted that the Black Seminoles "speak in the most contemptuous manner of the Americans, and threaten to have satisfaction for what has been done—meaning the destruction of the Negro Fort."[31] The Americans, in turn, wanted satisfaction for Seminole raids into Georgia and for the earlier American deaths on the Apalachicola River.

As the Patriots of 1812 had, Andrew Jackson blamed the weakened Spanish government for failing to control the unrest on the frontier. St. Augustine's governor, however, was at the time dealing with more serious problems. Claiming to represent various Spanish American nations, first Gregor MacGregor and then Luis Aury had "liberated" Amelia Island from the Spanish empire. Never one for diplomatic deliberations, and convinced the Spaniards would do nothing, Jackson decided to handle the border threat himself. He intended to "chastise a savage foe, who combined with a lawless band of negro brigands, had for some time been carrying on a cruel and unprovoked war against the citizens of the United States."[32] Once again, an American force crossed the international border to attack sovereign Spanish territory. Marching eastward, Jackson forced the surrender of the small Spanish garrison at San Marcos de Apalache. There he also captured the Red Stick Creek Prophet Francis (Hillis Hadjo) whose forces Jackson had decimated at Horseshoe Bend, Alabama, during the Creek War. After that disaster Francis had traveled with Colonel Nicolls to London and the Bahamas seeking British support, but they got little more than a reception. Jackson summarily executed Francis and, according to Daniel Penton, Traditional Chief of the Muscogee Nation of Florida, dumped the Prophet's body in a well. Jackson then organized a "field" trial for the two British subjects he had also captured at San Marcos—Arbuthnot and Ambrister. Jackson's officers interrogated the two men and several others and convicted them on charges of inciting and arming the Indians and blacks. Jackson executed them both—Arbuthnot by hanging and Ambrister by firing squad. In what would be a last letter to his son, Alexander Arbuthnot wrote, "The main drift of the Americans is to destroy the black population of Suwany. Tell my friend, Boleck [Bowlegs], that it is throwing away his people to attempt to resist such a powerful force."[33]

The blacks and Seminoles understood that all too well, but nonetheless they determined to put up a fierce resistance. A witness at Ambrister's trial later testified that the doomed man had told the black troops, who were by then under Nero's direction, that "it was useless to run, for if they ran any further, they would be driven into the sea."[34] Evidence at Ambrister's trial included a letter he had written Colonel Nicolls from the Suwannee stating that the three hundred blacks there "beg me to say, they depend on your promises, and expect you are the way out. They have stuck to the *cause,* and will always believe in the faith of you."[35]

Unfortunately, that faith was misplaced: the British government would fight no more wars in the South. The black and Indian soldiers they had trained were on their own when Jackson led more than 3,000 troops in a three-week campaign against the Seminole heartland. Joined by the Coweta Creek leader William McIntosh, who had also besieged Prospect Bluff, Jackson's troops on April 16, 1818, burned almost four hundred black and Seminole homes at Bowlegs' Town and Nero's Town on the Suwannee River. The American troops also destroyed large quantities of food supplies, and spirited away herds of carefully counted cattle and horses. From Bowlegs' Town, Jackson exulted prematurely: "I have reached and destroyed this and the other town in its vicinity [Mikasuki], and having captured the principal exciters of the war I think I may safely say, that the Indian war, for the present, is terminated."[36]

The blacks and Seminoles, who had been forewarned by Arbuthnot, put up a desperate fight, with three hundred of Nero's black warriors holding back a greatly superior force at the Suwannee to give women and children time to cross over to safety. Among the last defenders on the Suwannee were blacks like Nero and Fernando, who had already fought Jackson at Prospect Bluff. Although some reports said that Nero had been killed, he would appear again in the battles that followed.[37]

Andrew Jackson captured Fernando with weapon in hand and could have executed him on the spot. Instead, he claimed Fernando as his slave, renamed him Polydore, and took him back to Tennessee. When his former owner discovered Fernando's fate, she wrote Jackson to try and recover her slave. Jackson responded, adding to Fernando's history that after enlisting with the "notorious Woodbine" and Nicolls, he had also spent time with the "notorious Ambrister" before being captured on the Suwannee, "arms in his hands, under the character of a British soldier." Jackson added, "Our two governments being at peace, his life was forfeighted and he ought to have died."[38] Madam Satorios then wrote to Fernando (in Spanish) to chastise him for disloyalty. She called Fernando an ingrate, and after reference to her own Christian charity and Divine Providence, she continued in a kinder vein: "I do not doubt that you have experienced many troubles and scares and I hope that they have served as a lesson to you and that from this day forward you will seek liberty not in this miserable world, but in the next . . . God preserve your life many years and I hope you will treat your new master with fidelity and constancy until his death." It appears that Fernando, like other blacks who once lived among the Seminoles, was a literate man.[39]

After six years of freedom and warfare, Fernando was once again a slave, this time on the Hermitage, Andrew Jackson's plantation near Nashville, Tennessee. Polydore, as Jackson had renamed him, acquired a wife and children at the Hermitage. Although once again enslaved, his literacy, and perhaps other qualities as well, had at least ensured that he would not be a field hand. One of Jackson's acquaintances wrote him that "I saw your Servant Polidore [*sic*] yesterday and made particular Enquiry how your Black family were and how they Conducted, and if he can be relied upon, everything is going on well at your farm."[40] One can only wonder what the other slaves at the Hermitage learned from the multilingual and literate man who had once lived among the Seminoles and stood, gun in hand, against their "master." This example provides a reminder that the plantations of the antebellum South were not as homogeneous as popular imagery might suggest.

After the Suwannee River campaign Jackson marched westward, and in May 1818 he seized Spanish Pensacola, concluding the so-called First Seminole War. Jackson wrote President James Monroe that with permission, supplies, and troops, "I will assure you that Cuba will be ours in a few days."[41]

Although the Seminoles' northern settlements were ruined, their desperate resistance continued. Black and Indian refugees dispersed to western and southern Florida, joining others who had anticipated the attacks at Prospect Bluff and the Suwannee River and who had already resettled in traditional hunting villages near Tampa Bay. Harry, the literate shipwright once owned by Forbes & Company, was among the survivors of Prospect Bluff who had found refuge there. Utilizing the training he had received under Colonel Nicholls and Captain Woodbine, he was reported to be drilling one hundred warriors at Tampa Bay.[42] Captain James Gadsden described Tampa Bay as "the last rallying spot of the disaffected negroes and Indians and the only favorable point from whence a communication can be had with Spanish and European emissaries."[43] The desperate Seminoles and their black allies sent repeated diplomatic missions from Tampa to the British in the Bahamas and the Spaniards in Cuba. The Spaniards in St. Augustine gave them substantial food supplies and muskets, but the British sent only nominal gifts, not wanting to alienate the Americans who, by the terms of the Adams-Onís Treaty, were soon to take possession of Florida.[44]

In 1821 General Andrew Jackson became governor of the new United States territorial government of Florida—his reward for defeating the blacks and Indians who had blocked American expansion. Jackson recommended removing the remaining Creeks, Seminoles, and free blacks from the peninsula. As Jackson awaited a response to his proposal, several hundred Coweta warriors sponsored by Georgia speculators raided the Seminoles' Tampa Bay and Sarasota Bay settlements. After inflicting much destruction, the Cowetas returned with numbers of captured blacks as well as herds of cattle and horses. The black captives were sold back into slavery for a tidy profit. The remnant Seminoles and blacks who escaped capture were once again forced to flee—this time to the tip of the peninsula at Cape Florida. There, Cuban fishermen and Bahamian wreckers with whom they had long conducted trade carried hundreds "in a famishing state" to safety in Cuba and to Andros Island and

Bimini.[45] In Cuba the rescued may have encountered some of the black refugees that Whitten had shepherded from St. Augustine.

A number of the Black Seminoles had been killed during the war, and their numbers were further thinned by subsequent slaving raids, but some managed to survive and began to rebuild their lives farther south in the Florida peninsula. The remnants of Bowlegs' and Nero's people relocated their villages southward, but Bowlegs did not live long after this move. As was customary, on Bowlegs' death in 1821, his sister's son Micanopy succeeded him as the principal chief of the Seminoles. Micanopy's accession enhanced Abraham's importance, as well as his visibility in the written record. In recognition of his bravery during the First Seminole War Abraham adopted a new name, Sonanaffe Tustenuggee, meaning "Suwannee Warrior."[46] American military officials who had contact with Abraham described him as courtly and intelligent, "a perfect Talleyrand of the Savage Court." They recognized Abraham's influence with Micanopy, whom they still believed was his master, and they knew that Abraham would continue to promote resistance. "They [the Black Seminoles] fear being again made slaves, under the American government, and will omit nothing to increase or keep alive mistrust among the Indians, whom they in fact govern. If it should be necessary to use force with them, it is to be feared that the Indians would take their part. It will, however, be necessary to remove from the Floridas this group of lawless freebooters, among whom runaway negroes will always find refuge."[47]

The description of the Black Seminoles as lawless freebooters could hardly have been further from reality. Recognizing

Black Settlement Sites

Black settlement sites in Florida. Map by Jim Landers.

what had to be done, they got down to the hard work of clearing and planting the wilderness and building new villages, separate and autonomous, but near to those of the Seminoles. The
names of the new villages reflected the ethnic diversity that now
characterized the people living in them: Pilaklikaha, Mulatto

Girl's Town, King Heijah's Town, Bucker [Bukra] Woman's Town, Boggy Island, and Big Swamp.[48] Abraham governed the independent village of Pilaklikaha (Many Ponds) near present-day Bushnell, Florida, until the outbreak of the Second Seminole War. When the former slave trader turned settler Horatio Dexter visited Pilaklikaha in 1823, he reported that "about 100 Negroes belonging to Micanope and his family of different ages and sexes" had planted approximately 120 acres in corn, peanuts, and rice there. Dexter, like other Americans, could not see or acknowledge the independence of Abraham's villagers. Dexter also visited and reported on another black settlement at Boggy Island, where blacks allied to Sitarky had planted corn, rice, and sugar cane—the latter from plants that Dexter had provided during an earlier visit to the village.[49]

Meanwhile, the Americans who had acquired Florida in 1821 were also building a series of military forts in central Florida. Renewed conflict was almost inevitable as blacks, Indians, and Americans of racist sentiments began to live in closer proximity. In 1823 the victors forced upon the vanquished the Treaty of Moultrie Creek, which ceded the best Seminole lands to the U.S. government. The Seminoles had always prospered as pastoralists, but their cattle had been killed or stolen, and the lands they were allotted were so poor that they were soon starving.[50] In contrast, Dexter's descriptions of the Black Seminole villages he visited seem to suggest that they had made a better adjustment to relocation. The Seminoles attempted to negotiate their deteriorating situation by sending a formal delegation to Washington, D.C., in 1826, with Abraham accompanying Micanopy. An engraving commemorating the event shows Abra-

THE ILLUSTRATED LONDON NEWS.

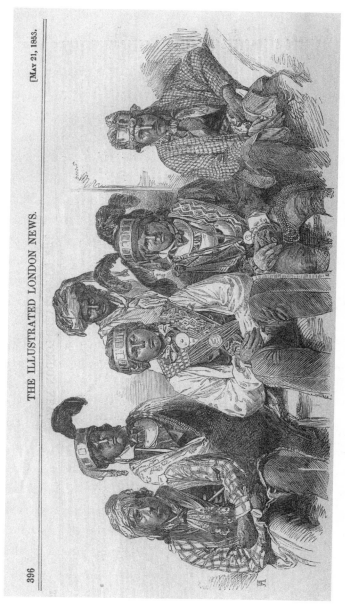

Seminole delegation to Washington, D.C., in 1826, showing Abraham in back center. *The Illustrated London News*, May 21, 1853. Copy in the Jean and Alexander Heard Library, Vanderbilt University.

ham positioned in the center of the image, behind Micanopy, reinforcing the Americans' perception that he guided Micanopy's politics.

By 1832 the increasingly desperate Seminoles had signed Payne's Landing Treaty and sent a delegation to Indian Territory to evaluate lands being offered them there—far way from white settlements. Abraham and another black interpreter, Lame Cudjo, made that journey, and it appeared that an agreement for relocation had been made. But many of the Seminole leaders, and all the Black Seminoles, resisted when the time came actually to depart. Again, American officers pointed to Abraham as the instigator of the resistance. Apparently they never noticed the irony of assigning so much power to one whom they consistently referred to as a slave. One official wrote that Abraham "dictated to those of his own color, who [in turn] to a great degree controlled their [Seminole] masters."[51]

In December of 1835, the Seminoles and their black allies rose in a series of concerted attacks on plantations along the St. Johns River and launched the Second Seminole War. Their lesser numbers dictated these guerrilla tactics, which also included the executions of targeted individuals they considered to have betrayed them. They knew better than to attempt attacks on the American forts near Tampa Bay or present-day Ocala, but in late December they wiped out a small patrol led by Brevet Major Francis L. Dade. The Dade Massacre, as it was thereafter known in American sources, was followed by major battles in the Withlacoochee Swamp during which the black and Seminole warriors managed to repulse major U.S. Army expeditions sent against them. They knew the terrain better, and they were fighting for their lives. The following month the *New York Observer* reported, "This is the last struggle of the Indians on our Atlantic frontier, and from the manner in which it has commenced it will be more bloody than any."[52] Brevet Major General Thomas Sidney Jesup took command of the war effort at the end of 1836, and before long he came to the conclusion that "this . . . is a negro war, not an Indian war; and if it be not speedily put down, the south will feel the effects of it on their slave population before the end of the next season."[53]

The beleaguered blacks and Seminoles managed to hold out in the swamps for two years against all odds, but despite their incredible bravery and persistence, the sheer weight of American military power eventually convinced Abraham and others that further resistance was futile. Abraham turned himself in to the U.S. forces and bowed to the inevitable. From Tampa, Abraham sent a dictated letter addressed to his old ally Wild Cat (Mad Panther or Cae Hadjo). Abraham reminded his old friend that when they had gone to Arkansas together to survey the land being offered them,

one rainy evening after passing a hill we sat down together on a bee tree which we had found & felled. The country was good and while sitting there a deer came close to us—We had no arms and could not shoot it,—You said—"Abraham, I used to think that all the whites hated us, but now I believe they wish us to live. This is a rich country and we will return home and tell the truth."

Fort Deynaud Florida
25th April 1838

General,

I have the honour to present my best respects to you. Myself and Tony Barnet have done every thing promised by us, and expect the General will do by us as he said at the beginning of this campaign. I send Tony to see you, and he can afterwards come and join me wherever I may be. We wish to get in writing from the General the agreement made with us. We will go with the Indians to our new home, and wish to know how we are to be protected, and who is to have the care of us on the road. We do not live for ourselves only, but for our wives & children who are as dear to us as those of every other men. When we reach our home we hope we shall be permitted to remain while the woods remain green, and the water runs.

Letter from Abraham to Colonel Thomas Sidney Jesup, April 30, 1838. Courtesy of the P. K. Yonge Library of Florida History, University of Florida.

I have charge of all the red people coming on to Pearce's Creek, and all are satisfied to go to Arkansas. They all wish to see you, and hope you will wait until they come to Tampa. Whoever is to be chief Interpreter we would wish to know. I cannot do any more than I have, I have done all I can, my heart has been true since I came in at Tohopokilika. I wish Tony to come to Pearce's Creek immediately. I hope Toskeeger is satisfied. All his Seminole Brethren are coming in. Holatoochee has done well. All the black people are contented I hope.

Your Servant

Abram
his + mark

Abraham contrasted that scene with what they found on their return to Tampa: "You and I sat down one day on a pine tree near this post—The country around was pine barren and we were hungry and had nothing to eat—You spoke of the same subject as when we sat together on the bee tree in the rich soil of Arkansas." Abraham advised Wild Cat to surrender and not to sacrifice himself for "crazy people," meaning the Mikasuki. "My heart is heavy for you and Micanopy and Jumper. If my advice was ever friendly to you—believe it is so now." He signed, as usual, with an X and the dictated, "Your friend Sonanaffe Tustenukke."[54]

Preparing finally to leave Florida, Abraham wrote to General Jesup saying that he was happy to hear of the peace and that another Black Seminole leader, Juan Cavallo (John Horse), had come in and was contented. He said that he hoped "all the black people are contented . . . I hope Toskeegee is contented. Hotatoochhee has done well. All the black people are contented I hope." Abraham asked that General Jesup put in writing all that they had agreed to and closed by saying,

> We will go with the Indians to our new home, and wish to know how we are to be protected, and who is to have the care of us on the road. We do not live for ourselves only, but for our wives and children who are as dear to us as those of any other men. When we reach our new home we hope we shall be permitted to remain while the woods remain green and the water runs. I have charge of all the red people coming out to Pease's Creek, and all are satisfied to go to Arkansaw.[55]

If General Jesup noticed the irony in the former slave's assumed leadership of the exiles, he did not remark on it. Official U.S. documents later listed Abraham on a "registry of Negro Prisoners captured by the Troops Commanded by Major General Thomas S. Jesup in 1836 and 1837; and owned by Indians, or who claim to be free." Beside Abraham's name is the notation "male, age 50, claims to be free." An added remark was "The principal negro chief. Supposed to be friendly to the whites."[56] It is clear from Abraham's letter to General Jesup that he considered himself responsible for the safety of all the émigrés, including the "red people" of whom he "had charge." Like Prince Whitten, Abraham would lead his followers into exile. For more than twenty years blacks and Seminoles had struggled to maintain their autonomy on the volatile Southern frontier, independent of both the Spaniards and the new American government—a nation apart. Such a position was difficult and eventually untenable, but it was not yielded without fierce resistance. The dream of a Black Seminole nation in Florida had ended.

6

Atlantic Creoles in Matanzas, Cuba

> Die at the hands of an executioner, if necessary, to break the
> yoke [of slavery].
>
> Gabriel de la Concepción Valdés, "El Juramento" (The Oath)[1]

IN 1844 THE FAMOUS mulatto poet Gabriel de la Concepción
Valdés, popularly known as Plácido, was condemned to be executed for his alleged participation in a slave uprising known afterwards as La Escalera, named for the ladder on which so many
were whipped to death. His well-known abolitionist beliefs also
condemned him. Plácido spent the last hours of his life visiting
with family members and friends in the prison chapel of San
Carlos de Matanzas, where he and his associates rapidly produced multiple copies of his inspirational poetry. The authorities later complained that the poems had been disseminated
widely across the island, keeping Plácido alive in the memories
of those for whom he died.[2]

Eighty years or so earlier, prior to the brief British occupation of 1762–1763, Cuba had relatively fewer slaves and many
more free blacks than other Caribbean islands. While the British were in residence, however, they introduced approximately
4,000 African slaves into Cuba and established local mercantile

Gabriel de la Concepción Valdés (Plácido), the famed
mulatto poet executed in 1844 in Matanzas, Cuba, for
his alleged participation in the La Escalera conspiracy.
From *Appleton's Cyclopaedia of American Biography*, ed.
James Grant Wilson and John Fiske (New York, 1887–
1889), vol. 6.

and slaving connections that endured. Thereafter, British and North American traders had an important presence in Cuba. In lesser numbers, Spanish slave traders also began to import Africans into Cuba after Spain purchased the African islands of Fernando Po and Annonbom from Portugal in 1778 and opened Spanish colonies to a "free trade" in slaves in 1789.[3]

The destruction of the sugar plantations in Saint Domingue in 1791 further stimulated large-scale sugar cultivation and the introduction of ever larger numbers of African-born slaves into Cuba. Between 1790 and 1820 Cuban planters imported approximately 325,000 slaves, following the old Spanish formula of one female for every three males—a threefold increase in slave imports in only thirty years.[4] The "Africanization" of Cuba continued apace in subsequent decades.[5]

Neither the British embargo of 1807, nor the U.S. embargo of 1808, nor the Mixed Commissions for the Suppression of the Slave Trade established by the British in Havana, Rio de Janeiro, Suriname, and Sierra Leone to decide whether captured ships were illegally slaving, deterred Cuban slave traders.[6] Fernando de la Maza Arredondo, head of the Havana-based company Arredondo and Son, became one of the primary links in the slave trade among Charleston, St. Augustine, and Havana, and, like others, he flouted the British and U.S. embargoes.[7] In 1810 the British ship *Dark*, captained by James Wilkins, captured several Cuban ships off the African coast, one of which, the *María Dolores*, belonged to Arredondo and Son. That ship left Havana in March of 1810 and took on tobacco and other trade goods in Florida for exchange on the African coast. The British seized the *María Dolores* at Gorée Island with a full complement of slaves, and despite protests by the ship's captain, the Sierra Leone Mixed Commission for the Suppression of the Slave Trade declared the ship a good prize. Arredondo and Son could absorb this loss, however, and the company continued to send ships to the African coast.[8]

Under duress, Spain signed a treaty with Great Britain in 1817 that prohibited the slave trade north of the equator and abolished that trade completely after 1820. But even after British naval forces began intercepting ships off the African coast in 1819, the Cuban slave trade continued with the clear collusion of Cuban officials, most of whom were members of the sugar plantocracy. Americans like the infamous slave trader and later U.S. Senator James DeWolf of Bristol, Rhode Island, made huge profits from the illicit trade. Some of the slaves imported by DeWolf were sent to his own sugar plantations in Cuba, which in turn supplied his distilleries in Bristol.[9] Cuban slave traders also became wealthy. Pedro Blanco, the "Mongo of Gallinas," operated one of the most successful trading operations on the West African coast. His baracoons on the small islands in the Rio Gallinas held up to 5,000 slaves at a time, and he reported in 1838 that "the United States was his best market."[10] After some forty years on the African coast, Blanco returned to Cuba in 1839 hoping to use his wealth to introduce his mixed-race daughter, Rosa, into Cuban society. This would have been possible earlier, perhaps, but by the 1830s race relations had hardened and such social mobility was impossible.[11] Although Blanco subsequently retired, many other slave traders continued to make huge profits smuggling Africans into Cuba until Cuban slavery was finally abolished in 1886.[12] Meanwhile, the free black communities which had long enjoyed various privileges in Cuba, and of which Plácido was a member, were undone by the campaigns to abolish the slave trade and slavery itself.

By the first quarter of the nineteenth century, the newly imported slaves had transformed the western province of Matanzas, on the northern coast of Cuba, from a cattle, timber, and tobacco frontier into a profitable sugar-growing region.[13] Wealthy and powerful scions of Havana, like Ricardo O'Farill y O'Daly, the *asientista* (holder of the slave import monopoly) for the English South Sea Company, established extensive new sugar estates in Matanzas. The planters also built a new port that opened Matanzas to international trade, and in 1819 the O'Farill family established the first steamship service between Havana and Matanzas, by then Cuba's second largest city.[14] U.S. capitalists invested in profitable sugar and coffee estates, slave trading, and merchant houses in Matanzas. Dispatches from the U.S. Consul posted in Matanzas after 1820 document the growing trade with cities in the United States and Europe. The local newspaper, *La Aurora de Matanzas,* which was launched in 1828, recorded the steady stream of ships going in and out of the port.[15] In 1836, construction began on the railroad line that would connect the impressive mechanized sugar estates of Matanzas to Havana. This was the first railroad to be built in Latin America. Not even Spain had a railroad at the time.[16]

By 1827 Matanzas was producing about one-fourth of the sugar grown in Cuba, and large numbers of slaves were required to grow that sugar. The demand for slaves was so great that Matanzas planters like Joaquín Madan and Zacarías Atkins organized their own direct trade in African slaves, although Havana-based traders also supplied the Matanzas slave market.[17] By 1827 the population of Matanzas included 16,671 whites, 2,602 free blacks and mulattoes, and 26,522 black slaves. Free and enslaved blacks thus formed two-thirds of the total population. This demographic trend only accelerated: in 1841 the census showed that Matanzas had a population of 27,148 whites, 4,705 free blacks and mulattoes, and 54,322 black slaves. Populations of color had almost doubled and now outnumbered whites more than two to one.[18]

These multiple transformations came, ironically, as enlightened liberals around the Atlantic world were promulgating the abolition of the slave trade and slavery and an end to monarchical government. Such rhetoric only made already fearful planters more repressive and slaves more restive. The confluence of demographic and economic shifts and revolutionary activity, or the suspicion of it, proved disastrous for Cuba's Atlantic Creoles.

While the countryside grew increasingly African, the city of Matanzas was home to a more creolized and international free black population. In 1817 free blacks and mulattoes formed about a fourth of the city's population, and slaves another fifth. Like the white population, they were a diverse lot, with origins in the French, British, and Spanish Caribbeans as well as Africa. Free people of color held occupational and social positions similar to those of their counterparts in Havana, St. Augustine, or New Orleans. They employed traditional means such as self-hire and *coartación* (graduated self-purchase) to acquire freedom, and once free they ran small businesses, farmed, and joined the institutions which offered them the most advantages—the church and the military.[19]

In 1726 the free people of color in Matanzas established the *cofradía* of the Santa Misericordia and another devoted to the Virgin of the Rosary, reforming the latter in 1736.[20] The head of the Santa Misericordia brotherhood was Captain Manuel de Soto of the *pardo* militia of Matanzas. Captain de Soto and his company were posted for some time in St. Augustine and had helped Captain Francisco Menéndez and the black militia of Gracia Real de Santa Teresa de Mose defend that frontier against British and English raiders. Despite that service, the black militia of Matanzas did not enjoy the status of its Havana counterpart: as of 1812, it still had not been granted the privilege of the *fuero militar*.[21]

The institutional opportunities for free blacks were more limited in Matanzas than in Havana because the former city was only about half the size. In the 1820s, Havana was the largest city in the Caribbean and the third largest in the Americas, with a population of over 100,000.[22] Matanzas had only really begun to take off as an urban center at the turn of the century. Nevertheless, many of the same patterns of social interaction noted in Havana could be found in Matanzas.

Politics, family, and social life were closely entwined in the free black community of Matanzas, and court records of various members of that community document a rich cultural life that might seem surprising in an area more noted for sugar plantations and rapidly growing slave populations. Like other Atlantic Creoles, the free blacks of Matanzas were fully engaged in the contemporary politics that surrounded them. They would have witnessed the gala celebrations staged in Matanzas to mark the birth of the Infanta Isabel in August of 1817. Officials duly reported every detail of the "jubilee of this loyal and most faithful citizenry of Matanzas." Many acts of charity were performed: the poor, the imprisoned, and the hospitalized were given "splendid" meals. For three nights the plazas were illuminated by "thousands" of lanterns, and of course the obligatory portraits of the Spanish monarchs were displayed, adorned with roses and laurels. Nightly balls allowed the elites of the town to show off their fanciest clothing while dancing to music provided by an orchestra. In the streets the lower classes also celebrated to nightly drumming and the sound of fusillades. To cap off the celebration, an armada of boats converged on the Yumurí and San Juan Rivers which bounded the town and staged a mock battle.[23] Although free persons of color outnumbered whites in the city, and must have been present at these celebrations, they are nowhere evident in this report. They had not yet had time to accumulate the wealth and status of their counterparts in Havana, and could not make the kinds of claims that men like Captain Barba could to the gratitude of the King. This left free persons of color even more vulnerable than their counterparts in Havana to the worsening repression of the nineteenth century.

In 1821 José Manuel Blonde, a mulatto barber and militiaman, was denounced by the priest of Matanzas and by several tavern-goers who heard him "spreading rumors of general and absolute liberty." They alleged that Blonde was a Methodist who had associations with individuals who had lived in England, "where Wilberforce said the trade should end and slaves should be freed." Blonde was also reported to have said that slaves were "flesh and bone [human] like others and should be treated as a father would treat a son and fed." It is clear that Blonde was closely following the news of the day and that he held opinions that made him an object of suspicion. Blonde's pronouncements included the report that Havana was in chaos after having received the news of the Sergeants' Revolt in Spain. He also reported that a proclamation from Mexico had invited Cubans to join them in independence. Upon his arrest Blonde was assigned a public defender, who admitted that Blonde made such statements but said that the reports were false and Blonde was drunk when he made them. Blonde's attorney argued that the jails would be filled to overflowing if all the drunks who misreported events were arrested.

Once sober, Blonde petitioned for his own release, signing his request with a flourish. Blonde complained that he was losing income from his barber shops (plural), as well as the rent he had paid in Havana for another shop. The zealous prosecutor interviewed several other witnesses during Blonde's trial. The white accusers stuck to their version of the events, while several free black artisans, including two black carpenters born in Havana, gave favorable assessments of Blonde's character but could not testify as to what he said. The prosecutor warned, "From a small spark of this nature, an electric fire could light that could result in the total dissolution of the social pact and tumble even the most solid political edifice." He cited a law that made it a crime to "copy, read, or even *hear read* [his underline] seditious papers" and that required those sentenced for this

crime to be judged as enemies of the state. He claimed it was
necessary for "the inexorable knife of the law to fall on such
delinquents." The court sentenced Blonde to six years in jail,
but fortunately for him, on the death of his original prosecutor,
a second, more moderate one reviewed his case, found that his
behavior had always been good, and decided that Blonde had
served enough time. After spending almost a year in jail, Blonde
was finally released.[24]

Political news traveled quickly between Havana and Matanzas by way of human conduits such as Blonde. It had become
easier to travel to and from Havana by water, and the shipping
companies that ran boats between the ports charged persons of
color a lower price for tickets. A weekly mail service was established in 1791, and by the turn of the century a biweekly service
was in operation. By 1828 the official government newspaper,
La Aurora, connected the townspeople of Matanzas to Havana
and the wider world.[25] These were times of swiftly shifting political currents, and the lives of free persons of color often depended on their interpretation and understanding of political
events.

In 1825, Cuba's Captain General created new Military Commissions in Matanzas and Havana designed to report possible
political conspiracies and keep the population in line—especially the population of color. Gatherings and activities that before would have gone unnoticed were now looked upon with
suspicion, and more free blacks were swept up in investigations.
Foreign elements were always regarded with even greater suspicion, so the black exiles from Florida who moved from Havana to Matanzas in 1827, although they may have had some

earlier Florida networks to build upon, must have experienced some of the institutional paranoia of the day.[26]

As part of that institutional structure, the free black militiamen were supposed to monitor their own communities and enforce the increasingly repressive laws. In 1831 the First Sergeant of the *pardo* battalion of Matanzas, Tomás Vargas, reported a suspicious gathering of between twenty and thirty free black men and women who had gathered in a house on Contreras Street to toast Simón Bolívar, the Liberator of New Granada, who had recently died.[27] Any mention of the independence leader was enough to trigger inquiries. Vargas found that the house was rented to a free mulatto carpenter, Bernardo Sevillán. Authorities alleged that free blacks congregated frequently at Sevillán's home behind closed doors and posted a lookout outside the house, thus raising suspicions. Those arrested in this investigation included all the captains and lieutenants of the free *pardo* and *moreno* militia of Matanzas and assorted other free people of color, men and women. Some of them were artisans such as masons, shoemakers, and cigar makers, and they came from Matanzas, Havana, and Gibacoa. They all claimed to be members of a subscription group practicing "some comedies for the Christmas season."[28] The group had elected a twelve-year-old girl to reign as queen of the festivities—they called her Claudia in honor of their patron saint—and each subscriber had paid five pesos to underwrite the costs of the theatrical production and the drinks to follow. The Matanzas players were rehearsing dramas such as *The Triumph of Ana María*, *The Duque of Viseo*, and even *Othello*.[29]

What worried the authorities most, however, were the kinds

of reading materials collected from the homes of this subscription group. Sevillán owned a volume entitled *Diccionario o nuevo vocabulario filosófico democrático, indispensable para todos los que desean entender la nueva lengua revolucionaria* (Dictionary or New Philosophical Democratic Vocabulary, Indispensable for All Those Who Wish to Understand the New Revolutionary Language). His fellow subscriber, Jorge López, owned works titled *Meditaciones sobre las ruinas* (Meditations on the Ruins), *El bosquejo ligerísimo de la revolución de Méjico* (The Quick Outline of the Mexican Revolution), *Guillermo Tell o la Suiza Libre* (William Tell or Free Switzerland), and the *Catecismo o Cantón constitucional para la educación de la juventud española* (The Constitutional Catechism for the Education of Spanish Youth). The authorities destroyed these incendiary materials and sentenced Sevillán and López to six months' labor on public works. López appealed his sentence on the grounds that he was a veteran lieutenant of the Loyal Battalion of Pardos and was thus entitled to a less degrading penalty. He won that appeal and spent the next six months in San Severino Castle rather than working shackled in public view, but even that sentence must have embittered the loyal militiaman. Fourteen years later, he would be executed during the repression of La Escalera.[30]

Clearly, free blacks in Matanzas were interested in and current with world events. Through the newspapers and travelers that came on ships, they were following debates on abolition, revolution, and constitutionalism—all subjects that terrified Cuban authorities. The arrest and investigation of the free mulatto Jorge Davison in 1837 yielded even more evidence that despite the authorities' best efforts at censorship, free persons of color

in Matanzas were receiving a wide range of abolitionist literature. They were also forming close, and potentially subversive,
associations through their leisure activities, including subscription societies, dances, and musical and theater groups.

The authorities had probably been watching Jorge Davison
for some time before they finally had grounds to arrest him in
1837. Davison was born free in St. Ann's, Jamaica, a port city
that had frequent commercial exchanges with Cuba.[31] He was a
tailor by trade and well traveled; he had lived for some time in
New Orleans before moving to Matanzas in 1829, but after three
years in Cuba he moved again, this time to New York. Davison
returned to Matanzas in 1835, allegedly because he could not
find employment as a tailor in the United States.[32] It would seem
a strange time for a free black man to return to Cuba, knowing,
as he would have, of the growing racial repression there.

Jorge's brother, H. W. Davison, an employee of the Anti-
Slavery Society in Philadelphia, was the source of his trouble,
for he sent Jorge an astounding array of newspapers, pamphlets,
and other literature via the ship *Carolina,* in from New York.
All of the material carried some discussion of slavery and the
abolition debates under way around the Atlantic world. Before
Davison even had time to read what his brother had sent him,
he was arrested on suspicion of "disseminating doctrines perni-
cious and dangerous to the slavery of this island" and also having gatherings of people of color in his home. Among the materials the authorities confiscated from Davison were *The New
York Mirror, The New York Weekly Messenger, The Examiner,*
and *The Transcript* (all New York papers), *The Boston Post* and
The Daily Evening Transcript of Boston, *The Daily Herald* of

New Haven, *The Mourning Courier and General Advertiser* of Providence, the *Diario de la Habana, The Norfolk and Portsmouth Herald and General Advertiser, The Alexandria Gazette, The American and Commercial Daily Advertiser* of Baltimore, *The Transcript* of Nassau, and *The Albion or British Colonial and Foreign Weekly Gazette.* This last paper carried a sale price of six dollars, a significant sum for the day. Davison's shipment also included various issues of *The Plain Dealer* of New York. One of them carried the *St. Augustine Herald*'s story of the "Dade Massacre," in which escaped slaves fighting along with the Seminoles wiped out a U.S. Army force in Florida. Another issue of the same paper carried an article entitled "Mr. Webster's Abolitionism."

Jorge's brother must have been sending him materials for some time before Jorge was finally arrested, because investigators found an extensive library in his home. Davison owned books such as *The Tale of a New Yorker, Three Experiments of Living, Society in America* by Harriet Martineau, an attack on slavery, and even a volume of Phyllis Wheatley poems, which is now sewn into the bound proceedings of his trial stored in the National Archive in Havana. Davison's library also held speeches in honor of George Thompson, with an appendix containing a remonstrance on the subject of slavery by the Paisley Emancipation Society and a pamphlet entitled *The War in Texas Instigated by Slave Holders, Land Speculators.* Davison may have been an avid reader, but it seems likely, as the authorities suspected, that this extraordinary collection was also meant to be shared.

Signing his complaint in a beautiful script, Davison challenged the seizure of the materials, some of which he said belonged to his wife, and also his arrest. He needed no translator and therefore must have been at least bilingual as well as literate. Davison named as his defender Don Juan Gregorio Reyes, a lieutenant in the Galician Regiment, with whom he may have had military connections; Reyes argued that his client was a "hard-working man, always occupied and never vagrant or attending parties."[33]

Jorge Davison was clearly an active member of an Atlantic network of abolitionists. Fortunately for him, his brother and his associates launched a publicity campaign to alert the world to Davison's arrest and to exert pressure on the Cuban government to free him. *The Colored American*, the African-American newspaper launched by abolitionist Samuel Cornish in New York in 1836, carried a report from Matanzas filed by William A. Gibbs, warning "all persons of color to beware the Island of Cuba." Gibbs had sailed to Havana from New York and had at the time of his report spent five weeks in Matanzas covering this story. He stated that Mr. George Davis (i.e., Jorge Davison) had been arrested and sent without trial to Havana, where Captain General Tacón had sentenced him to death. Gibbs then reported that the execution was carried out on September 10, and closed his report as follows:

I would say further for the benefit of the public, and the abolition cause, that those persons who have friends in this island should be very cautious how they write letters to them, for one work concerning abolitionism in Havana or Matanzas, will seal a man's doom forever. My business is not finished yet; but things here have arrived to such a pitch, that I find the country too hot to hold me.[34]

Fortunately for Davison, the report of his demise was premature. He spent ten months in jail in Matanzas and Havana, but his brother H. W. Davison was able to get the British Consul in Cuba to intervene in the case, and Davison was released. Davison's exultant brother reported that Jorge was finally "free from the grasp of tyranny" and had returned to St. Ann's, Jamaica, "where he may freely breathe his natal air." H. W. Davison compared his brother to William Lloyd Garrison, "the colored man's friend," who had also been jailed for espousing liberty and whose poem Davison quoted in a letter to Friend Cornish (the Reverend S. E. Cornish, one of the paper's editors).

> High walls and huge, the body may confine,
> And iron gates obstruct the prisoner's gaze . . .
> Yet scorns th' immortal mind this base control—
> No chains can bind it and no cell inclose;
> Swifter than light it flies from pole to pole,
> And in a flash from earth to heaven it goes.
> It leaps from mount to mount—from vale to vale,
> Wanders, plucking honied fruits and flowers,
> It visits home, to hear the fire-side tale,
> Or in sweet converse pass the joyous hours.[35]

Once home, Jorge Davison acted as an informal correspondent for *The Colored American* in Jamaica, sending Cornish articles and copies of the *Jamaica Morning Journal* and the *Colonial Reformer*, which were then published in *The Colored American*.[36]

Planters and government officials in Matanzas worried about the literate and politically engaged free blacks in their midst, but they were even more concerned about controlling the large enslaved populations that threatened to engulf them. Many of the newly imported slaves escaped their control altogether and formed large maroon communities or *palenques* between Matanzas and Ceiba Mocha. In 1817 officials in Matanzas began keeping systematic records of slave runaways; in the space of one month that year, 133 slaves deserted their plantations.[37] The provincial archives of Matanzas refer to twenty-two *palenques* known to be in existence between 1800 and 1850. El Palenque and El Espinal were two of the larger ones; El Espinal was said to be home to approximately 300 armed maroons. The first references to this large community date from 1828, and it was still in existence in 1852 after many expeditions failed to destroy it.[38] The maroons of Matanzas could simply melt away and hide in the numerous caves which dotted the nearby mountains and the local landmark, the Pan de Matanzas. To better secure the countryside, planters established regular patrol units, called the Santa Hermandad after their medieval precedents, and paid taxes to hire *rancheadores* or slave trackers to scour the mountains in search of the elusive maroons.[39]

Maroon life was not easy, but slaves ran away to escape the killing sugar regime. An old Cuban saying is that "Sugar is made with blood." During harvests the work was especially grueling because the cane had to be processed quickly or it was ruined; slaves worked up to nineteen hours a day. The shift in

Cuba to large-scale, industrialized monoculture on rural plantations meant that growing numbers of slaves no longer had access to a socially and legally obligated master. Instead, they worked for absentee owners and were supervised by overseers whose job it was to wring every ounce of work from the slaves. Far from the oversight of church or state, plantation slaves in Matanzas had few protectors. It is no wonder, then, that Matanzas experienced a number of significant slave revolts in the first half of the nineteenth century. The most serious of these was the 1825 uprising which began on the El Solitario coffee plantation outside Matanzas. An initial group of 19 rebels, including one alleged witch, Federico, El Brujo, grew to over 223 as the leaders gathered recruits from nearby plantations. Along the way the escaping slaves burned and looted twenty-four estates and killed sixteen white men, women, and children. Panicked whites poured into the city of Matanzas before troops squashed the uprising. The Military Commission of Matanzas blamed the trouble on foreign planters who allowed their slaves too much liberty to travel along the roads and gather on weekends for long nights of drumming, dancing, and feasting—the equivalent of the *tumbas* in Havana. Within days of the first uprising, another broke out which was also suppressed. In quick trials, the authorities sentenced the rebels; twenty-three slaves were executed by firing squads in the Plaza de la Vigia, in front of the military barracks near the entry to town. The heads and hands of several of the rebels were then posted in public places, to be left there as a warning to others "until time consumes them."[40]

The nearby refuge of the *palenques* may have seemed to some a better option than full-blown revolt.[41] The maroons, however, were also becoming more politicized. One of the most notorious maroons of the region was a man whom Spanish planters called José Dolores, but who called himself Mayumbe. For about two years beginning in 1842, Mayumbe led his maroons down from the hills to stage lightning strikes on the plantations below. The terrorized planters sent trackers to try to eliminate the menace, and they eventually wounded and caught one of Mayumbe's followers, a Congo woman who provided information about his tactics. Mayumbe was famous for a guerrilla strategy which Cubans referred to as "bite and run." He moved often and divided his followers into dispersed settlements. When pursuers located one of his camps on the edge of a coffee estate in nearby Limonar, they found that the maroons had already fled. That settlement had six buildings containing twenty-two beds—smaller than the settlements that trackers destroyed in the Savannah swamps. Mayumbe's most daring raid came in 1843, when he attempted to liberate the slaves of the Alcancía mill who had been imprisoned for their participation in an earlier rebellion. This earned him the nickname "Captain of the Cimarrones."[42]

One rebellion seemed to lead directly to another, and in March of 1843 a cycle of revolts broke out in Matanzas that then triggered the terrible repression known as La Escalera. The investigations of the Military Commissions into those uprisings uncovered a supposed connection between the free blacks of Matanzas and plantation slaves, many of whom turned out to be members of the Lucumí nation, like Aponte and Prieto. The rebellion allegedly involved witchcraft that would render the whites "stupid" and their weapons useless. At the signal of the drums, approximately 254 slaves on the Alcancía plantation set fire to the buildings on the estate and killed the white machinist and black overseers. The revolt spread quickly to four other estates before troops dispersed the rebels.

Slaves constructing the nearby railroad line rose next and succeeded in defeating one patrol before eventually being defeated themselves by the regular military troops, who caught up with them at the Jovellanos bridge. A number of slaves were killed in the fighting, and at least sixty others committed suicide on the spot rather than surrender. Slaves on nearby estates also committed suicide. At the base of the trees from which their slaves' bodies hung, planters found a number of African "fetishes." Alarmed by the seemingly endless cycle of revolts, the Spanish Crown installed a new Captain General, Leopoldo O'Donnell, whose charge it was to restore order at any cost.

O'Donnell soon won infamy as a "monster" for the regime of terror he launched against black rebels, real or suspected. He executed a number of the Alcancía rebels and sentenced others to long terms in prison or to hard labor in chains. O'Donnell deported two free blacks implicated in the revolt to prison in Africa, along with two slave conspirators. Despite the show trials and the public knowledge of the consequences of revolt, more serious revolts broke out in November. Two hundred and sixty slaves on the Triunvirato estate rose in protest against having to work on a rest day, and after attacking the administrator and overseers they marched to three other estates, gathering forces as they went. Notable in this revolt was the role played by Fermina, a female Lucumí slave from the Ácana estate, who urged the deaths of the white administrators. An enormous statue of her now overlooks the restored Triunvirato estate. In

Statue honoring slave rebels on the Triunvirato sugar estate, Matanzas. Photograph by the author.

February of 1844 the captured rebels were tried in absentia in Havana and the Military Commission sentenced to death all those identified as leaders, including Fermina. The executions took place on the Triunvirato plantation, where the assembled slaves could see each rebel shot in the back and their bodies burned.[43]

The repression that followed was known as La Escalera, named for the ladder on which slaves were tied face down *(boca abajo)* and whipped while being interrogated. Slaves from over 230 sugar and coffee plantations were implicated in this supposed conspiracy and arrested, as were many, if not most, of the free blacks of Matanzas. O'Donnell gave the Military Commis-

sioners a free hand to handle the matter, and a bloodbath followed. Torturers extracted the testimonies that led to approximately 1,800 persons being killed, imprisoned, or exiled. By the
end of 1844, the "year of the lash," "thousands of people of
color, free and slave, had been executed, banished, or imprisoned, or had simply disappeared." At least 78 individuals of
color were executed. An estimated 3,000 free and enslaved people of African descent, and some whites as well, died in the
wake of the long investigations that followed—executed, lan-
guishing in jail, or horribly whipped to death.[44]

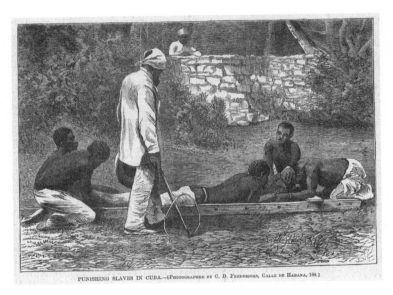

PUNISHING SLAVES IN CUBA.—[PHOTOGRAPHED BY C. D. FREDRICKS, CALLE DE HABANA, 108.]

Depiction of the ladder on which slaves were commonly whipped in Cuba.
Harper's Weekly, November 28, 1868, vol. 12, p. 753. Courtesy of "The Atlantic
Slave Trade and Slave Life in the Americas: A Visual Record" website, *http://
hitchcock.itc.virginia.edu/Slavery*, Virginia Foundation for the Humanities and
the University of Virginia Library.

Among the alleged leaders of the revolt were the most important members of the free black class in Matanzas. The U.S. consul, T. M. Rodney, reported back to the states: "It is generally supposed that the free mulattoes and blacks engaged in this affair, and it seems they are all engaged without an exception, will either be executed or driven from the island; the slaves will be dealt with severely, but only the prominent leaders will be executed."[45] British and American papers alike condemned the atrocities reported by eyewitnesses of varying nationalities, a number of whom compared the tortures to those of the Inquisition. The African American newspaper *The North Star* also reported on this event at length, alleging that "60,000 slaves were accessory" and were "hunted through the cane fields, and shot like wild beasts." The article continued, "Free negroes were the chief objects of suspicion, and were arrested and put to the torture on no other evidence of guilt than the fact that they were free." The author predicted that "it will not be strange if another insurrection shall not be attempted. They have the example and the sympathy, and may expect the aid of the 900,000 free blacks in St. Domingo, and the 400,000 in Jamaica."[46] This represented wishful thinking on the part of the author, for no help was forthcoming for the accused. In the end, thirty-eight free people of color, including one woman, were executed in 1844.[47]

Best known among the free persons to die was Gabriel de la Concepción Valdés, better known as Plácido, the gifted mulatto poet who was born in Havana and abandoned at the Casa Cuna, or state orphanage, by his mother, a Spanish ballerina. Like many other orphans from that institution, he took the surname of the beloved prelate, Don José Eusebio Valdés, who raised and educated him.[48] After moving to Matanzas, Plácido joined the vibrant, if small, community of educated and politically engaged liberals who discussed British abolitionism and its agent David Turnbull, the progress of the new republics in South America, and the developments in Santo Domingo and Jamaica. Plácido soon earned fame for his poetry and was acclaimed the "swan of the Yumurí" (the river bordering Matanzas), but he was also known for the company he kept—abolitionists and men associated with various aborted independence movements. He had already been arrested once before and was a predictable target for persecution. One of his most famous poems included the prophetic lines, "Die at the hands of an executioner, if necessary, to break the yoke [of slavery]."[49]

At least thirty-seven other free blacks also went to their deaths. These included men like the mulatto dentist Charles Blakely, a native of Charleston, and his protogé, the mulatto Andres Dodge. Both men were trained in London. Blakely practiced both in Havana and Matanzas and advertised in the official newspapers that he had been examined and certified by the Royal Protomedicato of Havana, the government institution charged with issuing medical credentials. Both men were well-to-do property owners whose clientele included whites. Blakely had also spent time in the 1830s in New York, where he may well have known the Davison brothers and other abolitionists with ties to Cuba.[50]

The governor of Matanzas complained to the Military Commission that when he had allowed friends and family a last visit with the condemned men, as was customary, the men had spent their last moments writing instead of saying goodbyes, confessing their sins, and commending their souls to God. They were copying Plácido's poems for distribution after his death. The governor was annoyed that government lawyers had discussed this with the prisoners and permitted it, which he felt discredited the government's sentences.[51]

Despite the governor's complaints, the condemned men did spend at least some time in confession and recording their last wills and testaments. These appear in the Cathedral burial records for Matanzas. A number of them named their heirs, left money to pay for masses for their souls, and made donations to charity. Santiago Pimienta, the mulatto son of a cleric who owned a ranch and slaves, left 200 pesos to commission a sculpture of St. John the Baptist for the church in the Pueblo Nuevo neighborhood on the outskirts of Matanzas, where other free black militiamen lived. He also left six ounces of gold to help establish a school for poor girls in Matanzas. Plácido left no bequests at all. The next morning the condemned men marched through the streets of Matanzas. Plácido recited a poem as he walked. At the place of execution in the barrio Versailles, the men had their hands tied behind them and were shot in the back. They were later buried in the cemetery of Matanzas.[52]

At least 739 Atlantic Creoles survived La Escalera by leaving Matanzas: 416 went to Mexico, while others from the decimated community fled to Brazil, Europe, and Jamaica. At least 92 went to Africa. A number of those had been born in Lagos and could recount stories of their original enslavement there by Spanish slavers.[53] Surprisingly, 40 free blacks from Matanzas headed north, to the United States.[54] It is possible that they returned to

Florida, seeking to recover their former properties and begin again, as the Senegalese plantation mistress Anna Kingsley did when she returned from Haiti.[55] This new wave of exiles once again had to remake their lives and identities in new locales.

Even before La Escalera, however, Cuban authorities had begun purging the island of free blacks they considered problematic. Jorge Davison was driven from Cuba, but he continued to advocate for abolition from safer territory in Jamaica. The free mulatto tailor and militiaman Bernardo Sevillán, if he survived, may have headed for independent Mexico, whose constitution he had been studying, and where slavery had been abolished. Starting in April 1839, Cuban authorities began to expel free blacks of foreign origins more systematically. Neighborhood commissioners had to account for all free blacks born outside of Cuba who were living among them, and advise whether or not they should be permitted to remain. Those so identified had to present themselves to the authorities and show cause why they should not be deported. Some men related how long they had lived in Spanish territories, while others presented proof of their military service in various Spanish posts. At least some of the Florida exiles who had traveled as children to Cuba in the exodus led by Prince Whitten, like Juan Romero, Diego Domingo, and Marcelino Mañes, were permitted to stay in Matanzas after proving their good conduct and presenting testimonials from Spanish military officers who had known them since childhood. Others were allowed to remain because they were already elderly, or were ill. But some, like Adam Rayt, who "always goes about with strangers and possesses the English language," and the literate and bilingual José Manuel Rivas, who was said to be frequently drunk and obscene, were expelled.[56] The mulatto shoemaker Jorge Seguí, son of the decorated veteran of the Black Auxiliaries of Carlos IV, Benjamin Seguí, was temporarily jailed for refusing to leave Cuba as ordered. He and Antonio Jacobo, son of the Black Auxiliary Jorge Jacobo, eventually secured important Spanish patrons and were allowed to remain in Cuba on the basis of the family's loyal military service.[57] They must have felt betrayed, nonetheless, by the Crown their families had so long served, and embittered by their reduced circumstances. The fate of their less well connected peers, dispersed across the Atlantic by this new diaspora, is still unknown.

After the horror of La Escalera, Cuba's remaining free blacks would quietly await a more propitious moment to challenge their oppressors. Although Spain finally abolished the slave trade in 1866, the end of slavery was still long in coming. Cuban slave interests stalled as long as they could. It would take an aborted bid for independence in the Ten Years' War (1868–1878), the Moret Free Womb Law of 1870, and a gradual emancipation law in 1880 to "break the yoke" and finally achieve abolition in 1886.[58]

Cuba's Atlantic Creoles had enjoyed a certain privilege in Cuba prior to the Age of Revolutions. Ironically, their race, their cosmopolitanism, their acquaintance with the powerful revolutionary concepts of the age, and their military engagement in the actual revolutions that reshaped the Atlantic world made them threatening to absolutist monarchs and racist plantation regimes alike. One could say they were undone by their very virtues.

Epilogue: Failed Promises of the Atlantic Revolutions

A loyal vassal of Your Majesty whose royal throne I will defend until I die . . . I had the honor of battling the enemy hordes that tried to take the Plaza of St. Augustine, Florida, which then belonged to the beneficent government of Your Majesty, King of Spain.

José Manuel Rivas, June 10, 1844, Havana[1]

IN 1844, in the wake of the La Escalera repression, fifty-year-old José Manuel Rivas appeared before authorities in Havana to present reasons why he should not be deported from Cuba, as required by an 1839 decree expelling "foreign" blacks. Although Rivas was born in Florida, "which was never one of the dissident colonies," he and other Atlantic Creoles from Venezuela, Puerto Rico, Brazil, or Tierra Firme (Venezuela or Colombia) were suddenly given fifteen days to leave Cuba. The real targets of the expulsion order were French-speaking individuals from Saint Domingue, suspected of harboring Jacobin sympathies, and English-speaking persons thought to be in league with British agents in Cuba who sponsored abolitionism. But even those Atlantic Creoles who were born in Spanish locales were now at risk of deportation.[2]

Rivas was born in St. Augustine, Florida, and as a young man he was part of the 1821 exodus to Cuba, heading a household that included his wife, his mother, two sisters, and four children. In 1844 the Rivas family lived in the Barrio de Colón in Havana, and Rivas worked as a stevedore on the docks. Although Rivas was illiterate, his occupation gave him access to sailors, passengers, and news from around the Atlantic. Only four years earlier authorities had uncovered the conspiracy allegedly led by the dock worker Margarita Blanco, and thus Rivas may have been under suspicion already. Three government officials who had served in St. Augustine testified that they had known Rivas for over a quarter of a century and that he was an honorable and hard-working man of good conduct. The barrio commissioner, however, gave a contrary account, stating that Rivas customarily became drunk, used excessive obscenities, and spoke English. These seemingly innocuous "crimes" were sufficient to ruin him. Rivas was ordered expelled.

Rivas's countryman Adam Rayt, also from Florida and also a dock worker, suffered a similar sentence for the same "crimes." Neither man accepted his expulsion without a fight. They promptly secured more testimonials about their service to Spain, not only in the free black militia of Florida, where they had fought Indians, Americans, and South American revolutionaries, but also in the Spanish expeditions to battle Bolívar in Tierra Firme. It was to no avail. Both men were expelled to the Isle of Pines off the southern coast of Cuba, where an earlier Captain General of Cuba had planned to quarantine the Black Auxiliaries of Carlos IV from Saint Domingue.[3] Despite a lifetime of service to Spain, Atlantic Creoles like Rivas and Rayt were now considered foreign elements in the communities they had inhabited for almost twenty-five years.

One might think that Atlantic Creoles would have been eager participants in the revolutions of their day, most of which promised freedom for the enslaved and racial equality for those already free. Even as monarchical systems broke down, however, for many Atlantic Creoles they still seemed their best hope. In fact, as we have seen, Rivas and Rayt and many of the Atlantic Creoles whose histories are recovered here pinned their hopes for freedom on a personal relationship with a distant monarch and on centuries-old legal, religious, and social constructs. This might seem to be anachronistic thinking, even retrograde, but for many of these individuals monarchy was, in fact, the best option. King Carlos and King Ferdinand of Spain, King George of England, and King Louis of France actually did free many enslaved persons, who became their loyal subjects and ardent defenders. The slave rebel Macaya compared the three European Kings to the three Magi of the Bible, writing in Saint Domingue that "these three kings are the descendants of those who, led by a star, came to adore God made man."[4] This interesting understanding of and reverence for kings suggests the powerful symbolic meaning they had for many African-born people and their descendants. On a more practical note, many Atlantic Creoles acquired freedom, property, and at least limited prosperity under the monarchical rule of Great Britain, France, or Spain.

Those Atlantic Creoles who had lived among and knew the

racial politics of the southern Patriots who helped create the United States of America understood that they could hope for none of those things under that new democracy. The very racial intransigence of Southerners predisposed Atlantic Creoles to the British and Spanish monarchies, at least initially. Moreover, Atlantic Creoles clearly read the signs of American expansionism and knew the U.S. government was bent on returning them to slavery. The Americans were equally determined to rid the land of the indigenous nations that stood in their way, and it is not surprising that both blacks and Seminoles rejected the democracy that demonized them.

Other Atlantic Creoles rejected any engagement at all in the revolutions swirling around them, choosing instead to recreate armed camps in the wilderness as maroons in Africa and the Americas had been doing for centuries. Some had witnessed their friends and family, dressed in fine red uniforms, left to die in misery along southern roadsides or in abandoned forts and thought it better to depend upon their own resources.

Atlantic Creoles in the Spanish world felt a renewed hope for change in 1812 with the promulgation of the Liberal Constitution that promised to erase lingering political inequality. Others cheered on the newly independent republics of Spanish America, whose constitutions also promised equality. But constitutional promises often proved emptier than those of monarchs. If governmental change turned out to be not really revolutionary, many Atlantic Creoles in Cuba believed at least in the radically transformative power of abolition and risked arrest, torture, or deportation to achieve it. However, this campaign also proved too weak to counter the power of restored absolutism and the capitalist systems dependent upon slavery.

Atlantic Creoles embodied the sometimes contradictory strands of revolution, counter-revolution, and social change, and often their perceptions of the political and philosophical struggles in which they engaged differed widely from those who have enjoyed more recognition and voice. Having risen from slavery by their wits and their courage, Atlantic Creoles and their descendants learned, by necessity, how to read shifting political landscapes and make daring choices. They based their alliances primarily on their desire for freedom and a measure of dignity. By comparing different imperial systems, analyzing new sources, and uncovering new narratives, we can better understand the agency and interconnectedness of Atlantic Creoles in the Age of Revolutions, and thus the revolutions themselves. The hopes of Atlantic Creoles for freedom and equality may not have been immediately fulfilled, but this does not diminish their importance to the causes they advanced.

Chronology

	North America	Hispaniola	Cuba
1565	Spanish found St. Augustine		
1670	English found Charleston	France gains Saint Domingue	
1685		French establish Code Noir regulating colonial slavery	
1693	Spain establishes religious sanctuary in Florida		
1700–1713			War of Spanish Succession; Bourbon reformers to throne; Britain gets *asiento*, or right to import slaves into Spanish Caribbean
1715–1717	Yamasse War begins in Carolina		
1738	Francisco Menéndez founds Gracia Real de Santa Teresa de Mose		
1739–1748	War of Jenkins Ear between Spain and Britain; Stono slave rebellion in Carolina		
1740	British siege of Florida		
1741	Spanish attack Georgia		
1745	French and Indian War begins		
1762			Britain seizes Havana; black militiamen win honors in Cuba's defense
1763	Spain cedes Florida to Britain		Spain regains Cuba and launches reforms

1764	Britain divides Florida into East and West
1774	First Continental Congress in Philadelphia; Prince Whitten arrives in Carolina
1775	American Revolution begins; SC Council of Safety elects Henry Laurens President; SC declares independence; Lord Dunmore offers to free slaves for military service to the British
1776	Congress declares American independence
1778	France and Spain join American cause; Britain launches Southern Campaign
1779	Loyalists from SC and GA flee to East Florida; British capture Savannah
1780	British capture Charleston and march inland; Spanish forces capture Mobile (British West Florida)
1781	Spanish forces seize Pensacola; American and French Forces capture British army at Yorktown; Cuban black militias win honors in Mississippi campaign

	North America	Hispaniola	Cuba
1783	Britain recognizes U.S. independence; Spain regains both Floridas		
1785	Whitten family receives sanctuary in Florida		
1789	Parisians launch French Revolution; George Washington becomes first President of the U.S.	Saint Domingue produces 40% of world's sugar; French National Assembly issues Declaration of the Rights of Man	
1790	Sec. of State Thomas Jefferson pressures Spain to revoke religious sanctuary policy	Abortive revolt of Vincent Ogé	
1791		May Decree of National Assembly; Slaves revolt in Saint Domingue	
1793		French Republic executes King Louis XVI; England and Spain declare war on France; Sonthonax abolishes slavery in Saint Domingue; Biassou, Jean-François, and Toussaint ally with Spain; Black Auxiliaries of Carlos IV formed	
1794		Toussaint allies with French Republic	
1795	Spanish and black militias defeat American "Jacobin" invaders	By Treaty of Basle, Black Auxiliaries of Carlos IV leave Saint Domingue	

1796	Biassou and troops arrive in Florida		
1800	William Augustus Bowles and State of Muskogee declare war on Spain		
1801	George Biassou dies in Florida	Napoleon sends troops to Saint Domingue	
1803	Creeks deliver Bowles to Spanish forces, ending the war; U.S. purchases Louisiana from France		
1804		Haiti becomes first independent black republic in western hemisphere	
1808	U.S. bans African slave trade		Napoleon invades Spain; Cubans proclaim loyalty to King Ferdinand VII
1810	U.S. seizes West Florida		
1812	War of 1812 between U.S. and Britain; "Patriots" invade Florida; Prince Whitten's forces defeat U.S. Marines		Spanish Córtes promulgates Liberal Constitution; Aponte's Conspiracy
1813	Andrew Jackson defeats Creeks at Horseshoe Bend		
1814	Andrew Jackson occupies Pensacola		Ferdinand VII restored; abrogates Liberal Constitution of 1812
1815	Andrew Jackson defeats British at New Orleans		

	North America	Hispaniola	Cuba
1816	U.S. Navy destroys Negro Fort on Apalachicola River		
1817	Gregor McGregor seizes Amelia Island and establishes the Republic of Florida; Luis Aury succeeds McGregor; finally U.S. forces eject Aury and occupy Amelia Island		
1818	Andrew Jackson invades Florida and launches First Seminole War		
1819	Adams-Onís Treaty sells Florida to the U.S.		
1820			Sergeants Revolt in Spain forces Ferdinand to restore the Liberal Constitution of 1812
1821	Prince Whitten leads Florida's free black militia to exile in Cuba; Andrew Jackson becomes the first governor of territorial Florida		
1844			La Escalera "Conspiracy"; Execution of Plácido

APPENDIX 2

Prince's Black Company

The information for these biographical sketches was derived from multiple sources, including the Catholic Parish Registers of St. Augustine; the East Florida Papers, PKY; Asuntos Politicos, ANC; and Patriot War Claims, NARA.

Abril (April/Eprel) served in Florida's free black militia with Prince.

Manuel Asendolf (Alcendolf/Holsendof) served in Florida's free black militia with Prince.

Placido Asil was born in "San Miguel on the coast of Guinea," was enslaved, and was taken to Saint Domingue. He fought with Jorge Biassou and emigrated to Florida in 1796. He served in Florida's free black militia with Prince.

Isaac Bacas was born a slave in Georgia but escaped with his family and received religious sanctuary in Florida. He served in Florida's free black militia with Prince and received a Spanish land grant for his services. He lived near Moses Creek, south of St. Augustine, near his sons, Andres and Justo, and his son-in-law, Juan Morel.

Andres Bacas was born a slave in Georgia but escaped with his family and received religious sanctuary in Florida. He served in Florida's free black militia with Prince and rose to First Corporal. He was the brother of Justo and the brother-in-law of Pedro Ysnardy and Juan Morel, who married his sisters. He emigrated to Cuba in 1821, at age 56, with his wife, Eva Fish, and their four children.

Justo Bacas was born a slave in Georgia but escaped with his family and received religious sanctuary in Florida. He served in Florida's free black militia with Prince. He was the brother of Andres and the brother-in-law of militiamen Pedro Ysnardy and Juan Morel, who married his sisters. He emigrated to Cuba in 1821, at age 58, with his mother, Ysabel Andros, and four children.

Guillermo Sanco Bacas was born in St. Augustine and emigrated to Cuba with his parents in 1821, at age 9–14. As an adult he lived in the Barrio Colón in Havana. When the government ordered the expulsion of foreigners in 1844, he petitioned to remain and was allowed to stay despite a report that he was "somewhat excessive with alcohol."

José Bonom served in Florida's free black militia with Prince. He rose to First Sergeant and emigrated to Cuba in 1821, at age 60, with his wife, Ignacia Travers, and two children.

Jary (Harry) Box served in Florida's free black militia with Prince.

Jorge Brus was born in Marmelade, Saint Domingue. He fought with Jorge Biassou and emigrated with him to Florida in 1796. He later served in Florida's free black militia with Prince. He rose to Corporal and emigrated to Cuba in 1821, at age 39, with his wife, Maria Carlota, and four children.

Cain (Caen/Quin/Sin) served in Florida's free black militia with Prince during the Indian wars of 1800–1803 launched by William Augustus Bowles and the State of Muskogee.

Esteban Cheves served in Florida's free black militia with Prince during the Indian wars of 1800–1803 launched by William Augustus Bowles and the State of Muskogee. He helped rescue Spanish dragoons at Fort Joaneda. For these services, he received a Spanish land grant in Florida.

Jacobo Clarke served in Florida's free black militia with Prince.

Jorge Clarke was a free mulatto carpenter and a slave runaway from Georgia. He served in Florida's free black militia with Prince and received a Spanish land grant for his services. His homestead was located 2 miles west of Fort Matanzas and 19 miles south of St. Augustine, on a creek about a mile from Matanzas River. He emigrated to Cuba in 1821.

Tomas Cook was born in "Guinea." He served in Florida's free black militia with Prince during the Indian wars of 1800–1803 launched by William Augustus Bowles and the State of Muskogee.

Felipe Edimboro (a.k.a. Sánchez) was a Congo, as was his wife, Filis, and both became slaves of the Spanish planter F. X. Sánchez. Edimboro sued Sánchez for his freedom, which was granted by the Spanish court. He later purchased the freedom of Filis and their children with funds earned from butchering and from parties hosted in St. Augustine. Edimboro served in Florida's free black militia with Prince and rose to Sergeant. He and his son, Sandy, were often posted among Seminole villages. Edimboro received a Spanish land grant for his military services and raised a herd of 40–50 cattle on his homestead, which was 4 miles west of St. Augustine, next to that of his son-in-law, Benjamin Wiggins. Edimboro also owned a garden in town.

Antonio (Sandy) Embara/Edimboro was born in St. Augustine on December 15, 1787, and baptized on January 31, 1788. He attended school with Prince Whitten's son, Glasgow, and grew up to serve in Florida's free black militia with Prince. He was often posted to the Seminole villages with his father, Felipe Edimboro. He rose to Corporal in the militia and emigrated to Cuba in 1821, at age 30, with wife, Ysabel Andros, and one child.

Marcelino Espinosa was born in Havana and began life as a slave. A mulatto, he obtained his freedom in Florida and became a tailor in St. Augustine. Felipe Edimboro and his wife, Filis, served as godparents for his daughter. He served in Florida's free black militia with Prince.

Scipio Fleming served in Florida's free black militia with Prince and received a Spanish land grant for his services. He lived at Padam Aram in 1812 on the east side of the St. Johns River, 5 or 6 miles from Francis Fatio's New Switzerland plantation.

Juan Antonio Florencia was the son of Mariana Bisit, who escaped from Georgia with her children and received religious sanctuary in Florida. Juan was baptized on November 9, 1789, at age 6. He attended school in St. Augustine with Glasgow Whitten and others in 1796 and served in Florida's free black militia with Prince during the Indian wars of 1800–1803 launched by William Augustus Bowles and the State of Muskogee. He later testified in support of Prince's Patriot War Claims against the U.S. government.

Simon Forrester served in Florida's free black militia with Prince.

Juan Fransua was born in Saint Domingue and emigrated to Florida with Jorge Biassou in 1796. He served in Florida's free black militia with Prince during the Indian wars of 1800–1803 launched by William Augustus Bowles and the State of Muskogee. He helped rescue Spanish dragoons at Fort Joaneda.

Tomas Herrera served in Florida's free black militia with Prince and was wounded in the Indian Wars of 1800–1803 launched by William Augustus Bowles and the State of Muskogee. He was hospitalized in St. Augustine.

Carlos Hill, the former slave of Charles Hill, bought his freedom in St. Augustine. He served in Florida's free black militia with Prince. In 1812 Patriot invaders from Georgia stole his wife and three children, and he never saw them again.

Juan Jorge Jacobo was born in Cap Français (Le Cap/Guarico). He was the brother-in-law and heir of Jorge Biassou, with whom he fought in Saint Domingue. He emigrated to Florida with Biassou in 1796 and became a Sergeant in Florida's free black militia. He fought with Prince in the Indian Wars of 1800–1803 and the Patriot War of 1812. Jacobo received a Spanish land grant and had a home and store in Fernandina, Amelia Island. He died in Fernandina in 1816.

Antonio Jacobo was the son of Jorge Jacobo. He emigrated to Cuba in 1821 and lived in the Barrio Colón near Guillermo Bacas and other members of Florida's free black militia. When the government ordered the expulsion of foreigners in 1844, Jacobo petitioned to stay but was denied on the basis that he was "constantly drunk and scandalous," that he "always associated with English speakers," and that he "was of bad conduct." He was jailed and was about to be deported to the Isle of Pines when he requested a passport to go to Veracruz, Mexico, instead.

Primus Jones served in Florida's free black militia with Prince.

Net Lesley served in Florida's free black militia with Prince and emigrated to Cuba in 1821, at age 38, alone.

Prince Leslie served in Florida's free black militia with Prince during the Indian wars of 1800–1803 launched by William Augustus Bowles and the State of Muskogee. He helped rescue Spanish dragoons at Fort Joaneda.

Juan Luis Loubel was born in Saint Domingue and emigrated to Florida with Jorge Biassou in 1796. He later served in Florida's free black militia with

Prince during the Indian wars of 1800–1803 launched by William Augustus Bowles and the State of Muskogee.

Abrahan (Ebran) McQueen (a.k.a. Hannahan) was the mulatto overseer on Zephaniah Kingsley's Fort George Island plantation. Hannahan's daughter became Kingsley's second wife, and Kingsley granted him his freedom. Hannahan served in Florida's free black militia with Prince during the Indian wars of 1800–1803 launched by William Augustus Bowles and the State of Muskogee. He received a Spanish land grant for his services and built a home in Fernandina. He emigrated to Cuba in 1821 but his wife, Basha, stayed in St. Augustine.

Pedro Miguel was born in Saint Domingue and fought with Jorge Biassou. He emigrated with Biassou to Florida in 1796 and became a Corporal in Florida's free black militia. He served with Prince in 1812 and emigrated to Cuba in 1821, age 71, alone. He was later hanged in Havana.

Jacob Moore served in Florida's free black militia with Prince.

Juan Moore served in Florida's free black militia with Prince.

Tomas Moore (Mur) served in Florida's free black militia with Prince.

Isaac Morel served in Florida's free black militia with Prince.

Juan Morel served in Florida's free black militia with Prince. He lived next to Isaac Bacas and married his daughter Catalina (Kitty) Bacas, becoming a brother-in-law of fellow militiamen Andres and Justo Bacas, and of Pedro Yysnardy who married another Bacas daughter, Teresa. Juan's family emigrated to Cuba in 1821, when he was 60.

Augustine Net served in Florida's free black militia with Prince.

Jare (Harry) Panchita served in Florida's free black militia with Prince.

Tomas Pellicer served in Florida's free black militia with Prince during the Indian wars of 1800–1803 launched by William Augustus Bowles and the State of Muskogee. He rose to Corporal and emigrated to Cuba in 1821, at age 62, with his wife, Ricarda Kiata, and three children.

Sambo Pevet served in Florida's free black militia with Prince during the Indian wars of 1800–1803 launched by William Augustus Bowles and the State of Muskogee.

Pedro Pons served in Florida's free black militia with Prince during the Indian wars of 1800–1803 launched by William Augustus Bowles and the State of Muskogee. He helped rescue Spanish dragoons at Fort Joaneda. He emigrated to Cuba in 1821, at age 60, with his wife, María Encarnación Fernández.

Tony Primus was born free in St. Augustine and served in Florida's free black militia with Prince.

Adam Rayt served as a soldier in Florida's free black militia with Prince during the Indian wars of 1800–1803 launched by William Augustus Bowles and the State of Muskogee. In 1812 he accompanied Prince in expeditions to round up cattle during the Patriot invasion and was targeted for retribution by the rebels. He emigrated to Cuba in 1821. Like other free black militiamen from Florida, he lived in the Barrio Colón and worked as a stevedore on the docks of Havana. He later served with Spanish royalist forces fighting revolutionaries in the Costa Firme (Venezuela), and when the government ordered the expulsion of foreigners in 1844, he petitioned to remain. Like Rivas, he secured testimonials from Florida's former governor José Coppinger and Colonel Tomás Llorente, with whom he had served, but the Barrio commissioner reported that he used English and associated with foreigners, and his petition was denied.

Jose Antonio Rivas was born in "Guinea" and served in Florida's free black militia with Prince and his sons, Jose Antonio and Jose Manuel, during the

Indian wars of 1800–1803 launched by William Augustus Bowles and the State of Muskogee.

Jose Antonio Rivas 2nd (a.k.a. Antonio Capo) served in Florida's free black militia with Prince during the Indian wars of 1800–1803 launched by William Augustus Bowles and the State of Muskogee.

Jose Manuel Rivas was born ca. 1794 in St. Augustine and served in Florida's free black militia with Prince and his father and brother during the Indian wars of 1800–1803 launched by William Augustus Bowles and the State of Muskogee and against the Patriots in 1812. He emigrated to Cuba in 1821, as a single man. There he lived in the Barrio Colón near Guillermo Bacas and Antonio Jacobo. Like other free black militiamen from Florida, he worked on the docks of Havana. He later served with Spanish royalist forces fighting revolutionaries in the Costa Firme (Venezuela). When the government ordered the expulsion of foreigners in 1844, Rivas petitioned to stay. Colonel Tomás Llorente and Lieutenant Pedro Miranda, with whom he had served in Florida, and Florida's royal notary, Juan Entralgo, all testified on his behalf, stating that they had known him since he was a child, that he was a hard worker, and that he was never known to join in "reunions with persons of color." The Barrio commissioner, however, reported that Rivas was "frequently drunk, used obscene language and also English words," and his petition was denied. Rivas appealed, this time directly to the Queen, sending her another testimonial from Florida's former governor, José Coppinger. The outcome of his appeal is unknown.

Pedro Rivas was born free in St. Augustine and emigrated to Cuba in 1821 at age 9. He was living in Matanzas when the government ordered the expulsion of foreigners in 1844. He petioned to remain and was allowed to stay because he was the sole support of his elderly father.

Abraham (Ebran a.k.a. Jacobo) Roque, a.k.a. Abraham Richo, was formerly a slave in St. Augustine but bought his freedom from Roque Leonardy ca.

1803–1804. He served in Florida's free black militia with Prince and emigrated to Cuba in 1821 at age 60 with his wife, Ygnacia Sánchez, age 41, and one child, Sayrus Roque, age 12. All were dead by 1830.

Sanco (a.k.a. Sanco Davis) served as a soldier in Florida's free black militia with Prince and received a Spanish land grant for his services. His homestead was located on the back side of Cabbage Swamp, 1½ miles from Pablo Road and 20 miles from St. Augustine.

Diego Domingo Sanco (a.k.a. Domingo Davis, and who may be the same person as Sanco Davis) emigrated to Cuba in 1821 with his wife, Gracia Bacas, and four children. They lived in the Barrio Colón near Gracia's father, Guillermo Bacas, and other Florida militiamen. When the government ordered the expulsion of foreigners in 1844, the Barrio commissioner stated that Sanco's conduct was good and he was permitted to stay.

Jorge Sanco served in Florida's free black militia with Prince and emigrated to Cuba in 1821, at age 24, with his mother (?), Maria Rosa, age 50, and five children.

Benjamín Seguí was a mulatto born in Saint Domingue. He fought with Jorge Biassou in Saint Domingue and emigrated with him to Florida in 1796. He then served in Florida's free black militia with Prince and rose to Sub-Lieutenant. He emigrated to Cuba in 1821, at age 51, with his wife, Francisca Fish, and three children, including sons Jorge and Alejandro Seguí.

Alejandro Pita Seguí was a mulatto born in St. Augustine and served in Florida's free black militia with his father Benjamín and Prince. He emigrated to Cuba in 1821 and lived in the Barrio Colón with other members of the free black militia of Florida. When the government ordered the expulsion of foreigners in 1844, he secured a passport to go to Veracruz, Mexico. At that time an unnamed brother (possibly Jorge) and uncle were in jail in Matanzas.

Jorge Seguí was a mulatto born in St. Augustine and served in Florida's free black militia with his father Benjamín and Prince. He emigrated to Cuba in 1821, at age 35, where he joined the free black militia and firefighters unit in Havana. In 1835 he petitioned not to be exiled as ordered by the Spanish government.

Bob Tomquins (Tompkins?) was a river pilot and served in Florida's free black militia with Prince.

Ramon Vicente served in Florida's free black militia with Prince.

Antonio Vilar served in Florida's free black militia with Prince during the Indian wars of 1800–1803 launched by William Augustus Bowles and the State of Muskogee.

Luis Viles served in Florida's free black militia with Prince.

Francisco Whitten (a.k.a. Domingo/Glasgow) was born a slave in South Carolina but became free when his family received religious sanctuary in Florida in 1785. He was baptized on August 16, 1788, and attended school in St. Augustine. He became a shoemaker and served in Florida's free black militia with his father, Prince.

Benjamin Wiggins was the free mulatto son of the Englishman Jacob Wiggins and the Senegalese Nancy Wiggins. He served in Florida's free black militia with Prince and married Felipe Edimboro's daughter, Nicolasa. He was an Indian translator and river pilot and received a Spanish land grant for his military services. He kept herds of cattle and horses on his homestead, which was next to that of his father-in-law, Felipe Edimboro. In 1812, Patriot invaders ruined his homestead.

Teodoro Xavier served in Florida's free black militia with Prince during the Indian wars of 1800–1803 launched by William Augustus Bowles and the State of Muskogee. He helped rescue Spanish dragoons at Fort Joaneda.

Pedro Ysnardy was the illegitimate mulatto son of Florida's royal treasurer, Miguel Ysnardy. He served in Florida's free black militia with Prince and rose to Corporal. He emigrated to Cuba in 1821, at age 48, with his wife, Teresa Bacas. He was brother-in-law to the Bacas brothers, Andres and Justo, and to Juan Morel, and the son-in-law of Isaac Bacas.

Juan Zamorano served in Florida's free black militia with Prince during the Indian wars of 1800–1803 launched by William Augustus Bowles and the State of Muskogee. He helped rescue Spanish dragoons at Fort Joaneda.

Pedro Zamorano served as a soldier in Florida's free black militia with Prince and emigrated to Cuba in 1821, at age 50, with his wife, Josefa Rait.

Sairus (Sayrus) Zamorano served as a soldier in Florida's free black militia with Prince and emigrated to Cuba in 1821, at age 59, with his wife, Maria Margarita, and nine children

Juan Zauly (Howley) served as a soldier in Florida's free black militia with Prince and received a Spanish land grant for his services. He lived near Five Miles, on the King's Road, and worked at cooperative farming with Abraham McQueen and Abraham Richo. He emigrated to Cuba in 1821.

APPENDIX 3

Registry of Negro Prisoners

Registry of negro prisoners captured, &c.—Continued.

No.	Names.	Sex.	Tribe, town, or owner.	Estimated age.		Remarks.
				Years	Mths.	
80	Ben	Male	Holatoochee	22	0	
81	Jacob	..do	....do	24	0	Most intrepid and hostile warriors.
82	Muredy	..do	Micapotoka	20	0	
83	Murray	..do	....do	35	0	Owned by Colonel Crowell, and claimed by Nelly Factor, the best guide in the nation.
84	Prince	..do	....do	35	0	
85	Toney	..do	....do	25	0	Hostile; either qualified to take the lead in an insurrection.
86	Toby	..do	....do	32	0	
87	Peter	..do	....do	15	0	
88	Pompey	..do	....do	60	0	
89	Jacob, 2d	..do	Sauathithka	20	0	
90	Dally	..do	....do	22	0	
91	Mundy	..do	Micapotoka	1	0	Died May 11, 1837.
92	George	..do	....do	1	0	Died May 23, 1837.
93	Philips	..do	....do	4	0	Died May 17, 1837.
94	Morris	..do	....do	1	0	Died May 31, 1837.
95	Lydia	Female	Nusalocco	80	0	Died May 11, 1837.
96	Abram	Male	Claims to be free	50	0	The principal negro chief, supposed to be friendly to the whites; said to be a good soldier and an intrepid leader; he is the most cunning and intelligent negro we have seen; he is married to the widow of the former chief of the nation.
97	Tony Barnet	..do	....do	36	0	
98	Polly Barnet	Female	....do	36	0	
99	Beckey	..do	....do	2	0	
100	Grace	..do	....do	6	0	
101	Lydia	..do	....do	5	0	
102	Mary Ann	..do	... do	3	0	
103	Martinas	Male	....do	1	0	

Note.—In addition to the above, ninety-three negroes, the property of citizens, were taken and secured by the troops.

THOMAS S. JESUP, *Major General, Commanding.*

Notes

Introduction

1. Ira Berlin, *Many Thousands Gone: The First Two Centuries of Slavery in North America* (Cambridge, Mass., 2000), 64.

2. Peter Wood, *Black Majority: Negroes in Colonial South Carolina from 1670 through the Stono Rebellion* (New York, 1974), 28–34, 55. On contemporary Mandinga life along the Gambia, see Douglas Grant, *The Fortunate Slave: An Illustration of African Slavery in the Early Eighteenth Century* (New York, 1968), 11–25.

3. Jane Landers, *Black Society in Spanish Florida* (Urbana, Ill., 1999), 25.

4. Berlin, *Many Thousands Gone*, 24.

5. Richard Jobson, *The Golden Trade; or, A Discovery of the River Gambra, and the Golden Trade of the Aethiopians* (London, 1968), 51; Donald R. Wright, *The World and a Very Small Place in Africa* (Armonk, N.J., 1997); Charlotte A. Quinn, "Niumi: A Nineteenth-Century Mandinga Kingdom," *Africa: Journal of the International African Institute* 38 (October 1968): 443–455.

6. Scholars hotly debate the origins and meaning of these African ethnonyms. I have used them throughout as they appear in Spanish documents. See, for example, Paul E. Lovejoy, "Identifying Enslaved Africans in the African Diaspora," in Lovejoy, ed., *Identity in the Shadow of Slavery* (London,

2000); Gwendolyn Midlo Hall, *Slavery and African Ethnicities in the Americas: Restoring the Links* (Chapel Hill, N.C., 2005); Philip D. Morgan, "The Cultural Implications of the Atlantic Slave Trade: African Regional Origins, American Destinations and New World Developments," *Slavery and Abolition* 18:1 (1997): 122–145.

7. Landers, *Black Society,* 35–45.

8. Ibid., 59–66.

9. See Olaudah Equiano, *The Life of Olaudah Equiano, or Gustavus Vassa, the African, Written by Himself* (London, 1789); "Narrative of the Enslavement of Ottobah Cugoano, a Native of Africa; published by himself, in the Year 1787," in *The Negro's Memorial, or Abolitionist's Catechism* (London, 1825); *The Biography of Mahommah Gardo Baquaqua: His Passage from Slavery to Freedom in Africa and America,* ed. Robin Law and Paul Lovejoy (Princeton, N.J., 2001); Randy J. Sparks, *The Two Princes of Calabar: An Eighteenth-Century Odyssey* (Cambridge, Mass., 2004).

10. R. R. Palmer, *The Age of Democratic Revolution: Political History of Europe and America, 1760–1800,* 2 vols. (Princeton, N.J., 1959–1964); Eric J. Hobsbawm, *The Age of Revolution [Europe], 1789–1848* (London, 1962).

11. Benjamin Quarles, *The Negro in the American Revolution* (New York, 1961); Sylvia R. Frey, *Water from the Rock: Black Resistance in a Revolutionary Age* (Princeton, N.J., 1991); Simon Schama, *Rough Crossings: Britain, the Slaves and the American Revolution* (New York, 2006); Gary Nash, *The Forgotten Fifth: African Americans in the Age of Revolution* (Cambridge, Mass., 2006); Cassandra Pybus, *Epic Journeys of Freedom: Runaway Slaves of the American Revolution and Their Global Quest for Liberty* (Boston, 2006); David Patrick Geggus, *Haitian Revolutionary Studies* (Bloomington, Ind., 2002); Laurent Dubois, *Avengers of the New World: The Story of the Haitian Revolution* (Cambridge, Mass., 2004); Madison Smartt Bell, *Toussaint Louverture: A Biography* (New York, 2007).

1. African Choices in the Revolutionary South

1. Memorial of Juan Bautista Whitten, July 31, 1819, East Florida Papers (hereafter cited as EFP), microfilm reel 14, P. K. Young Library of

Florida History, University of Florida, Gainesville, Florida (hereafter cited as PKY).

2. Berlin, *Many Thousands Gone,* 64–76.

3. Philip D. Morgan, *Slave Counterpoint: Black Culture in the Eighteenth-Century Chesapeake and Lowcountry* (Chapel Hill, N.C., 1998), 444–445. The practice of throwing dead slaves into the Charleston harbor was still common in 1807, and Juries of Inquests ruled these deaths a "visitation of God." *Charleston Courier,* April 8, 21, and 22, 1807, and August 24, 1807, cited in Elizabeth Donnan, *Documents Illustrative of the History of the Slave Trade to America,* vol. IV (Washington, D.C., 1935), 526–527.

4. Equiano, *Life of Olaudah Equiano;* "Narrative of the Enslavement of Ottobah Cugoano; *Biography of Mahommah Gardo Baquaqua;* Sparks, *Two Princes of Calabar.*

5. After analyzing more than 27,000 slave trading voyages, David Eltis and his collaborators found that the 1770s and 1780s were high points in the "Guinea" trade. David Eltis, Stephen D. Behrendt, David Richardson, and Hebert S. Klein, *The Trans-Atlantic Slave Trade: A Database on CD-ROM* (Cambridge, Mass., 1999). That data has now been updated online at *www. slavevoyages.com/tast/index.faces.* See also David Eltis and David Richardson, eds., *Extending the Frontiers: Essays on the New Transatlantic Slave Trade Database* (New Haven, Conn., 2008).

6. Morgan, *Slave Counterpoint,* 241, 244, 245.

7. Robert Higgins, "Charleston: Terminus and Entrepôt of the Colonial Slave Trade," in *The African Diaspora: Interpretive Essays,* ed. Martin L. Kilson and Robert I. Rothberg (Cambridge, Mass., 1976), 129; Converse D. Clowse, *Measuring Charleston's Overseas Commerce, 1717–1767: Statistics from the Port's Naval Lists,* 31, Table A-21; Peter H. Wood, *Black Majority: Negroes in Colonial South Carolina from 1670 through the Stono Rebellion* (New York, 1974), 132.

8. Data from the Trans-Atlantic Slave Trade Database [TSTD2], *www .slavevoyages.com,* cited in David Eltis, Philip Morgan, and David Richardson, "Agency and Diaspora in Atlantic History: Reassessing the African Contribution to Rice Cultivation in the Americas," *American Historical Review* (December 2007), Table 1, 1336.

9. Darold D. Wax, "'The Great Risque We Run': The Aftermath of Slave Rebellion at Stono, South Carolina, 1739–1745," *Journal of Negro History* 68, no. 2 (Summer 1982): 136–147.

10. Henry Laurens to John Knight, March 17, 1773, and *South Carolina Gazette*, September 20, 1773, cited in Donnan, *Documents*, vol. IV, 459, 464. On Laurens's long association with Oswald, Grant, and Company, owners of an important slave factory at Bance Island in the Sierra Leone River, see Donnan, *Documents*, vol. IV, 347, 429. A Philadelphia merchant visiting Charleston in January 1774 also reported that almost 10,000 Africans had been imported into Carolina in 1773. William Pollard to Messrs B. and J. Bower, Manchester, cited in H. Roy Merrens, ed., *The Colonial South Carolina Scene: Contemporary Views, 1698–1774* (Columbia, S.C., 1977), 275–278.

11. Non-Importation Agreement, 1774, and *South Carolina Gazette*, May 16, 1774, cited in Donnan, *Documents*, vol. IV, 467, 470–471.

12. *South Carolina Gazette*, September 26, 1775; *http://timmonstree.org/maps/Mouzon-SC-Map-2-Georgetown.jpg* (accessed 8/30/08). In other sources, Whitten appears as Witten.

13. Alexander Semple to Lt. McFernan, December 16, 1786, To and From the U.S. 1784–1821, EFP, microfilm reel 41, PKY.

14. Morgan, *Slave Counterpoint*, 58–79, and *Henry Laurens Papers*, II, 230, 357, cited in Morgan, *Slave Counterpoint*, 68; John Tozer, "Postillion," to the Royal Africa Company, May 2, 1704, T 70/13, f.61 Voyage id, 15005, cited in David Eltis, *The Rise of African Slavery in the Americas* (Cambridge, Mass., 2000), 165; Walter Rodney, "Upper Guinea and the Significance of the Origins of Africans Enslaved in the New World," *The Journal of Negro History* 54 (1969): 327–345.

15. European accounts of this region span the sixteenth through the eighteenth centuries, and all note the presence of these peoples. This leads Michael Gomez to argue that ethnicity in Senegambia was "unambiguous," and he uses the term "Gambian" as eighteenth-century South Carolinians did. Michael A. Gomez, *Exchanging Our Country Marks: The Transformation of African Identities in the Colonial and Antebellum South* (Chapel Hill,

N.C., 1998), chap. 3. Other scholars generally agree that ethnic identifications in Africa, as well as in the Americas, were fluid and contingent, and must be used with care. Joseph Miller describes terms like "Kongo" as an "ethno-linguistic abstraction" and a creation of the Atlantic slave trade. Joseph Miller, "Retention, Reinvention, and Remembering: Restoring Identities through Enslavement in Africa and Under Slavery in Brazil," in José C. Curto and Paul E. Lovejoy, eds., *Enslaving Connections: Changing Cultures of Brazil and Western Africa During the Age of Slavery* (Amherst, N.J., 2004), 81–121. Robin Law makes a similar argument about "Yoruba" in "Ethnicity and the Slave Trade: 'Lucumi' and 'Nago' as Ethnonyms in West Africa," *History in Africa* 24 (1997): 205–219, and about "Mina" in "Ethnicities of Enslaved Africans in the Diaspora: On the Meanings of 'Mina' (Again)," *History in Africa* 32 (2005): 247–267.

16. Eltis, *Rise of African Slavery; South Carolina Gazette,* December 20, 1773. The revolt aboard the *New Britannia* occurred on January 18, 1768. Captain Ebenezer Daniel of the sloop *Charming Salley* reported the attack on Fort James. *South Carolina Gazette and Country Journal,* January 31, 1769.

17. "Charleston, S.C. in 1774 as Described by an English Traveller," *Historical Magazine,* 9 (November 1865), 341–347, reproduced in Merrens, *Colonial South Carolina Scene,* 280–289.

18. Peter H. Wood, "'Taking Care of Business' in Revolutionary South Carolina: Republicanism and Slave Society," in Jeffrey J. Crow and Larry E. Tise, eds., *The Southern Experience in the American Revolution* (Chapel Hill, N.C., 1978), 268–293; Morgan, *Slave Counterpoint,* 250–251; W. Robert Higgins, "The Ambivalence of Freedom: Whites, Blacks and the Coming of the American Revolution," in Higgins, ed., *The Revolutionary War in the South: Power, Conflict, and Leadership* (Durham, N.C., 1979), 43–63; Robert Olwell, "'Loose, Idle and Disorderly': Slave Women in the Eighteenth-Century Charleston Marketplace," in David Barry Gaspar and Darlene Clark Hine, eds., *More Than Chattel: Black Women and Slavery in the Americas* (Bloomington, Ind., 1996), 97–110.

19. John Chestnut to Robert Henry, April 15, 1794, cited in Morgan, *Slave Counterpoint,* 238–239. On the mobility and independence of black

boatmen on the Cooper River, see Higgins, "Ambivalence of Freedom," 57, and Philip D. Morgan and George D. Terry, "Slavery in Microcosm: A Conspiracy Case in Colonial South Carolina," *Southern Studies* 21 (1982): 121–145. See also Wax, "'The Great Risque We Run.'"

20. Robert Stansbury Lambert, *South Carolina Loyalists in the American Revolution* (Columbia, S.C., 1987), 168.

21. Mouzon Map of 1775, *www.gaz.jrshelby.com/canty.htm* (accessed 6/30/08). The Canteys (also spelled Canty) were one of the oldest European families in South Carolina, having arrived on the "first fleet from Barbados" in 1670, and they became important military and political figures in Charleston and later in the inland districts. See Walter B. Edgar, ed., *Biographical Directory of the South Carolina House of Representatives*, vol. 2 (Columbia, S.C., 1974), cited in Thomas J. Kirkland and Robert M. Kennedy, *Historic Camden, Colonial and Revolutionary*, vol. 1 (Columbia, S.C., 1905), 354–357.

22. Camden Jury complaint, April 1773, cited in Kirkland and Kennedy, *Historic Camden*, 95–99; James H. O'Donnell III, "The South on the Eve of the American Revolution: The Native Americans," in Higgins, *Revolutionary War in the South*, 64–78.

23. William Stephens, *A Journal of the Proceedings in Georgia* (Savannah, 1740), 592.

24. "A Teacher's Journal, 1740," *Colonial South Carolina Scene*, 130–137; Higgins, "Ambivalence of Freedom," 57. One slave in the 1749 plot told his master that "they would run away to Augustine," upon which the master allegedly responded that "they might go and be damned." Morgan and Terry, "Slavery in Microcosm," 144; Wax, "'The Great Risque We Run.'"

25. Landers, *Black Society*, chap. 2.

26. Daniel E. Meaders, "South Carolina Fugitives as Viewed Through Local Colonial Newspapers with Emphasis on Runaway Notices, 1732–1801," *The Journal of Negro History* 60 (April 1975): 288–319.

27. Morgan, *Slave Counterpoint*, 97.

28. Wood, *Black Majority*, 108–110.

29. This data comes from Berkeley County probate inventories for 1769–1779 analyzed by George D. Terry, "'Champaign Country': A Social History of an Eighteenth-Century Lowcountry Parish in South Carolina: St. Johns Berkeley County" (Ph.D. diss., University of South Carolina, 1981), 249, cited in Olwell, *Masters, Slaves, and Subjects*, 45.

30. Mark Catesby, "The Manner of Making Tar and Pitch," cited in Merrens, *Colonial South Carolina Scene*, 106–108; Morgan, *Slave Counterpoint*, 215.

31. In Spanish Florida Prince began his own timbering business, hiring as his crew other freed runaways from South Carolina. Claim of Prince Whitten, March 28, 1848, Settled Miscellaneous Treasury Accounts, No. 98273, Treasury Accounts, September 6, 1790–September 29, 1894, Office of the First Auditor, Records of the Accounting Officers of the Department of the Treasury, Record Group 217, National Archives and Record Administration (hereafter cited as NARA). I would like to thank Frank Marotti for generously sharing this file with me.

32. Donnan, *Documents*, vol. IV, 470. Camden signatories included Samuel and John Cantey. Kirkland and Kennedy, *Historic Camden*, 107–108.

33. Frey, *Water from the Rock*, 54. During the Stamp Act crisis of 1765, slaves marched through the streets of Charleston shouting "Liberty!" Memories of those public marches must have still been alive when war finally broke out. Wood, "'Taking Care of Business,'" 277.

34. Peter H. Wood, "'Impatient of Oppression': Black Freedom Struggles on the Eve of White Independence," *Southern Exposure* 12, 6 (November-December 1984), 14.

35. Ibid., 15.

36. Josiah Smith to James Poyas, May 18, 1775, cited in Frey, *Water from the Rock*, 57.

37. Colonel William Thompson reported to South Carolina's Council of Safety on July 22, 1775, that "King Prow and about 59 of the Catawbas are at Camden on a friendly visit." Kirkland and Kennedy, *Historic Camden*, 117. The Catawbas were allies of inland settlers during their wars against the

Tuscaroras and Yamasees and had served the colonists as slave catchers since at least 1772. "The Tuscarora Expedition Letters of John Barnwell," *South Carolina Historical and Genealogical Magazine* 9, 1 (1908): 28–54.

38. Lord William Campbell, British Public Records Office (hereafter cited as BPRO), Trans., 35: 184–188, 207–208, cited in Wood, "'Taking Care of Business,'" 283–285, 292 n. 49; Olwell, *Masters, Slaves, and Subjects,* 236.

39. Meaders, "*South Carolina Fugitives.*"

40. Rachel N. Klein, "Frontier Planters and the American Revolution: The South Carolina Backcountry, 1775–1782," in Ronald Hoffman, That W. Tate, and Peter J. Albert, eds., *An Uncivil War: The Southern Backcountry during the American Revolution* (Charlottesville, 1985), 37–69.

41. In one famous incident Patriot James Cantey refused to yield a shipment of gunpowder to his Loyalist uncle, Daniel McGirtt. Walter Edgar, *Partisans and Redcoats: The Southern Conflict that Turned the Tide of the American Revolution* (New York, 2001), 32–33; Frey, *Water from the Rock,* 132.

42. On the disaffected Loyalists, Brown, Cunningham, and McGirtt (or McGirt), see Rachel N. Klein, *Unification of a Slave State: The Rise of the Planter Class in South Carolina Backcountry, 1760–1808* (Chapel Hill, N.C., 1990), 98–108.

43. Laurens reported only three or four "Negroes killed" at Sullivan's Island. Henry Laurens to Richard Richardson, December 19, 1755, Papers of Henry Laurens, 10, 576, cited in Olwell, *Masters, Slaves, and Subjects,* 241.

44. Henry Laurens to Stephen Bull, March 16, 1776, Papers of Henry Laurens, 11, 172, cited in Olwell, *Masters, Slaves, and Subjects,* 242–243.

45. On the reluctant revolutionaries of Charleston see Olwell, *Masters, Slaves, and Subjects,* 243.

46. Alexander Semple to McFernan, December 16, 1786, EFP, microfilm reel 41, PKY.

47. Archibald Campbell to [?], January 9, 1770, Prioleau papers, South Carolina Historical Society, cited in Philip D. Morgan, "Black Society in the Lowcountry," in Ira Berlin and Ronald Hoffman, eds., *Slavery and Freedom in the Age of the American Revolution* (Charlottesville, 1983), 83–141; Olwell,

Masters, Slaves, and Subjects, 245. Among the surrendered Patriots were three Cantey brothers: James, Zachariah, and Philip.

48. Jerome J. Nadelhaft, *The Disorders of War: The Revolution in South Carolina* (Orono, Maine, 1981), 52–64; Klein, *Unification of a Slave State,* 102–104.

49. Edgar, *Partisans and Recoats,* 132–134.

50. *Letters of Eliza Wilkinson,* ed. Caroline Gilman (New York, 1969), 29, 62.

51. Colonel Otho Williams, Adjutant General to Gates's army, disparaged the attire and arms of Marion's multiracial force. William Gilmore Simms, *The Life of Francis Marion* (Freeport, N.Y.), 106, 178.

52. Nathanael Greene, December 1780, cited in Robert Stansbury Lambert, *South Carolina Loyalists in the American Revolution* (Columbia, S.C., 1987), 198, 199–215.

53. Frey, *Water from the Rock,* 132–133.

54. Nadelhaft, *Disorders of War,* 60–62; Certificate of John McKinnon, November 27, 1782, Charles Town, cited in The On-Line Institute for Advanced Loyalist Studies, *www.royalprovincial.com/military/mems/sc/clm johnston.htm* (accessed 6/28/08).

55. Colonel John Watson to General Francis Marion, Cantey's House, March 9, 1781, and General Francis Marion to Colonel Peter Horry, October 29, 1781, in Robert Wilson Gibbes, A *Documentary History of the American Revolution* (Columbia, S.C., 1857), vol. 3, no. 52, p. 33. The Swamp Fox was still in residence at Mount Hope when Cornwallis surrendered at Yorktown in October 1781, and the Patriots quickly organized a celebratory ball at the Cantey plantation. Francis Marion to Peter Horry, Cantey's House, October 29, 1781, ibid., no. 202, p. 200.

56. Frey, *Water from the Rock,* 133–134.

57. Many captured Patriots also died of smallpox and typhus aboard prison ships in the Charleston harbor or in makeshift prisons at Camden. Elizabeth A. Fenn, *Pox Americana: The Great Smallpox Epidemic of 1775–82* (New York, 2002), chap. 4.

58. Philip D. Morgan and Andrew Jackson O'Shaughnessy, "Arming

Slaves in the American Revolution," in Christopher Leslie Brown and Philip D. Morgan, eds., *Arming the Slave from Classical Times to the Modern Age* (New Haven, Conn., 2006), 180–208; Frey, *Water from the Rock*, 99–100, 138–139.

59. Johnston alleged that after Cornwallis's surrender, General Howe inquired after him and would have hanged him if friends had not concealed him aboard the *Rhinocerus*, on which he escaped to England. Claims and Memorial petition of Thomas Johnston of South Carolina, London, July 21, 1786, BPRO, Audit Office, Class 13, vol. 70b, part 1, folios 301–302, cited in The On-Line Institute for Advanced Loyalist Studies, *www.royalprovincial .com/military/mems/sc/clmjohnston.htm* (accessed 6/28/08).

60. Governor Rutledge's order of June 28, 1781, to Francis Marion. On October 6, 1782, Governor John Mathews ordered Marion to execute any blacks taken in arms. Quarles, *Negro in the American Revolution*, 128; Deposition of J. Doyle, Major, BPRO, Audit Office, Class 13, vol. 4, folio 321, cited in The On-Line Institute for Advanced Loyalist Studies, *www.royalpro vincial.com/military/mems/sc/clmjohnston.htm* (accessed 6/28/08).

61. On the use of black troops in Georgia and South Carolina, see Frey, *Water from the Rock*, 99–100, 138–140; Quarles, *Negro in the American Revolution*, 127, 149–151; Klein, *Unification of a Slave State*, 105–107; Olwell, *Masters, Slaves, and Subjects*, 256–260; Foner, *Blacks in the American Revolution*, 59–67; Berlin, *Many Thousands Gone*, 291–301; Morgan and O'Shaughnessy, "Arming Slaves," in Brown and Morgan, eds., *Arming the Slave*, 180–208.

62. Frey, *Water from the Rock*, 137; Nadelhaft, *The Disorders of War*, 50–65; Klein, *Unification of a Slave State*, 97–108; Lambert, *South Carolina Loyalists*, 216–226; Edward Cashin, *The King's Ranger: Thomas Brown and the American Revolution on the Southern Frontier* (Athens, Ga., 1989).

63. Berlin, *Many Thousands Gone*, 304.

64. Lambert, *South Carolina Loyalists*, 220–221. On blacks among and plunder by McGirtt's and Cunningham's bands, see August 18, 1779, September 17, 1779, and Aedanus Burke to Governor Guerard, July 27, 1785, in *The Pennsylvania Gazette;* Francis Marion to Governor John Matthews, August 30, 1782, cited in Frey, *Water from the Rock*, 138.

65. Alexander Semple to McFernan, December 16, 1786, EFP, microfilm reel 41, PKY. On the widespread plundering of slaves in South Carolina, see Frey, *Water from the Rock*, 122–137; Klein, *Unification of a Slave State*, 106–107; and Berlin, *Many Thousands Gone*, 296–298. On the efforts of slave owners to be compensated for slaves lost to the British, see John H. Bracey, Jr., Sharon Harley, and August Meier, eds., *Race, Slavery, and Free Blacks: Series I, Petitions to Southern Legislatures, 1777–1867*, ed. Loren Schweninger and Robert Shelton (Bethesda, Md., 1998).

66. Lambert, *South Carolina Loyalists*, 219; Statement of Prince, January 9, 1789, Census Returns, 1784–1814, EFP, microfilm reel 148, PKY.

67. J. Leitch Wright, Jr., *Florida in the American Revolution* (Gainesville, Fla., 1975). On British plantation development in Florida, see Daniel L. Schafer, "'Yellow Silk Ferret Tied Round Their Wrists': African Americans in British East Florida, 1763–1784," in David R. Colburn and Jane L. Landers, eds., *The African American Heritage of Florida* (Gainesville, Fla., 1995), 71–103; "Family Ties That Bind: Anglo-African Slave Traders in Africa and Florida, John Fraser and His Descendants, " *Slavery & Abolition* (December 1999); and "'A Swamp of an Investment?': Richard Oswald's East Florida Plantation," in Jane G. Landers, ed., *Colonial Plantations and Economy in Florida* (Gainesville, Fla., 2001), 11–38.

68. Twenty-eight of Alexander Patterson's slaves "eloped" during the evacuation. Robert Robinson's slave, Jack, ran away on the day of Robinson's departure for Halifax "for his dread of encountering so cold a climate." Wilbur Henry Siebert, ed., *Loyalists in East Florida, 1783–1785: The Most Important Documents Pertaining Thereto, Edited With an Accompanying Narrative*, 2 vols. (Deland, Fla., 1929), 125, 140.

69. Weed was among the founders of the frontier town of St. Marys, which became the southernmost port of the United States and where the new U.S. government established a garrison. Between 1786 and 1788 the Georgia Assembly granted Weed more than 80,000 acres in Camden County. *www.camdencounty.org/ccnews/jacob_weed.html* (accessed 9/18/08).

70. Semple to McFernan, December 16, 1786, EFP, microfilm reel 41, PKY. Semple operated a dry goods store on Cumberland Island which was frequented by Floridians living along the St. Marys River. Susan R. Parker,

"Men without God or King: Rural Settlers in East Florida, 1784–1790," *Florida Historical Quarterly* 69 (October 1990): 135–155.

71. Carlos Howard to Luis de las Casas, July 2, 1791, Cuba 1439, Archivo General de Indias, Seville, Spain (hereafter cited as AGI); Helen Hornbeck Tanner, "Zéspedes and the Southern Conspiracies," *Florida Historical Quarterly* 38 (1959): 15–28.

72. Carlos Howard to Luis de las Casas, July 2, 1791, Cuba 1439, AGI; Robert Francis Crider, "The Borderland Floridas, 1815–1821: Spanish Sovereignty under Siege," (Ph.D. diss., Florida State University, 1979), 9–10.

73. Memorial of the Italians, Greeks, and Minorcans, July 12, 1784, and July 13, 1784, and Zéspedes to Bernardo de Gálvez, October 20, 1784, cited in Joseph Byrne Lockey, *East Florida, 1783–1785: A Collection of Documents Assembled and Many of Them Translated* (Berkeley, 1949), 232–233, 285–286. For the history of this community, see Patricia C. Griffin, *Mullet on the Beach: The Minorcans of Florida, 1768–1788* (Jacksonville, Fla., 1991), and "Blue Gold: Andrew Turnbull's New Smyrna Plantation," in *Colonial Plantations and Economy of Florida*, 39–68. Intimately tied to the urban economy, the Minorcans clustered near St. Augustine and along the North and Matanzas Rivers. Susan R. Parker describes the coastal estuaries north and south of St. Augustine as a "Minorcan littoral." Parker, "Men Without God," 138.

74. Memorials of Francis Philip Fatio, February 23, 1785, and James Clarke, February 26, 1785, cited in Lockey, *East Florida*, 464–465. For more on Fatio, see Susan R. Parker, "Success through Diversification: Francis Philip Fatio's New Switzerland Plantation," in *Colonial Plantations and Economy of Florida*, 69–82.

75. Landers, *Black Society*, 205–209.

76. On British plantation development and the African slave trade to Florida, see Schafer, "'Yellow Silk Ferret,'" "Family Ties," and "'A Swamp of an Investment,'" and David Hancock, *Citizens of the World: London Merchants and the Integration of the British Atlantic Community, 1735–1785* (Cambridge, Mass., 1995).

77. Vicente Manuel de Zéspedes to Joseph de Ezpeleta, October 2, 1788, Cuba 1395, AGI.

78. Proclamation of Vicente Manuel de Zéspedes, July 26, 1784, cited in Lockey, *East Florida,* 240–241. Royal slaves traditionally labored on public works, in mines, and in galleys. See María Elena Díaz, *The Virgin, The King, and the Royal Slaves of El Cobre: Negotiating Freedom in Colonial Cuba, 1687–1780* (Stanford, Calif., 2000).

79. Patrick Tonyn to Lord Sydney, December 6, 1784, cited in Lockey, *East Florida,* 339. Most of the declarations simply stated the name and race of the petitioner, who showed the Spanish notary documents signed by British military authorities attesting to his or her free status. More complete declarations gave information on previous owners, family composition, occupations, reasons for escaping, and employment in St. Augustine. Census Returns, 1784–1814, EFP, microfilm reel 148, PKY.

80. "Principe" stated that he ran three years before his registration date of November 14, 1788, from Pedro Whitten of South Carolina. He made no mention of Young or Weed. Census Returns, 1784–1814, EFP, microfilm reel, 148, folio 183, PKY.

81. List of the free blacks who have presented themselves to the Government and the names of the subjects with whom they are staying as required by the edict of February 18, 1792, EFP, Miscellaneous Papers, 1784–1821, microfilm reel 174, folio 1488, PKY.

82. Ira Berlin, Steven F. Miller, and Leslie S. Rowland have argued that British slaves understood their society "in the idiom of kinship" and that, for slaves, "familial and communal relations were one." Mediterranean cultures also viewed society as an extension of family structures. Institutions of extended kinship like *parentela,* which included blood relations, fictive kin, and even household servants and slaves, and *clientela,* which bound more powerful patrons and their personal dependents into a network of mutual obligations, were deeply rooted in Hispanic society. Lyle N. McAlister, *Spain and Portugal in the New World, 1492–1700* (Minneapolis, 1984), 39–40.

83. Alice Bellagamba, "A Matter of Trust: Political Identities and Interpersonal Relationships along the River Gambia," *Paideuma* 46 (2000): 37–61.

84. Landers, *Black Society,* 76–79.

85. Maureen Flynn, *Sacred Charity: Confraternities and Social Welfare in Spain, 1400–1700* (Ithaca, N.Y., 1989); Alonso de Sandoval, *Un tratado sobre la esclavitud* (Madrid, 1987). A number of recent works have addressed the experiences of black Catholics in Africa. See, for example, Linda Heywood and John Thornton, *Central Africans, Atlantic Creoles and the Making of the Foundation of the Americas, 1585–1660* (New York, 2007); John Thornton, *The Kongolese Saint Anthony: Dona Beatriz Kimpa Vita and the Antonian Movement, 1684–1706* (Cambridge, 1998); Miller, "Retention, Reinvention, and Remembering." For Mexico, see Nicole Von Germeten, *Black Blood Brothers: Confraternities and Social Mobility for Afro-Mexicans* (Gainesville, Fla., 2006); Herman L. Bennett, *Africans in Colonial Mexico: Absolutism, Christianity, and Afro-Creole Consciousness, 1570–1640* (Bloomington, Ind., 2003); Joan Cameron Bristol, *Christians, Blasphemers, and Witches: Afro-Mexican Ritual Practice in the Seventeenth Century* (Albuquerque, N.M., 2007).

86. Baptisms of Polly and Glasgow, August 16, 1788, St. Augustine Catholic Parish Registers (hereafter cited as CPR), Black Baptisms, vol. 1, p. 41, no. 85 and no. 86, microfilm reel 284 J, PKY. Glasgow's godparents were Domingo Martineli and his wife, Mariana Cavedo, and Polly's godfather was Pedro Cosifacio. Newcomers Prince Paten and Flora Spole had six of their children baptized in a five-year period. In the same period, Juan and Mila Right baptized four children, Antonio and Anna Overstreet baptized five, and Antonio and Ester Capo also baptized five children. Ibid.

87. One eighteenth-century Cuban example of this *doctrina* exam consisted of twenty-six questions with set answers on the nature of the Trinity, creation, immaculate conception, Christ's death and resurrection, sin, confession, and salvation. *Doctrina Para Negros*, trans. and ed. Javier Laviña (Barcelona, 1989).

88. The fact that more black adults than white were converted over the course of the second Spanish regime in Florida (1784–1821) probably reflects the efforts of fugitives from the United States, like the Whittens, to secure and protect their freedom. Unlike some whites, the fugitives had no intention of returning to a land of slavery, and thus had more to gain by the

conversion that guaranteed them sanctuary. Baptisms of Prince and Judy, January 11, 1792, CPR, Black Baptisms, vol. 1, microfilm reel 284 J, PKY.

89. Godparents typically gave gifts at the baptism and were expected to provide for the spiritual and material care of their god-"child" in the event of the parents' death, but more important were the ties that bound the members of the newly-linked "family." Such extended kinship may have had even stronger significance for adult converts, many of whom were uprooted and kinless *bozales* (recently arrived and unacculturated Africans). Joseph Miller argues that Africans understood Christianity as a form of healing, as well as of social integration. Miller, "Retention, Reinvention, and Remembering."

90. Black parents may have considered the Whittens good role models, or they may have hoped for more tangible aid for their children. Whitten's origins may have also made him a desirable choice of godfather for some African-born parents. CPR, Black Baptisms, microfilm reel 284 J, PKY.

91. Michael Gannon, *Cross in the Sand: The Early Catholic Church in Florida, 1513–1870* (Gainesville, Fla., 1965), 99.

92. Other formerly enslaved students included Antonio Capo, whose father, Antonio, was Guinea-born and whose mother, Ester, was born in Virginia, and Antonio Florencio, the mulatto son of Mariana Bisit, of New York. Roster of school boys by Josef Monasterio, March 25, 1796, SD 2531, AGI.

93. Rules and instructions to be observed by the Government in the direction of schools, 1786, SD 2588, AGI.

94. William Pengree to Carlos Howard, July 10, 1787, EFP, microfilm reel 82, PKY. Pengree, a Loyalist who remained in Florida after the cession, was a wealthy planter. James Robertson Ward, *Old Hickory's Town: An Illustrated History of Jacksonville* (Jacksonville, Fla., 1985).

95. Ambrosio Nelson to Governor Zéspedes, April 20, 1787, EFP, microfilm reel 77, PKY. While living in St. Augustine, Prince entered into a work contract with the Minorcan carpenter Francisco Pellicer. Contract with Francisco Pellicer, January 9, 1789, Census Returns, 1784–1814, EFP, microfilm reel 148, p. 183, PKY.

96. Memorial by Prince Witten, November 12, 1789, EFP, microfilm reel 148, PKY. Prince signed with an X, and the governor ordered McGirtt to appear and respond to Prince's complaint.

97. Death of Juan Fatio, free black, natural son of Prince and Judith Witten, born July 20, 1789, CPR, Black Baptisms, vol. 1, p. 53, no. 103, microfilm reel 284 J, and CPR, Deaths, vol. 2, p. 11, no. 27, microfilm reel 284-L, PKY.

98. Petition of Prince, free black, November 12, 1789, EFP, microfilm reel 77, PKY.

99. Some years later, Judy also filed suit against McGirtt, asking to be paid for laundry she claimed to have washed for his imprisoned brother, Daniel. Judy could not sign her petition but added her mark. Memorial of Rafaela Lluly, August 9, 1796, and response of James McGirtt on petition of Judith, alias Rafaela, July 15, 1797, EFP microfilm reel 79, PKY.

100. Memorial of María Witten [*sic*], August 27, 1798, and responses by don José and don Bernardino Sánchez, Memorials 1784–1821, EFP, microfilm reel 79, PKY. For more on how African American women used the Spanish legal system, see Landers, *Black Society*, chap. 5, and "African-American Women and their Pursuit of Rights through Eighteenth-Century Texts," in Anne Goodwyn Jones and Susan Donaldson, eds., *Haunted Bodies: Gender and Southern Texts* (Charlottesville, Va., 1997), 56–76.

101. Report of Domingo Rodríguez de León, December 9, 1789, SD 2558, AGI.

102. Victor M. Uribe-Uran, "The Birth of a Public Sphere in Latin America During the Age of Revolution," *Comparative Studies in Society and History* 42, no. 2 (April 2000): 425–457. Uribe-Uran frames this period as the birth of a public sphere and of challenge to monarchy and old hierarchies, but at least for some new Spanish subjects, it was a period of welcome incorporation.

103. Royal decree of May 17, 1790, included in Captain General Luís de las Casas to Governor Manuel de Zéspedes, July 21, 1790, Letters from the Captain General, 1784–1821, EFP, microfilm reel 1, PKY; Thomas Jefferson to Juan Nepomuceno de Quesada, December 17, 1790, and August 9, 1791,

Letters To and From the United States, 1784–1821, EFP, microfilm reel 41, PKY; Revocation of sanctuary notice of Governor Juan Nepomuceno de Quesada, August 23, 1790, *Georgia Gazette*, September 23, 1790, p. 2; Luis de las Casa to Juan Nepomuceno de Quesada, November 11, 1790, Miscellaneous Papers, EFP microfilm reel 174, PKY.

104. Petition of Juan Bautista Whiten [*sic*] to quarry coquina stone on Anastasia Island, August 22, 1797 (Francisco Whiten signed "for my father who does not know how"), EFP, microfilm reel 79, PKY; Manuel Romero to Enrique White, reporting he owed Prince fourteen pesos for cutting wood for the construction of the San Juan Battery, November 12, 1803, EFP, microfilm reel 57, PKY; Census of 1793, Census returns 1784–1814, EFP, microfilm reel 148, PKY.

105. Baptism of Francisco Xavier Quinty [*sic*], November 23, 1794, CPR, Black Baptisms, vol. 2, p. 34, no. 65, microfilm reel 284J, PKY.

106. Declaration of Manuel Fernández Bendicho, February 22, 1792, EFP microfilm reel 174, PKY.

107. Census of 1793, Census Returns, 1784–1814, EFP, microfilm reel 148, PKY.

108. An extensive literature on black military service in the Spanish colonies includes Joseph P. Sánchez, "African Freedmen and the Fuero Militar: A Historical Overview of Pardo and Moreno Militiamen in the Late Spanish Empire," *Colonial Latin American Historical Review* 3 (1994): 165–184; Lyle N. McAlister, *El fuero militar en la Nueva España (1764–1800)* (Mexico City, 1982); Allan J. Kuethe, *Military Reform and Society in New Granada, 1773–1808* (Gainesville, Fla., 1978), 8–27, 38–39; Christon I. Archer, *The Army in Bourbon Mexico, 1760–1810* (Albuquerque, N.M., 1977), 4, 224–231; Christon I. Archer, "Pardos, Indians and the Army of New Spain: Inter-Relationships and Conflicts, 1780–1810," *Journal of Latin American Studies* 6, 2 (1974): 231–255; Leon Campbell, "The Changing Racial and Administrative Structure of the Peruvian Military Under the Later Bourbons," *Americas* 32 (1975): 117–133; Margarita Gascón, "The Military of Santo Domingo, 1720–1764," *Hispanic American Historical Review* 73 (1993): 431–452.

109. Ben Vinson, III, *Bearing Arms for His Majesty: The Free-Colored Militia in Colonial Mexico* (Stanford, Calif., 2001), 25.

110. Herbert S. Klein, "The Colored Militia of Cuba: 1568–1868," *Caribbean Studies* 6 (July 1966): 17–27; Pedro Deschamps Chapeaux, *Los Batallones de Pardos y Morenos Libres* (La Habana, 1976); Landers, *Black Society*, chaps. 9 and 10.

111. See David P. Geggus, ed., *The Impact of the Haitian Revolution in the Atlantic World* (Columbia, S.C., 2001); David Patrick Geggus, *Haitian Revolutionary Studies* (Bloomington, Ind., 2002); Laurent Dubois, *Avengers of the New World: The Story of the Haitian Revolution* (Cambridge, Mass, 2004); Laurent Dubois, *A Colony of Citizens: Revolution and Slave Emancipation in the French Caribbean, 1787–1804* (Chapel Hill, N.C., 2004).

112. Royal Order, May 18, 1791, cited in Richard K. Murdoch, "The Genesis of the Genêt Schemes," *The French-American Review* (April-June 1949): 81–97.

113. France's grand scheme included revolutionizing Louisiana, Canada, and Spanish possessions in North America, including Mexico. Richard K. Murdoch, *The Georgia-Florida Frontier, 1793–1796: Spanish Reaction to French Intrigue and American Designs* (Berkeley, 1951), 9–72, and "Elijah Clarke and Anglo-American Designs on East Florida, 1791–1798," *Georgia Historical Quarterly* 3 (September 1951): 173–190.

114. "Proposals for Enlistment in the French Service," cited in Murdoch, *Georgia-Florida Frontier*, 19. The commanding officers were to receive commissions after becoming French citizens, and their payment would be large tracts of land.

115. Ibid., 23.

116. Governor Sebastián Kindelán to Governor George Matthews, November 14, 1795, and response, November 15, 1795, Cuba 1439, AGI.

117. War Council, St. Augustine, June 1795, Cuba 1428, AGI, cited in Charles E. Bennett, *Florida's "French" Revolution, 1793–1795* (Gainesville, Fla., 1981), 179.

118. Leslie also commanded a unit of black slaves attached to the artil-

lery. He may have been selected because he could underwrite the unit's expenses, or he might have been chosen because he had a black consort and mulatto children. Report of Gonzalo Zamorano, April 30, 1794, EFP, Letters with the Accountant of the Exchequer, 1784–1821, microfilm reel 26, PKY; Accounts of 1795, Accounts of the Royal Treasury, 1784–1796, SD 2635 and 2636, AGI.

119. Accounts of 1795, SD 2635, AGI. Black sailors also served on river boats during this invasion. Libros de Asientos, Cuba 486, AGI.

120. David Patrick Geggus, "Slavery, War, and Revolution in the Greater Caribbean, 1789–1815," in David Barry Gaspar and David Patrick Geggus, eds., *A Turbulent Time: The French Revolution and the Greater Caribbean* (Bloomington, Ind., 1997), 1–50.

121. Included in Carlos Howard to Bartolome Morales, Letters from the St. Johns and St. Marys Rivers, July-September 1795, EFP, microfilm reel 52, PKY.

122. Juan Nepomuceno de Quesada to Luis de Las Casa, October 26, 1795, Letters to the Captain General, 1784–1823, EFP, microfilm reel 10, PKY.

2. The Counter-Revolution in Saint-Domingue

1. Jorge Biassou to Captain General Joaquín García, July 15, 1793, Guerra Moderna (hereafter cited as GM) 7157, no. 7, Archivo General de Simancas (hereafter cited as AGS). This document is also signed by Field Marshall Belair.

2. Méderic-Louis-Elie Moreau de Saint-Mery, *A Civilization That Perished: The Last Years of White Colonial Rule in Haiti*, trans. Ivor D. Spence (New York, 1985), 114–127, 131–137, 145–148; Madison Smartt Bell, *Toussaint Louverture: A Biography* (New York, 2007), 63–64.

3. Bell, *Toussaint Louverture*, ch. 1; Jorge Biassou to Captain General Joaquín García, July 15, 1793, GM 7157, no. 7, AGS.

4. Toussaint to Biassou, Grande-Rivière, October 15, 1791. The letter is signed General Doctor. Général Nemours, *Toussaint Louverture fonde*

à Saint-Domingue la liberté et l'égalité (Port-au-Prince, 1988). *http://thelouvertureproject.org/index.php?title=Toussaint_letter_to_Biassou_during _Boukman_Rebellion* (accessed 6/5/09).

5. Toussaint to Biassou, October 4, 1791, and October 25, 1791, cited in Bell, *Toussaint Louverture*, 24–25. In the first example, Toussaint closes by saying, "I wish you the most perfect health and am for life your friend."

6. Biassou's father, Carlos, may also have worked on the plantation. Communications from Madison Smartt Bell, September 25, 2005, and from David Patrick Geggus, September 15, 2008; I am indebted to both for their assistance, their friendship, and their fine scholarship. An older account claims that the godfathers of Biassou and Toussaint were both slaves at the Hospital of the Fathers of Charity and places Biassou at the Bréda plantation for some time. Stephen Alexis, *Black Liberator, The Life of Toussaint Louverture* (London, 1949), 12–13, 30.

7. Jorge Biassou to Captain General Joaquín García, July 15, 1793, GM 7157, no. 7, AGS.

8. Bell, *Toussaint Louverture*, 64–65. The beloved Jesuit Father Pierre Boutin, like Fathers Sandoval and Claver in Cartagena, was noted for his efforts to evangelize Africans and learn African languages. Moreau de Saint-Mery, *A Civilization That Perished*, 116–117, 120.

9. Baron Alexandre-Stanislas de Wimpffen, *Voyage à Saint-Domingue*, in *Haiti au XVIII siècle: Richesse et esclavage dans une colonie française*, ed. Pluchon, 239–240, cited in Stewart R. King, *Blue Coat or Powdered Wig: Free People of Color in Pre-Revolutionary Saint Domingue* (Athens, Ga., 2001), 23.

10. Vincent Olivier, a respected free black veteran of the 1697 French attack on Cartagena, lived in Le Cap and helped recruit more than one thousand blacks for the expedition to Savannah. King, *Blue Coat or Powdered Wig*, 65–77, 226–265; David Geggus, "The Arming of Slaves in the Haitian Revolution," in Brown and Morgan, *Arming the Slaves*, 209–232.

11. Bell, *Toussaint Louverture*, 14; King, *Blue Coat or Powdered Wig*, xv; Samuel G. Perkins, "Insurrection in St. Domingo," *Massachusetts Historical Society Proceedings*, 1885–1886, 2nd Ser. II, 307–390.

12. The rebels also demanded that the Spanish government (which had been covertly supplying them for some time) guarantee their terms. Gérard M. Laurent, T*oussaint Louverture à travers sa correspondance* (Madrid, 1953), in Bell, *Toussaint Louverture*, 38–41.

13. Laurent Dubois and John D. Garrigus, eds., *Slave Revolution in the Caribbean, 1789–1804: A Brief History with Documents* (Boston, 2006), 26.

14. In 1789 Grégoire published his famous *Lettre aux gens de couleur et nègres libres*. John D. Garrigus, *Before Haiti: Race and Citizenship in French Saint-Domingue* (New York, 2006), 259.

15. Geggus, *Haitian Revolutionary Studies*, 84; Carolyn E. Fick, "The Saint-Domingue Slave Insurrection of 1791: A Socio-Political and Cultural Analysis," *Journal of Caribbean History* 25: 1 and 2 (1991): 1–40.

16. Dubois, *Avengers of the New World*, chap. 4.

17. After carefully analyzing the main primary accounts, David Geggus has shown that scholars have mistakenly collapsed two meetings into one: the famous Bois Caïman ceremony was held on August 22, 1791. David Geggus, "The Bois Caïman Ceremony," *Journal of Caribbean History* 25: 1 and 2 (1991): 41–57. For a detailed discussion of contemporary ritual practices performed at nighttime gatherings, see Gabriel Deben, "Night-Time Meetings in Saint-Dominge (La Marmelade, 1786)," translated by John Garrigus from *Annales historiques de la révolution française* 44 (April–June 1972): 273–284, *www.vancouver.wsu.edu/fac/peabody/voodoo.htm* (accessed 9/28/2006).

18. Dubois, *Avengers of the New World*, 94–97.

19. "St. Domingo Disturbances," *Philadelphia Aurora*, October 10, 1791, entry for August 27, 1791, cited in Fick, "The Slave Insurrection of 1791," 19.

20. Fick, "The Slave Insurrection of 1791," 23.

21. Dubois, *Avengers of the New World*, 102–109.

22. Procès-verbal d'interrogatoire, subi par le curé du Dondon par devant nous commissaire de la république délégué aux Iles françaises de l'Amérique sous le vent, Interrogation of Guillaume Silvestre de la Haye, February 1, 1793. I am indebted to Madison Smartt Bell for this reference.

23. M. Gros, *An Historick Recital of the Different Occurrences in the Camps of Grand-Reviere, Dondon, Sainte-Suʒanne and others from the 26th of October, 1791 to the 24th of December, of the Same Year* (Baltimore, 1792), 21–22, 31. Most contemporary accounts agree that the insurgents, Africans and creoles alike, proclaimed themselves devoted to Louis XVI, some carrying flags decorated with the fleur-de-lis and others calling themselves *gens du roi*. Dubois, *Avengers of the New World*, 106.

24. Jorge Biassou to Captain General Joaquín García, July 15, 1793, GM 7157, no. 7, AGS.

25. Dubois, *Avengers of the New World*, 106; Fick, "The Slave Insurrection of 1791," 24.

26. Jorge Biassou to Captain General Joaquín García, July 15, 1793, GM 7157, no. 7, AGS; Toussaint to Georges Biassou, October 15, 1791, cited in Bell, *Toussaint*, 25.

27. Gros, *An Historick Recital*, 22–23, 40, 42. Two of Toussaint's letters to Biassou from this period are signed Médecin Général, but Madison Smartt Bell points out that the language is of one equal to another. This familiar tone might derive from their long acquaintance. Toussaint to Biassou, October 4, 1791, and October 15, 1791, from the private collection of Gérard Berthélemy, cited in Bell, *Toussaint Louverture*, 24–25.

28. Thomas Madiou, *Histoire d'Haiti* (Port-au-Prince, Haiti, 1922–1923). C. L. R. James describes Biassou as "a fire-eater, always drunk, always ready for the fiercest and most dangerous exploits." C. L. R. James, *The Black Jacobins: Toussaint L'Ouverture and the San Domingo Revolution* (London, 1980), 93–94, 106. Carolyn E. Fick agrees with these characterizations and goes so far as to assert that "among the prominent leaders, it was now Biassou, the fiery and impassioned voodoo adept who, in his more impulsive moments, best incarnated the aspirations and mentality of the insurgent slaves." *Making of Haiti: The Saint Domingue Revolution from Below* (Knoxville, Tenn., 1990), 115. To say that Biassou might "incarnate" the "mentality" of the slaves would be a leap in any case, but certainly not because of his impulsive and fiery nature. One might equally argue that Biassou's actions exhibit pragmatic and assiduous pursuit of self-interest.

29. Michel-Rolph Trouillot, "From Planters' Journals to Academia: The

Haitian Revolution as Unthinkable History," *Journal of Caribbean History* 25, 1 and 2 (1991): 81–99, and *Silencing the Past: Power and the Production of History* (Boston, 1995); Alfred N. Hunt, *Haiti's Influence on Antebellum America: Slumbering Volcano in the Caribbean* (Baton Rouge, La., 1988).

30. Gros, *An Historick Recital*, 57.

31. *Philadelphia General Advertiser*, No. 322, Tuesday, October 11, 1791, cited in Dubois and Garrigus, eds., *Slave Revolution in the Caribbean*, 97–99.

32. Gros, *An Historick Recital*, 34.

33. Ibid., 35.

34. The masses of rebels mistakenly thought that the commander of Saint Domingue troops near Le Cap, Anne-Louis de Tousard, had been killed, and they staged a celebratory dance or *calenda*. For three days they enjoyed themselves while regaling their white prisoners with tales of their great war exploits. Ibid., 34–35; Fick, "The Slave Insurrection of 1791," 25.

35. Fick, "The Slave Insurrection of 1791," 29.

36. Gros, *An Historick Recital*, 40, 47.

37. Jean-François and Toussaint both recognized that they were betraying their compatriots. Dubois, *Avengers of the New World*, 125–128; James, *Black Jacobins*, 104–106.

38. Gros, *An Historick Recital*, 42.

39. Jean-François, General, and Biassou, General to the Commissioners, December 12, 1791, and Biassou and Jean-François to the Commissioners, December 21, 1791, in Dubois and Garrigus, eds., *Slave Revolution in the Caribbean*, 100–102.

40. Gros, An *Historick Recital*, 44–47.

41. Letter of Dr. Arthaud, Archives de France, Centre des Archives d'Outre-mer, Aix-en-Provence, F3/197. I am indebted to David Geggus for this reference.

42. Bell, *Toussaint Louverture*, 38.

43. Ibid., 27.

44. Dubois, *Avengers of the New World*, 147.

45. Ibid., 41.

46. Biassou (from San Miguel) to Captain General Joaquín García, August 24, 1793, GM 7157, no. 6, AGS.

47. Moreau de Saint-Mery, *A Civilization That Perished*, 121.

48. Dubois, *Avengers of the New World*, 157–160.

49. Robin Blackburn, "*The Black Jacobins* and New World Slavery," in Selwyn R. Cudjoe and William E. Cain, eds., *C. L. R. James, His Intellectual Legacies* (Amherst, Mass., 1995), 81–97, 86; James, *Black Jacobins*.

50. Dubois, *Avengers of the New World*, 160.

51. Captain General Joaquín García to the Duque de Alcudia, December 12, 1795, cited in Emilio Rodríguez Demorizi, *Cesión de Santo Domingo a Francia* (Ciudad Trujillo, D. R., 1958), 46–48.

52. David Patrick Geggus, "Slavery, War, and Revolution in the Greater Caribbean, 1789–1815," in Gaspar and Geggus, *A Turbulent Time*, 1–50.

53. Julius S. Scott, III, "The Common Wind: Currents of Afro-American Communication in the Era of the Haitian Revolution," Ph.D. diss., Duke University, 1986); Geggus, "Slavery, War, and Revolution."

54. I am indebted to James G. Cusick for a personal communication on Florida captains like José Saby and Sebastián Ortegas who sailed for Guarico (Le Cap) in 1787. See James G. Cusick, "Across the Southern Border: Commodity Flow and Merchants in Spanish America," *Florida Historical Quarterly* 69, no. 3 (1991): 277–299.

55. Landers, *Black Society;* Stephen Webre, "Las compañías de milicia y la defensa del istmos centroamericano en el siglo XVII: el alistamiento general de 1763," *Mesoamérica* 14 (1987): 511–529; Peter M. Voelz, *Slave and Soldier: The Military Impact of Blacks in the Colonial Americas* (New York, 1993), chaps. 1 and 2.

56. Herbert S. Klein, "The Colored Militia of Cuba: 1568–1868," *Caribbean Studies* 6 (July 1966): 17–27; Pedro Deschamps Chapeaux, *Los Batallones de Pardos y Morenos Libres* (Havana, 1976).

57. The three chiefs swore submission and vassalage to the Spanish King in the house of Don Matias de Armona on November 8, 1793. Estado (hereafter cited as ES) 13, AGI. Twelve other sub-chiefs received medals of silver and documents attesting to their meritorious service. Captain General Joaquín García to the Duque de la Alcudia, February 18, 1794, ES 14, doc. 86, AGI.

58. James, *Black Jacobins,* 124, 155.

59. Father Josef Vásquez to the Vicar of Santiago, December 12, 1793, ES 11, doc. 98, AGI.

60. Jorge Biassou (from San Miguel) to Captain General Joaquín García, August 24, 1793, GM 7157, no. 6, AGS.

61. Bell, *Toussaint Louverture,* 18–19.

62. Jorge Biassou (from San Miguel) to Captain General Joaquín García, July 15, 1793, GM 7157, no. 7; August 23, 1793, GM 7157, no. 8; August 24, 1793, GM 7157, no. 6; September 25, 1793, GM 7157, no. 13; Captain General Joaquín García to Jorge Biassou, October 29, 1793, GM 7157, no. 15, AGS.

63. King Carlos IV, March 1, 1794, GM 7159, no. 11 and no. 14; Council of State, September 26, 1794, GM 7159, no. 61, AGS. The King and Council of State were convinced that Biassou's three white secretaries, the Frenchmen Cavaux de Franqueville and LaPlace and the Canary Islander José de los Reyes, were behind Biassou's torrent of complaints, and they ordered them summarily arrested and sent to prison in Puerto Rico.

64. Comandante Guiambois to General Biassou, August 5, 1793, GM 7157, no. 11, AGS; Geggus, *Haitian Revolutionary Studies,* 8.

65. Thomas O. Ott, *The Haitian Revolution, 1789–1804* (Knoxville, Tenn., 1973), 83–84; Fick, *Making of Haiti,* 184; Bell, *Toussaint Louverture,* 92.

66. Spanish authorities and most historians place the blame for the Bayajá massacre on Jean-François, but Jean-François accused Biassou and his men of the atrocities. Jean-François claimed that "although General Viasou [*sic*] made war under the same banners as we, my conduct, the direction of my troops, their discipline, and their military operations have always been better." He argued that if "disorders" occurred after Biassou's troops arrived on the scene and he should be found culpable, Biassou should be punished as required by the law. Jean-François to Captain General Luis de Las Casas, January 12, 1796, ES 5-A, doc. 28, AGI.

67. James, *Black Jacobins,* 151; Geggus, "Slavery, War, and Revolution"; Scott, "The Common Wind."

68. James, *Black Jacobins,* 123–151; Memorial of Jean-François, January

14, 1796, ES 5-A, doc. 28, AGI; the Marqués de Casa Calvo to Captain General Luis de Las Casas, December 31, 1795, ES 5-A, doc. 23, AGI.

69. The Marqués de Casa Calvo to Captain General Luis de Las Casas, December 31, 1795, ES 5-A, doc. 23, AGI; Jane G. Landers, "An Eighteenth-Century Community in Exile: The Floridanos of Cuba," *New West Indian Guide* 70, no. 1 & 2 (Spring 1996): 39–58.

70. Marqués de Casa Calvo to Captain General Luis de Las Casas, December 31, 1795, ES 5-A, doc. 23, AGI.

71. Captain General Joaquín García to the Duque de la Alcudia, February 18, 1794, ES 14, doc. 86, AGI; Captain General Joaquín García to Captain General Luis de Las Casas, January 25, 1796, ES 5-A, doc. 36, AGI.

72. Petition of Jorge Biassou, September 14, 1796, Cuba 1439, AGI.

73. Complaint of Jorge Biassou, May 31, 1794, ES 13, doc. 11, AGI.

74. The leaders evacuated with General Jean-François included Field Marshalls Benjamin and Juan Jacque, Inspector Bernardino, Major General Agapito, Lieutenant Ambrosio Noesi, Intendant Legui, Aides de camp, Lefebre, Watable, Basaña and Delie, the General's Secretary, Perró, Brigadiers, Gil and Paul Mercure, and Colonels Desombray, Hiler Sabanó, and Paul Picard. Report by Captain General Luis de las Casas, January 13, 1796, ES 5-A, doc. 28, AGI. Brigadier Narciso Gil was consulted by members of the Aponte conspiracy in Havana in 1812 and later played a role in the 1812 rebellion in Santo Domingo. Geggus, "Slavery, War, and Revolution," 15. Jorge Biassou had already departed for Havana from Ocoa with his wife and twenty-three dependents. Luis de Las Casas to Duque de Alcudia, January 8, 1796, ES 5-A, doc. 24, AGI. Historians following the trails of other exiles include Renée Soulodre-La France, "The King's Soldiers: Black Auxiliaries in the Spanish and British Empires," paper delivered at the American Historical Association, New York, 2009, and Jorge Victoria Ojeda, S*an Fernando Aké: microhistória de una comunidad afroamericana en Yucatán* (Mérida, Yucatan, 2001). See also Rina Cáceres and Paul Lovejoy, eds., *Haití: revolución y emancipación* (Costa Rica, 2008).

75. White fears of such men and their "notions" are described in Trouillot, "From Planters' Journals to Academia." See also David Geggus, "Racial

Equality, Slavery, and Colonial Secession during the Constituent Assembly," *American Historical Review* 94 (December 1989): 1290–1308, and Geggus, "Slavery, War, and Revolution"; Jane G. Landers, "Rebellion and Royalism in Spanish Florida: The French Revolution on Spain's Northern Colonial Frontier," in Gaspar and Geggus, *A Turbulent Time*, 156–177.

76. Rodríguez Demorizi, *Cesión de Santo Domingo*, 75; Captain General Luis de Las Casas to Captain General Joaquín García, January 10, 1796, ES 5-A, doc. 40, AGI.

77. Petition of Jean-François, January 12, 1796, ES 5-A, doc. 28, AGI.

78. Captain General Luis de Las Casas to Jean-François, January 15, 1796, ES 5-A, doc. 28, AGI.

79. Captain General Joaquín García to the Duque de Alcudia, February 2, 1796, ES 5-A, doc. 36, AGI.

80. One account states that Jean-François ended his days as the governor of Oran in 1820. Alexis, *Black Liberator*, 76.

81. Captain General Luis de Las Casas to Captain General Joaquín García, February 17, 1796, ES 5-A, doc. 52, AGI.

82. Marqués de Casa Calvo to Captain General Luis de Las Casas, January 12, 1796, ES 5-A, doc. 28, AGI; Geggus, *Haitian Revolutionary Studies*, 8, 11.

83. Captain General Joaquín García had suggested the Isle of Pines as a place to "confine" the blacks he was sending to Cuba. Captain General Luis de Las Casas to the Duque de Alcudia, January 18, 1796, ES 5-A, doc. 24, AGI.

84. Accounts of the Royal Treasury, 1796–1814, Account of 1796, SD 2636, AGI. Members of Biassou's immediate family included his wife, Romana; her mother, Ana Gran Pres; her sisters, Barbara and Cecilia Gran Pres; and her brother, Juan Jorge Jacobo, Biassou's military successor. All were free blacks from Guarico (Le Cap). In the "extended" family were Juan Luis Menar, a free mulatto from Guarico (Le Cap), who married Barbara Gran Pres; Placido Asil, a free black from San Miguel on the coast of Guinea, who married Biassou's slave Isabel, a black from Villa de Granada; Jorge Brus, a free mulatto from Marmelade, and his wife, María Car-

lota, a free black from Guarico (Le Cap); Pedro Miguel, a free black; Benjamín Seguí, a free mulatto; Peter Yon Frances, ethnicity not given; Leon Duvigneau, a free mulatto, and his black slave wife, Simonett. This group was identified by searching the black baptisms, marriages, and burials for the post-1796 period. CPR, microfilm reels 284 J, K, and L, PKY. This represents only a partial accounting of the refugees, since others may not have been recorded in these registers.

85. Governor Juan Nepomuceno de Quesada to Captain General Luis de Las Casas, January 25, 1796, Cuba 1439, AGI.

86. Testamentary Proceedings of Jorge Viassou [*sic*], July 15, 1801, EFP, microfilm reel 138, PKY. An account of Biassou's dress in the early days of the slave revolt also stressed his flamboyant style: "Biassou wore a richly embroidered orange-coloured costume and sumptuous black silk scarf, spangled with silver." Alexis, *Black Liberator*, 43.

87. Governor Juan Nepomuceno de Quesada to Captain General Luis de Las Casas, March 5, 1796, Cuba 1439, AGI.

88. Ibid.

89. Landers, *Black Society*.

90. In their first year in the colony, both Biassou and Pedro Miguel complained directly to the captain general of Cuba, who returned the appeals to Florida's new governor, Enrique White. White stiffly admonished all involved that future correspondence should be directed through proper channels, meaning himself. Governor Enrique White to Captain General Luis de Las Casas, March 15 and July 15, 1796, Cuba 1439, AGI.

91. Governor Juan Nepomuceno de Quesada to Captain General Luis de Las Casas, March 5, 1796, EFP, microfilm reel 10, PKY. Biassou had proof of having received 320 pesos monthly through February 1796, but other documents indicated he had once been paid 250 pesos monthly. Treasury officials seized this excuse to pay the lower rate. Gonzalo Zamorano to Interim Governor Bartolomé Morales, January 25, 1796, Cuba 1439, AGI; Accounts of the Royal Treasury, 1784–1795, Santo Domingo (hereafter cited as SD) 2635, and 1796–1819, SD 2636, AGI.

92. Jorge Biassou to Captain General Luis de Las Casas, January 31,

1796, Cuba 1439, AGI. The governor had assigned to Biassou an interpreter from the Cuban Third Battalion who translated Biassou's French dictation into Spanish, which a Spanish amanuensis in turn wrote down for Biassou. Because Biassou could not write in any language, he customarily marked his correspondence with a specially made black stamp.

93. Landers, *Black Society;* McAlister, *Spain and Portugal in the New World,* 3–8, 32, 133–152.

94. In addition to land grants, incentives for relocation included municipal charters specifying exemptions and privileges, royal subsidies, and tax relief. Numerous examples of homesteading and repopulation plans can be found documented in Ministerio de Cultura, *Documentación Indiana en Simancas,* 250–257.

95. Jane Landers, "Gracia Real de Santa Teresa de Mose: A Free Black Town in Spanish Colonial Florida," *American Historical Review* 95 (February 1990): 9–30.

96. Jane G. Landers, "La cultura material de los cimarrones: los casos de Ecuador, La Española, México y Colombia," in Rina Cáceres, ed., *Rutas de la esclavitud en África y América Latina* (San José, Costa Rica, 2001), 145–156.

97. Petition of Juan [*sic*] Buissou [*sic*], July 7, 1797, Spanish Florida Land Records, Florida State Archives, Tallahassee (hereafter cited as SFLR), record group 599, series 992, box 1, folder 32. After Biassou's death in 1806, his brother-in-law and military heir Juan Jorge Jacobo laid claim to Biassou's lands. Landers, "Rebellion and Royalism." Jacobo must have abandoned the claim, since Governor Coppinger later granted the acreage as a service grant to Estéban Arnau. Claim of Joseph F. White, *Spanish Land Grants in Florida,* vol. 1 (Tallahassee, Fla., 1940), 339.

98. There is no record of the captain general's response. Petition of Jorge, November 20, 1798, EFP, microfilm reel 10, PKY.

99. Testamentary Proceedings of Jorge Viassou [*sic*], July 15, 1801, EFP, microfilm reel 138, PKY.

100. Fernando Ortiz, *Los cabildos y la fiesta afrocubanos del Día de Reyes* (Havana, 1992). In the 1790s, when Biassou's entourage left for Florida, the

adult slave population of Saint Domingue was 60 to 70 percent African-born, and a majority of the slaves had arrived within the previous ten years from the lower Guinea coast or the coast of Angola. John K. Thornton, "African Soldiers in the Haitian Revolution," *Journal of Caribbean History* 25 (1991): 58–80.

101. Witnesses at the marriage of Jorge Jacobo and María Rafaela Kenty included the groom's sister and Biassou's wife, Romana, and the bride's brother, Francisco. Marriage of Jorge Jacobo and María Rafaela Kenty, April 12, 1796, Black Marriages, CPR, microfilm reel 284 L, PKY. When the couple's children were born, the maternal grandfather, Juan Bautista (Prince) Whitten, and the paternal grandmother, Ana Gran Pres, served as godparents for María del Carmen, and the maternal uncle, Francisco Whitten, and the paternal aunt, Barbara Gran Pres, served as godparents for the next child, Julian. Another militiaman from Saint Domingue, Benjamín Seguí, was Catalina Melchora Jacobo's godfather. Black Baptisms, vol. 2, CPR, microfilm reel 284 J, entries no. 176, 563, 670, 799, and vol. 3, microfilm reel 284 J, entry no. 31, PKY.

102. Marriage of Francisco Whitten and María Francisca Fatio, January 26, 1799; Marriage of Juan Bautista Whitten and María Rafaela Kenty, July 7, 1798. When Francisco Whitten married on January 26, 1799, his marriage sponsors were Felipe Edimboro and Romana Jacobo (a.k.a. Biassou), who had also served the same roles at his parents' wedding the previous year. Black Marriages, CPR, microfilm reel 284, PKY. Scholars working on other Spanish colonies have found similar patterns of social advancement, family linkages, and multi-generational patterns of service among free black militiamen. See George Reid Andrews, "The Afro-Argentine Officers of Buenos Aires Province, 1800–1860," *Journal of Negro History* 64 (1979): 85–100, and Chapeaux, *Batallones de pardos y morenos libres*, 56–62.

103. Heinl and Heinl, *Written in Blood*, 63; Governor Enrique White to Captain General Luis de Las Casas, October 1796, Cuba 1439, AGI.

104. Alí, at least, never left the island, but his loyalty apparently paid off in the end. He died in 1844, in his nineties, as Governor of the District of Santo Domingo. Captain General Joaquín García to the Duque de Alcudia,

October 28, 1797, in *Cesión de Santo Domingo a Francia*, 254–257; Geggus, *Haitian Revolutionary Studies*, 201.

105. Decoration of Benemerito Boeff by Captain General Joaquín García, August 22, 1794, Cuba 168, AGI; Criminal Proceedings Against Louis Boeff, December 24, 1796, Cuba 169, AGI.

106. Juan Bautista alleged that English-speaking black militiamen always wanted to fight with him because they knew him to be valiant. Those men replied that Bautista was the instigator. These charges seem to indicate some division among St. Augustine's black community along language lines. Memorial of Juan Bautista, June 25, 1798, EFP, microfilm reel 79, PKY. Biassou stated that he had been too ill to handle the insult previously, but he did not want to give the town more to talk about, and hoped the governor would support his authority. The governor must have avoided this thicket. It is interesting that Biassou accused Juan Bautista of chronic drunkenness, a charge that Spanish officials leveled against Biassou. Perhaps the charge against Juan Bautista was true, but Biassou may also have been using a standard European slur to discredit the soldier. Memorial of Jorge Biassou, June 26, 1798, ibid.

107. Governor Enrique White to Conde de Santa Clara, May 24, 1799, GM 6921, AGS.

108. Memorials of Jorge Biassou, November 2, 1799, and December 6, 1799, EFP, microfilm reel 2, PKY.

109. Although he was given an impressive military funeral, Biassou died deeply in debt, and his many creditors began clamoring to be paid. Biassou's greatest asset was his pension, and he had borrowed heavily against it. There was far from enough to pay the bakers, tailors, storekeepers, and landlords who had allowed him credit, so the governor ordered Biassou's gold medal melted and the proceeds applied toward his debts. Testamentary Proceedings of Jorge Biassou, EFP, microfilm reel 138, PKY. Biassou's widow, Romana, remained in Havana. Ill and destitute after Biassou's death, she requested a widow's pension, or half of his monthly salary of 250 pesos. She received considerably less—a pension equal to that of a captain's widow. Petition of Romana Jacobo, October 12, 1801, SD 1268, AGI, and Marqués

de Someruelos to Cavallero, October 22, 1801, ibid. I am indebted to Julius S. Scott for the reference on Romana Biassou.

110. Biassou's burial entry noted that he was a native of Guarico and the son of the negroes Carlos and Diana. He received no sacraments "due to the unexpectedly rapid death which overtook him." Burial of Jorge Biassou, July 14, 1801, Black Burials, CPR, microfilm reel 284 L, PKY. The accounts of Biassou's death have been inconsistent. Some versions follow James's erroneous story that Biassou was murdered and that Toussaint awarded a pension to his widow. *Black Jacobins,* 254. Others say that Biassou died in a drunken brawl in St. Augustine. Heinl and Heinl, *Written in Blood,* 70.

3. Maroons, Loyalist Intrigues, and Ephemeral States

1. Interview of "Samson," in Vicente Sebastian Pintado to José de Soto, May 6, 1815, SD 2580, AGI.

2. Benjamin Quarles, "Lord Dunmore as Liberator," *William and Mary Quarterly* 15 (1958): 494–507.

3. J. Leitch Wright, "Lord Dunmore's Loyalist Asylum in the Floridas," *Florida Historical Quarterly* 46 (April 1971): 370–379; Herbert Aptheker, "Maroons Within the Present Limits of the United States," *Journal of Negro History* 24 (April 1939): 167–184. Because Aptheker's important study relied solely on English-language sources, even this number seriously undercounts the phenomenon.

4. *The Independent Journal or the General Advertiser* (New York), June 20, 1787; Quarles, *Negro in the American Revolution,* 174. This may be the same large maroon community described in the *Charleston Morning Post,* October 26, 1786, and cited in Morgan, "Black Society in the Lowcountry," 139; Census Returns, 1784–1814, EFP, microfilm reel 148, PKY. Berlin, *Many Thousands Gone,* 170.

5. Thomas Jefferson to Governor Juan Nepomuceno de Quesada, Philadelphia, March 10, 1791, GM 6928, AGS. See also Richard K. Murdoch, "The Return of Runaway Slaves, 1790–1794," *Florida Historical Quarterly* 38 (October 1959): 96–113.

6. For detailed discussions on the issue of reciprocal return of runa-

ways, see Governor Manuel de Zéspedes to Marques de Sonora, May 14, 1786; Decree, May 8, 1788, and Governor Zéspedes to Joseph de Espeleta, October 2, 1788 and February 4, 1789, all in Miscellaneous Papers, EFP, microfilm reel 174, PKY.

7. Titus's fellow runaway was "Tise, about the same age, 5 feet 4 or 5 inches high, of a dark complexion, and rather stout." *Savannah Gazette of the State of Georgia,* July 28, 1785, in Lathan A. Windley, ed., *Runaway Slave Advertisements: Documentary History from the 1730s to 1790—Volume 4, Georgia* (Westport, Conn., 1983).

8. Ibid., Savannah, May 20, 1789, *Georgia Gazette 1788–1790.*

9. List of Fugitive Negroes who have come into the Province of East Florida since the promulgation of his Catholic Majesty's Order on the 2 of September, 1790, To and From the United States, EFP, microfilm reel 41, PKY. Titus appeared first on the list, followed by Tice, Jeffrey, John, Summer, Lester, Sue, Beck, Beck's two children, Rose, and Rose's child, Marguerite. Brian Morel presented documents that claimed he owned Febe [*sic*], Jorge, and Reyna; that John Morel owned Miguel, Cato, and Tytus [*sic*]; that Richard Wylly owned Abraham, Monday, and Bentura; that William Bryan owned Tony; and that John Houston Johnston owned Adam and Sam. Only Titus appeared on both lists. Report of Carlos Howard, October 18, 1791, EFP, microfilm reel 174, PKY.

10. James Seagrove to Governor Enrique White, July 4, 1797, EFP, microfilm reel 42, PKY.

11. Ibid.

12. Ibid.

13. Landers, *Black Society,* chap. 1; Wood, *Black Majority,* 3–5; William S. Willis, "Divide and Rule: Red, White, and Black in the Southeast," *Journal of Negro History* 48 (July 1963): 157–176.

14. In earlier challenges to the U.S. boundary commissioners, Bowles had titled himself Director of Affairs, Creek Nation, but the Cussettas referred to Bowles as "the lying captain." "A Talk, received by Major Call, November 6, 1791," in *Pennsylvania Gazette,* December 21, 1791. For more recent studies of Indian diplomacy in the Southeast, see Gregory Evans Dowd, *A Spirited Resistance: The North American Indian Struggle for Unity,*

1745–1815 (Baltimore, 1992), and Claudio Saunt, *A New Order of Things: Property, Power, and the Transformation of the Creek Indians, 1733–1816* (Cambridge, 1999).

15. Lyle N. McAlister, "The Marine Forces of William Augustus Bowles and his 'State of Muskogee,'" *Florida Historical Quarterly* 32 (July 1953): 3–27; McAlister, "William Augustus Bowles and the State of Muskogee," *Florida Historical Quarterly* 40 (April 1962): 317–328.

16. McAlister, "William Augustus Bowles"; J. Leitch Wright, *William Augustus Bowles, Director General of the Creek Nation* (Athens, Ga., 1967). In 1792 William "Bloody Bill" Cunningham, Bowles, and seventy-four "renegade Indians" had seized the stores of the Panton, Leslie & Co. at Apalachee, so their alliance dates at least to that time, but probably even earlier. *The Pennsylvania Gazette*, March 7, 1792.

17. Savannah, April 11, 1800, *Pennsylvania Gazette*, April 23, 1800.

18. McAlister, "Marine Forces."

19. West Florida's governor, Vicente Folch, retook the fort and sank one of Bowles's ships, but Bowles escaped. Savannah, July 24, 1800, in *Pennsylvania Gazette*, August 13, 1800.

20. U.S. Commissioner James Seagrove to John McQueen, June 24, 1800, EFP, microfilm reel 42, PKY. Robert Allen had served as interpreter on June 5, 1799, when Methlogey, "second chief of the Mackasooky Indians," complained to James Seagrove about the boundary line that American surveyors were drawing through Creek lands. The British Captain Nicolls was also present. *Pennsylvania Gazette*, July 17, 1799, *www.accessible.com/accessible/text/gaze4/00000828/00082885.htm* (accessed 8/22/2004).

21. McAlister, "Marine Forces."

22. Andrew Atkinson to Governor Enrique White, June 28, 1800, EFP, microfilm reel 55, PKY.

23. Francis Fatio to Governor Enrique White, June 25, 1800, and Fernando de la Puente to Governor Enrique White, June 24, 1800, EFP, microfilm reel 55, PKY.

24. "Extract of a letter from a gentleman in Augustine, June 24, 1800," *Pennsylvania Gazette*, July 23, 1800, *www.accessible.com/accessible/text/gaze4/00000833/00083331.htm* (accessed 5/7/2006).

25. Instructions for General Biassou, Matanzas, July 1, 1800, War Orders for Picolata, July 1, 1800, Orders for General Biassou, 1801, and Governor Enrique White to Juan McQueen, September 12, 1801, EFP, microfilm reel 55, PKY.

26. Governor Enrique White's talk to the Indians, St. Augustine, July 18, 1800, *Pennsylvania Gazette,* September 3, 1800. The Spanish/Seminole alliance held and, in 1802, Chief Payne traveled to Mikasuki to try to recover a white family and some stolen slaves. Bowles's allies would not release them. Governor Enrique White to Captain General Marques de Someruelos, June 10, 1802, EFP, microfilm reel 10, PKY.

27. Nathaniel Hall to Captain John McQueen, August 11, 1801, David Garvin to Captain John McQueen, and John McQueen to Governor Enrique White, September 3, 1801, and September 7, 1801, EFP, microfilm reel 56, PKY. Newspapers from as far away as Philadelphia and Connecticut reported the hostilities instigated by "That infamous fellow Bowles," and charged that the Spanish military force in Florida was "by no means equal to meet a hundred Indians in the woods." "Extract of a letter from a gentleman in the town of St. Marys, February 10, 1802," *Philadelphia Gazette and Daily Advertiser,* March 10, 1802, and *Connecticut Journal,* March 11, 1802, Florida Newspaper Collection, PKY, *http://fulltextt6.fcla.edu/cgi/t/text/text-idx?c =flnp&idno= UF00002343* (accessed 6/10/2009).

28. Petition of Jorge Jacobo, February 9, 1802, Cuba 357, AGI.

29. Junta de Guerra, January 29, 1802, Cuba 357, AGI; Report of Sergeant Martin Oderiz, February 19, 1802, and Report of John McQueen, April 7, 1802, EFP, microfilm reel 56, Bundle 137G11, Container 20, Library of Congress (hereafter cited as LC).

30. Order of Governor Enrique White to the various army posts, June 11, 1802, and Review lists of the free black militia of St. Augustine, 1802, Papeles Procedentes de Cuba, 357, AGI; Expenses of the Free Black Militias, August 4 and September 24, 1802, Cuba 433, AGI; Wright, *William Augustus Bowles,* 16.

31. March 31, 1802 Summary of John Kelsall, Judge of the Vice-Admiralty, cited in McAlister, "Marine Forces."

32. David H. White, "The Spaniards and William Augustus Bowles in

Florida, 1797–1803," *Florida Historical Quarterly* 54, no. 2 (October 1975): 145–155.

33. John Kinnard to Governor Enrique White, May 8, 1802, and Order of Governor Enrique White to the various army posts, June 11, 1802, EFP, microfilm reel 56, Bundle 137G11, Container 207, LC; Expenses of the Free Black Militias, August 4 and September 24, 1802, Cuba 433, AGI; Wright, *William Augustus Bowles,* 16.

34. Treaty Between Spain and the Seminoles, August 30, 1802, PPC 142, AGI, cited in David Hart White, *Vicente Folch, Governor in Spanish Florida, 1787–1811* (Washington, D.C., 1981), 63.

35. "A Journal of John Forbes, May, 1803: The Seizure of William Augustus Bowles," *Florida Historical Quarterly* 9 (April 1931): 279–289; McAlister, "William Augustus Bowles."

36. The U.S. promised to honor the rights that free blacks had enjoyed under the Spaniards. Kimberly S. Hanger, *Bounded Lives, Bounded Places: Free Blacks in Colonial New Orleans, 1769–1803* (Durham, N.C., 1998).

37. Frank Lawrence Owsley, Jr., and Gene A. Smith, *Filibusters and Expansionists: Jeffersonian Manifest Destiny, 1800–1821* (Tuscaloosa, Ala., 1997), 7–9.

38. Andrew McMichael, "The Kemper 'Rebellion': Filibustering and Resident Anglo American Loyalty in Spanish West Florida," *Louisiana History* 43, no. 2 (Spring 2002): 133–165; F. Andrew McMichael, *Atlantic Loyalties: Americans in Spanish West Florida, 1785–1810* (Athens, Ga., 2008); Paul E. Hoffman, *Florida's Frontiers* (Bloomington, Ind., 2002), 243–281.

39. For the most detailed account of the Patriot War, and the only one to so fully use Spanish sources, see James G. Cusick, *The Other War of 1812: The Patriot War and the American Invasion of Spanish Florida* (Gainesville, Fla., 2003). For an older, but still valuable, account see Rembert W. Patrick, *Florida Fiasco: Rampant Rebels on the Georgia-Florida Frontier* (Athens, Ga., 1954).

40. Ludovick Ashley to the commandant of Amelia Island, March 6, 1812, Cuba 1789, AGI; Rembert W. Patrick, ed., "Letters of the Invaders of East Florida, 1812," *Florida Historical Quarterly* 28 (July 1949): 53–60;

T. Frederick Davis, ed., "United States Troops in Spanish East Florida, 1812–13," *Florida Historical Quarterly* 9 (July 1930): 3–23; Davis, ed., "United States Troops in Spanish East Florida, 1812–13," *Florida Historical Quarterly* 9 (April 1931): 259–278; Kenneth Wiggins Porter, *The Negro on the American Frontier* (New York, 1971).

41. Mary R. Bullard, *Cumberland Island: A History* (Athens, Ga., 2003), 55.

42. Testimony of Jacob Summerlin to the Legislative Council of East Florida, Box 60, File 2, Names, Buckner Harris, Georgia Department of Archives, Atlanta, Georgia. I am indebted to Canter Brown, Jr., for this reference.

43. Their commander, Bernardo de Gálvez, nominated a number of the black militia for royal commendations, and the Crown acknowledged their contribution with silver medals and promotions. Landers, "Transforming Bondsmen into Vassals," in Brown and Morgan, eds., *Arming the Slaves*, 120–145; Hanger, *Bounded Lives, Bounded Places*, 109–135; Vinson, *Bearing Arms for His Majesty*, 7–8.

44. Report of Fernando de la Puente, August 19, 1809, EFP, microfilm reel 68, PKY.

45. Lists of the Free Black Militia of St. Augustine, October 12, 1812, Cuba 357, AGI.

46. Black Marriages, CPR, microfilm reel 284 L, PKY, and Black Baptisms, CPR, microfilm reel 284 J, PKY.

47. Testimony of Juan Antonio Florencio, Claim of Prince Whitten (deceased), Patriot War Claims, Treasury Department, First Auditor's Office, No. 98273, NARA. I am indebted to Frank Marotti for guiding me to this source. Copies of a number of these claims are also held at the St. Augustine Historical Society. The recorder inserted the annotation that Florencio was a mulatto.

48. Governor Sebastián Kindelán to Captain General Juan Ruiz de Apodaca, November 17, 1812, Cuba 1790, AGI.

49. Nominations for Promotions, September 30, 1812, Cuba 357, AGI; Governor Sebastián Kindelán to Captain General Juan Ruiz de Apodaca,

August 19, 1812, Cuba 1789, AGI. A promotion from sergeant first-class to captain represented a salary raise of 75 percent for Jorge Jacobo, and Whitten earned a 73 percent raise. These gains, however, must be considered in the context of paper scrip, inflated prices, and inadequate supplies. Moreover, as it did for white officers, the government deducted sums from the black officers' salaries to pay for their coverage in a military pension fund, the *Montepío militar,* and for an insurance program for disabled troops, *Ynvalidos.* The black unit, like the white, also had to pay for its own hospitalizations. Review lists for the Free Black Militia of St. Augustine, 1812, Cuba 357, AGI.

50. Duvigneau signed with a flourish. Review Lists of Free Black Militia of St. Augustine, March 16 and April 30, 1812, Cuba 357 and January 1813, Cuba 433, AGI.

51. Claim of Prince Whitten, Patriot War Claims, NARA.

52. Although mortally wounded by eight bullets, Marine captain John Williams lived long enough to describe the night battle and the death and scalping of his sergeant. Captain John Williams to Lieut. Samuel Miller, Adjutant, September 15, 1812, Letters Received, no. 44, Marine Corps 1812 Archives, National Archives; "United States Troops in Spanish East Florida, 1812–1813," *Florida Historical Quarterly* 9 (January 1931): 135–155.

53. Governor Sebastián Kindelán to Captain General Juan Ruiz de Apodaca, August 2, 1812, Cuba 1789, AGI.

54. In the name of the captive king Fernando VII, the Spanish Junta offered the insurgents a general amnesty. Looking for a graceful out, the United States asked Kindelán to honor the offer, and he did, granting the rebels three months within which to register for pardon. Major General Thomas Pinckney to Governor Sebastián Kindelán, March 20, 1813, and Kindelán to Pinckney, March 31, 1813, cited in Davis, "United States Troops in Spanish East Florida, 1812–13, V," *Florida Historical Quarterly* 10 (1931): 24–34.

55. Testimony of John Leonardy and Juan Antonio Florencia, March 20, 1846, Patriot War Claims, Treasury Department, First Auditor's Office. No. 98273, Claim of Prince Whitten, Patriot War Claims, NARA.

56. Ibid.

57. Captain General Juan Ruiz de Apodaca wrote more than fifty letters on the same subjects to the Minister of War in 1813 and 1814. Cited are those of March 15, 1813, August 6, 1813, August 9, 1813, and November 11, 1814, Indiferente General 1603, AGI.

58. During the Creek War (1813–1814), Americans under the command of Andrew Jackson waged a series of pitched battles against the nativist Creeks or Red Sticks. On March 27, 1814, at Horseshoe Bend, the already decimated Red Sticks lost about another eight hundred warriors, or half their remaining force. The survivors, including the Prophet Francis, fled to Spanish Florida. Some made a final stand at Prospect Bluff, and Andrew Jackson later executed the Prophet. Gregory Evans Dowd, *A Spirited Resistance: The North American Indian Struggle for Unity, 1745–1815* (Baltimore, 1992), 185–190. Other important works that explore the grim, centuries-long efforts of Southeastern Indians to hold their lands include Claudio Saunt, *A New Order of Things;* Kathryn E. Holland Braund, *Deerskins and Duffels: The Creek Indian Trade with Anglo-Americans, 1683–1815* (Lincoln, Neb., 1993); and Joel Martin, *Sacred Revolt: The Muskogees' Struggle for a New World* (Boston, 1991).

59. Zephaniah Kingsley, *A treatise on the patriarchal system of society as it exists in some governments and colonies in America and in the United States under the name . . .*, 4th ed. (London, 1834), 17 n. 3.

60. Admiral Cockburn to Admiral Cochrane, February 28, 1815, cited in Bullard, *Cumberland Island*, Appendix A, 122–125.

61. John Forbes of Forbes & Company lost seventy-seven slaves from his San Pablo plantation. Pedro Capo found that his runaway slave had enlisted in the British service. Documents related to the Actions of English troops in Fernandina and Apalachicola in the year 1814, SD 2580, AGI.

62. Nathaniel Millett, "Defining Freedom in the Atlantic Borderlands of the Revolutionary Southeast," *Early American Studies: An Interdisciplinary Journal* 5.2 (2007), 367–394; James W. Covington, "The Negro Fort," *Gulf Coast Historical Review* 5 (Spring 1990): 72–91; Owsley and Smith, *Filibusters and Expansionists,* chap. 6; John D. Milligan, "Slave Rebelliousness and

the Florida Maroon," *Prologue, The Journal of the National Archives* 6 (Spring 1974): 5–18.

63. Colonel Edward Nicolls to Colonel Benjamin Hawkins, April 28 and May 12, 1815, and Colonel Benjamin Hawkins to Colonel Edward Nicolls, May 28, 1815; *Niles Weekly Register,* June 10, 1815.

64. Alexander Arbuthnot to Edward Nicolls (from Nassau), August 26, 1817, in James Parton, *Life of Andrew Jackson,* 3 vols. (Boston, [18--?]–1885), 414–416.

65. Report of José de Soto, May 4, 1815, SD 2580, AGI.

66. Doyle signed his letter, "In hopes that you may yet hang the Scoundrel." Edmund Doyle to Captain R. C. Spencer, undated, cited in "The Panton, Leslie Papers, Letters of Edmund Doyle," 242. Despite Doyle's negative assessment, which was shared by the United States Indian agent, Benjamin Hawkins, Nicolls demonstrated concern for their black and Indian allies on a number of occasions. He offered to pay the remaining 200 pesos that the mulatto Carlos owed his owner for his freedom, but Pintado felt he had no authority to accept it. List of the Slaves Belonging to Owners in Pensacola, December 30, 1814, and March 4 and May 6, 1815, SD 2580, AGI.

67. Inhabitants of West Florida to José de Soto, May 6, 1815, SD 2580, AGI.

68. Milligan, "Slave Rebelliousness," 11.

69. On post-1808 slave smuggling into Texas and Louisiana and links to Florida, see Ernest Obadele-Starks, *Freebooters and Smugglers: The Foreign Slave Trade in the United States after 1808* (Fayetteville, Ark., 2007), chaps. 1–2.

70. Vicente Sebastián Pintado to José de Soto, April 29, 1815, SD 2580, AGI.

71. Pensacola residents claimed the loss of 136 slaves, including 78 men, 23 women, 8 boys, 4 girls, and 23 whose sex was not given. List of the Slaves Belonging to Owners in Pensacola, May 4 and May 6, 1815, SD 2580, AGI.

72. Aptheker, "Maroons Within the Limits."

73. Admiral Cockburn to Admiral Cochrane, Cumberland Island, Janu-

ary 26, 1815, *Cockburn Papers*, vol. 25: 50–52, cited in Bullard, *Cumberland Island*, 57.

74. Pintado confronted Captain Woodbine about the slaves he allegedly lured from East Florida, and Woodbine stated that 78 slaves belonging to the Indians accompanied him to Prospect Bluff, but that none came directly from St. Augustine. Vicente Sebastián Pintado to José de Soto, April 29, 1815, SD 2580, AGI.

75. Vicente Sebastián Pintado to José de Soto, May 6, 1815, and Owner's declarations, May 8, 1815, SD 2580, AGI.

76. Colonel D. L. Clinch to Colonel R. Butler, August 2, 1816, Record group 45, U.S. Navy 1775–1910, Subject File J, Box 181, National Archives.

77. Report of a Gentleman from New Orleans, *Niles Weekly Register*, September 14, 1816; Report of the Attack of Major M'Intosh, *Niles Weekly Register*, August 31, 1816.

78. Clinch to Butler, August 2, 1816. This letter is also reprinted in the *National Intelligencer*, November 15, 1819, and in James Grant Forbes, *Sketches Historical and Topographical of the Floridas: More Particularly of East Florida* (New York, 1821), 102.

79. Ibid.

80. Jay Kinsbruner, *Independence in Spanish America: Civil Wars, Revolutions, and Underdevelopment* (Albuquerque, 2000); Karen Racine, *Francisco de Miranda: A Transatlantic Life in the Age of Revolution* (Wilmington, Del., 2003).

81. For the definitive works on the Kingsleys, see Daniel L. Schafer, "Shades of Freedom: Anna Kingsley in Senegal, Florida, and Haiti," in *Against the Odds: Free Blacks in the Slave Societies of the Americas*, ed. Jane G. Landers (London, 1996), 130–154; Schafer, "Zephaniah Kingsley's Laurel Grove Plantation, 1803–1813," in Landers, *Colonial Plantations and Economy*; and Schafer, *Anna Madgigene Jai Kingsley, African Princess, Florida Slave, Plantation Owner* (Gainesville, Fla., 2003).

82. Fenda and John Fraser filled their coastal baracoons with slaves purchased from native chiefs such as Mongo Barkey of Bashia Branch and

Mongo Besenty of Bahia, "Principal Merchants of the Rio Pongo." Claims of John Fraser, Works Projects Administration, *Spanish Land Grants in Florida* (hereafter *SLGF*), (Tallahassee, 1942), vol. 3, 141–145.

83. Schafer, "Shades of Freedom," 137 n. 152. Fraser's agent at Bangra, Charles Hickson, probably facilitated this process. *SLGF*, vol. 3, 145. When Fraser drowned in 1814, three of his daughters still lived at Bangra, but Fraser's will decreed that his five children should share equally in his sizeable estate, which included 158 African-born slaves. Testamentary Proceedings of John Fraser, 1814, EFP, microfilm reel 134, PKY, and Notarized Documents, January 24, 1816, EFP, microfilm reel 55, PKY; Daniel L. Schafer, "Family Ties That Bind: Anglo-African Slave Traders in Africa and Florida, John Fraser and His Descendants," *Slavery and Abolition: A Journal of Slave and Post-Slave Studies* 20 (1999): 1–21.

84. John Fraser to Governor Enrique White, April 28, 1810, and Fernando de la Maza y Arredondo to Governor Enrique White, December 20, 1810, EFP, microfilm reel 133, PKY, cited in Schafer, "Family Ties That Bind." Fraser's captains included Francisco Ferreyra, Lorenzo Seguí, and Bartolomé Mestre. After Seguí's death on the African coast, James (Santiago) Cashen made several voyages to the Rio Pongo. Puerto Rican officials impounded the 92 slaves from his first voyage, and on the second only 28 slaves arrived alive. Cuba 419 A, AGI; SD 2533, AGI.

85. Landers, *Black Society*, 237–244.

86. W. E. B. Du Bois, *The Suppression of the African Slave-Trade to the United States of America, 1638–1870* (New York, 1896), 110.

87. List of ships, owners, and captains, 1811–1812, in Varios, EFP microfilm reel 84, Bnd 298 C16, Library of Congress. The brigantine *Don Alonso* sailed for Liverpool with 10,000 pounds of cleaned cotton, 25,000 pounds of rice, and thousands of casks on board. Registration of the *Don Alonso*, January 25, 1810, Cuba 419, AGI.

88. *United States v. Ferreira*, Senate Miscellaneous Documents, no. 55, 36th Congress, 1st Session, 17–18.

89. Free Blacks and Mulattoes of Fernandina and Amelia Island, 1814, and 1814 Census of Fernandina, EFP, microfilm reel 148, PKY; Memorials

for City Lots in Fernandina, 1809–1821, *SLGF,* vol. 1, series 996; Landers, *Black Society,* 237–244.

90. When Spanish forces besieged Cartagena in 1815, Bolívar sought sanctuary and support in Haiti, the first black republic in the hemisphere. President Petión promised Bolívar arms and support in return for slave emancipation. Bolívar subsequently emancipated his own slaves and incorporated many into his army, as would later his arch-enemy, the Spanish General Pablo Morillo. David Bushnell, *Simón Bolívar, Liberation and Disappointment* (New York, 2004), 74–79, 111–112.

91. The deputies who commissioned MacGregor claimed to represent Mexico, Río de la Plata (modern Argentina), New Granada (modern Colombia), and Venezuela. Parton, *Life of Andrew Jackson,* 421–423; David Bushnell, "The Florida Republic: An Overview," and Charles H. Bowman, Jr., "Amelia Island and Vicente Pazos of Upper Peru," in *La República de las Floridas: Texts and Documents,* compiled by David Bushnell (Mexico City, 1986), 7–18, 39–50.

92. Spain had diverted most of its resources to the wars in South America, and Florida's government had to depend on what it had, despite repeated requests for aid. Tulio Arends, *La República de las Floridas, 1817–1818* (Caracas, 1986), 33–41.

93. *Niles Weekly Register,* September 22, 1817.

94. Parton, *Life of Andrew Jackson,* 422–423.

95. Resolution on Elections for Amelia Island, November 16, 1817, cited in Arends, *La República de las Floridas,* 170–172.

96. *Charleston Courier,* April 14, 1817, cited in Bowman, "Amelia Island"; Parton, *Life of Jackson,* 425; Arends, *La República de las Floridas,* 160–161.

97. *Narrative of a Voyage to the Spanish Main in the Ship "Two Friends,"* facsimile reproduction of the 1819 edition, introduction and index by John H. Griffin (Gainesville, Fla., 1978), 94.

98. List of the Black Militia of Fernandina, August 12, 1811, EFP, microfilm reel 61, PKY; Review lists for Fernandina's Black Militia, Cuba 353, AGI; Rufus Kay Wyllys, "The Filibusters of Amelia Island," *Georgia Historical Quarterly* 12 (December 1928): 297–325.

99. *Baltimore Patriot*, December 12, 1817, cited in Arends, *La República de las Floridas*, 95.

100. John Houston McIntosh to Secretary of the Treasury William H. Crawford, July 10, 1817, *Savannah Republican*, November 8, 1817.

101. *Columbia Museum and Savannah Daily Gazette*, December 1, 1817, cited in Bowman, "Amelia Island."

102. *Niles Weekly Register*, November 29, 1817; T. Frederick Davis, "MacGregor's Invasion of Florida," *Florida Historical Quarterly* 7 (1928): 3–71.

103. James Monroe, December 2, 1817, *Message from the President of the United States to Both Houses of Congress at the Commencement of the First Session of the Fifteenth Congress*. The naval force consisted of the *U.S.S. John Adams, Saranac, Enterprise, Prometheus, Lynx,* and *Gunboat 168*. War Department Orders, November 12, 1817, and Navy Department Orders, November 14, 1817, cited in Davis, "MacGregor's Invasion," 39–42; Bowman, "Amelia Island."

104. Letters of Captain John H. Elton to the Secretary of the Navy, October 19, 1817, November 15, 1817, and January 3, 1818, cited in *Nile's Weekly Register*, November 29, 1817.

105. *Niles Weekly Register*, February 21, 1818.

106. *Savannah Republican*, May 2, 1818. Even after Spain formally ceded Florida to the United States in 1819, traders made a mockery of the inadequately supported slave trade embargo. In 1820 a U.S. Treasury cutter patrolling off the coast of St. Augustine captured the *Antelope*, a slaver incoming from Cabinda and carrying 280 Africans aboard with a commission from José Artigas, father of the as yet unsecured nation of Uruguay. A Portuguese spokesman complained that its commission was no better than one issued by the Seminole Indians. In fact, some of the liberated Africans from the seized ships ran almost immediately for the hinterlands, where they might have found refuge with the Seminoles. John T. Noonan, Jr., *The Antelope: The Ordeal of the Recaptured Africans in the Administrations of James Monroe and John Quincy Adams* (Berkeley, 1977), 4, 135–138, 145, 152; Obadele-Starks, *Freebooters and Smugglers*; Frances J. Stafford, "Illegal Im-

portations: Enforcement of the Slave Trade Laws Along the Florida Coast, 1810–1828," *Florida Historical Quarterly* 46 (October 1967): 124–140.

107. Bowman, "Amelia Island"; Protest by Vicente Pazos to Secretary of State John Quincy Adams, February 7, 1818, in Arends, *La República de las Floridas*, 200–218. As "deputed agent of the authorities acting in the name of the republics of Venezuela, New Granada and Mexico," Vicente Pazos submitted a memorial to the U.S. Congress on March 6, 1816, which argued that "in this free, this enlightened, friendly and neutral country" they should be allowed a "redress of grievances." The House of Representatives refused to receive his petition. *Niles Weekly Register* (1814–1837), April 11, 1818, *American Periodical Series Online, http://proquest.umi.com/pqdweb?index=7 &did=811813102&SrchMode=2&sid=2&Fmt=10&VInst=PROD&VType =PQD&RQT=309&VName=HNP&TS=1245850212&clientId=2335* (accessed 6/23/09).

On January 10, 1817, Aury's black troops from Saint Domingue killed their former leader after losing a naval engagement with the Spaniards. Julio F. Guillén, *Indice de los papeles de la sección de corso y presas, Archivo General de Marina* (Madrid, 1953), 151.

108. Commodore J. D. Henley to the Secretary of the Navy, Benjamin W. Crowninshield, December 24, 1817, and "América del Norte," *Correo del Orinoco*, March 27, 1819, in Arends, *La República de las Floridas*, 184–185, 228–236.

4. Black Militiamen and African Rebels in Havana

1. Pedro Deschamps Chapeaux, *El negro en la economía Habanera del siglo XIX* (Havana, 1971), 122–125.

2. Ibid.

3. Pedro Deschamps Chapeaux, *Los Batallones de Pardos y Morenos Libres* (Havana, 1976), 27–33. Havana's earliest black hermitage was Espiritu Santo, created in 1638 and devoted to the Holy Spirit. By 1648 the devotion had become so strong and the neighborhood around it had grown so populated that church officials declared Espiritu Santo an auxiliary parish, and by

1661 the brothers had an auxiliary church. M. Cuadrado, *Obispado de la Habana: Su historia a través de los siglos, Libro 1, Parte 1, De las parroquias* (Havana, n.d.), 252–253.

4. Murdo MacLeod, "Self-Promotion: The 'Relaciones de méritos y servicios' and Their Historical and Political Interpretation," *Colonial Latin American Historical Review* 7:1 (Winter 1988): 25–42; Deschamps Chapeaux, *Batallones de Pardos y Morenos*, 43.

5. Allan J. Kuethe, *Cuba, 1753–1815: Crown, Military, and Society* (Knoxville, 1986); Matt D. Childs, *The 1812 Aponte Rebellion and the Struggle against Atlantic Slavery* (Chapel Hill, N.C., 2006), 79–87.

6. The *pardo* units wore white uniforms with a green collar, gold buttons, and short black boots. A few years later they changed to white trousers, dress coat, and waistcoat, bright green lapel and collar, gold buttons, and black boots. The *moreno* units wore a red waistcoat with blue lapel and collar, white buttons, red tie, white pants, black cap, and short black boots. Deschamps Chapeaux, *Batallones de Pardos y Moreno*, 43.

7. Ibid., 23, 46–49; Childs, *The 1812 Aponte Rebellion*, 86; Sherry Johnson, The *Social Transformation of Eighteenth-Century Cuba* (Gainesville, Fla., 2001), 68.

8. Blacks also enlisted in large numbers in the other areas governed by the Reglamento, or Cuban military code. These included Florida, Puerto Rico, Louisiana, and Panama. Klein, "Colored Militia."

9. Johnson, *Social Transformation*, 63.

10. Ibid., 67–68; Deschamps Chapeaux, *Batallones de Pardos y Morenos*, 52–59; Deschamps Chapeaux, *El negro en la economía*, 59–86; Landers, *Black Society*, 101–106; Hanger, *Bounded Lives, Bounded Places*, chap. 4.

11. Deschamps Chapeaux, *Batallones de Pardos y Morenos*, 29–30; Gloria García, *Conspiraciones y revueltas: La actividad política de los negros en Cuba (1790–1845)* (Santiago, Cuba, 2005), 13.

12. Kuethe, *Cuba, 1753–1815*, 74.

13. For example, the *moreno* sergeant Juan Felipe de los Santos served for more than twenty-five years and listed the expeditions at Mobile, Pensacola, and a corsairing expedition among his services of note. Despacho de

Sub/te de Vandera, June 1, 1802, Cuba 1667, AGI. For other black service records see Cuba 1798, AGI; Hanger, *Bounded Lives, Bounded Places,* 109–135; Landers, *Black Society,* 198–200; Vinson, *Bearing Arms for His Majesty,* 7–8. On geopolitical literacy see Philip Troutman, "Grapevine in the Slave Market: African American Geopolitical Literacy and the 1841 Creole Revolt," in Walter Johnson, ed., *The Chattel Principle: Internal Slave Trades in the Americas* (New Haven, Conn., 2004), 202–233. Francisco Miranda also fought at Pensacola and spent time in Havana, so it is at least possible that the Cuban militiamen may have exchanged political ideas with the "precursor" to Venezuelan independence. Racine, *Francisco de Miranda,* 21–24.

14. See Julius S. Scott, "The Common Wind: Currents of Afro-American Communication in the Era of the Haitian Revolution" (Ph.D. diss., Duke University, 1986); Peter Linebaugh and Markus Rediker, *The Many-Headed Hydra: Sailors, Slaves, Commoners and the History of the Revolutionary Atlantic* (Boston, 2000); Jeffery W. Bolster, *Black Jacks: African American Seaman in the Age of Sail* (Cambridge, Mass., 1997).

15. Deschamps Chapeaux, *Batallones de Pardos y Morenos,* 50; Johnson, *Social Transformation,* 66–67; Klein, "Colored Militia of Cuba"; Landers, *Black Society,* 198–200.

16. Hanger, *Bounded Lives, Bounded Places,* 109–135; Vinson, *Bearing Arms for His Majesty,* 7–8; Landers, *Black Society,* 61–68, 246–248.

17. Deschamps Chapeaux, *Batallones de Pardos y Morenos,* 56–60.

18. Deschamps Chapeaux, *El negro en la economía,* 103–183.

19. Africans also organized informal or unauthorized *cabildos* that functioned as the licensed *cabildos* did. Jane Landers, "Cimarrón and Citizen: The Evolution of Free Black Towns," in Jane Landers and Barry M. Robinson, eds., *Slaves, Subjects, and Subversives: Blacks in Colonial Latin America* (Albuquerque, 2006), 111–145; Jane Landers, "Conspiradores esclavizados en Cartagena en el siglo XVII," in *Afrodescendientes en las Américas: trayectorias sociales e identitarias: 150 años de la abolición de la esclavitud en Colombia,* ed. Claudia Mosquera, Mauricio Pardo, and Odile Hoffman (Bogotá, Colombia, 2002), 181–193.

20. For black brotherhoods in other Spanish colonies, see José Luis Sáez,

La iglesia y el negro esclavo en Santo Domingo: Una historia de tres siglos (Santo Domingo, 1994), and Von Germeten, *Black Blood Brothers.*

21. To date, scholars have depended almost exclusively on the state archives of Cuba to explicate how Africans and their descendants understood, defined, and redefined ethnicities in *cabildos de nación.* Matt D. Childs, "'The Defects of Being a Black Creole': The Degrees of African Identity in the Cuban *Cabildos de Nación, 1790–1820,*" in Landers and Robinson, eds., *Slaves, Subjects, and Subversives,* 209–245; Philip A. Howard, *Changing History: Cuban Cabildos and Societies of Color in the Nineteenth Century* (Baton Rouge, La., 1998); Stephan Palmié, *Wizards and Scientists: Explorations in Afro-Cuban Modernity and Tradition* (Durham, N.C., 2002).

22. For more detail on the *cabildos de nación* and *cabildos de criollos,* see Rafael L. López Valdés, *Pardos y morenos, esclavos y libres en Cuba y sus instituciones en el Caribe Hispano* (San Juan, Puerto Rico, 2007), 171–283.

23. Bishop Pedro Agustín (Morrell de Santa Cruz) to the Captain General, December 6, 1755, SD 515, no. 51, AGI.

24. Fernando Ortiz, *Los cabildos y la fiesta afrocubanos del Día de Reyes* (Havana, 1992), 7–16.

25. Ibid.; Judith Bettelheim, *Cuban Festivals: A Century of Afro-Cuban Culture* (Kingston, Jamaica, 2001).

26. Ortiz, *Los cabildos,* 25–64. See also Ortiz's original article annotated and translated by Jean Stubbs, "The Afro-Cuban Festival 'Day of Kings,'" in *Cuban Festivals, An Illustrated Anthology,* ed. Judith Bettelheim (New York, 1993), 3–47; "Los cabildos Afrocubanos," in *Orbita de Fernando Ortiz,* ed. Julio Le Riverand (Havana, 1973), 121–134.

27. Lydia Cabrera, "Babalú Ayé-San Lázaro," in *La enciclopedia de Cuba* (San Juan, 1975–1977), vol. 6, 268–282. Robert Farris Thompson compares nineteenth-century Cuban costuming with contemporary costumes from Nigeria and Calabar and demonstrates the continuities of form and design in *Flash of the Spirit: African and Afro-American Art and Philosophy* (New York, 1984), 260–267. For comparison see Michael Mullin, *Africa in America: Slave Acculturation and Resistance in the American South and the British Caribbean, 1736–1831* (Urbana and Chicago, 1992).

28. Ecclesiastical Sources for Slave Societies Database (hereafter cited as

ESSS), *http://lib11.library.vanderbilt.edu/diglib/esss,* DSCNO538 (accessed 9/4/08).

29. Geggus, "Slave Resistance in the Spanish Caribbean in the Mid-1790s."

30. Childs, *The 1812 Aponte Rebellion.*

31. Oscar Grandío Moráguez, "The African Origins of Slaves Arriving in Cuba, 1789–1865," in David Eltis and David Richardson, eds., *Extending the Frontiers: Essays on the New Transatlantic Slave Trade Database* (New Haven, Conn., 2008), 176–201.

32. Childs, *The 1812 Aponte Rebellion,* 50, 61; Landers, *Black Society,* 176–178.

33. Jay Kinsbruner, *Independence in Spanish America: Civil Wars, Revolutions, and Underdevelopment* (Albuquerque, 2000), 35–37; Larry R. Jensen, *Children of Colonial Despotism: Press, Politics, and Culture in Cuba, 1790–1840* (Tampa, Fla., 1988), 3–21. Cuba's late-eighteenth-century papers included the *Guía de Forasteros,* the *Gaceta de Havana,* and the *Papel Periódico de la Habana,* although the first two were short-lived. The *Aurora: Correo Político-económico de la Habana,* the *Mensajero Político Económico-literario de la Habana,* and the *Diario de la Habana* were Cuba's most important nineteenth-century newspapers.

34. Johnson, *Social Transformation,* 14.

35. List of Contributions, Amelia Island, June 25, 1810, EFP, microfilm reel 115.

36. José M. Portillo Valdés, *Crisis Atlántica: Autonomía e Independencia en a Crisis de la Monarquía Hispánica* (Madrid, 2006); Kinsbruner, *Independence in Spanish America,* 35–37.

37. Memorial of Antonio Flores, 1759, and response of the Council of the Indies, February 28, 1760, SD 1455, AGI.

38. Deschamps Chapeaux, *El negro en la economía,* 122–125.

39. Ibid.

40. Declaration of Captain Gabriel Dorotea Barba, December 4, 1809, Cuba 357, AGI. The exotic remained popular in Havana, among both black and white literati. In 1827 the *Diario de la Habana* announced that the Teatro Mecánico y Pintoresco on San Ignacio Street would open the drama *Aradin*

Barbarroja, which featured "beautiful seascapes, Turkish galleys, the fortress [of Orán}, battles, swimming men, fires and many other things." In 1833 the same paper carried an article on the Turkish Mufti, and in 1838 Cubans could read Silvestre de Balboa's republished seventeenth-century poem, *Espejo de paciencia,* in which Salvador Golomón, a "brave negro," "dignified Ethiope," and "good soldier," rescues Havana's bishop from a French pirate, fighting like "a furious lion" with his machete and lance. In 1842 Juan Francisco Manzano, the celebrated poet and former slave, published his first tragedy, *Zafira,* a five-act play that also featured the Berber pirate Barbarroja and a brave "Arab" slave, Noemí. In his autobiograpy, Manzano recalled going to the theater with his owners as a child. Roberto Friol, *Suite para Juan Francisco Manzano* (Havana, 1977), 67–87. I am indebted to my colleague William Luis for this reference; Alejo Carpentier and Alan West-Duran, "Music in Cuba," *Transition* 9: 1 and 2 (2000): 172–228, *http://muse.jhu .edu/journals/transition/v009/9.1carpentier.html* (accessed 6/21/2009).

41. Petition of Gabriel Dorotea Barba, October 1, 1811, and Bishop's response, November 2, 1811, Ecclesiastical Sources for Slave Societies Database, *http://lib11.library.vanderbilt.edu/diglib/esss,* DSCNO523, (accessed 9/4/08).

42. In June of 1811, Arango met secretly with William Shaler, U.S State Department official, to discuss Cuba's possible annexation. José Luciano Franco, *Las conspiraciones de 1810 y 1812* (Havana, 1977), 14.

43. Childs, *The 1812 Aponte Rebellion,* 69.

44. Captain General Someruelos, February 11, February 20, March 5, 1812, SD 1284, AGI, cited in Jensen, *Children of Colonial Despotism, 39.*

45. Franco, *Las conspiraciones,* 16; Childs, *The 1812 Aponte Rebellion,* 164–166; Jensen, *Children of Colonial Despotism,* 38.

46. Childs, *The 1812 Aponte Rebellion,* 157–162.

47. List of the blacks in the Castillo del Morro to be sent to the Presidio of Saint Augustine, Florida, September 16, 1812. Cuba 1789, AGI. Eighteen men appeared on this list. They were sentenced to ten years and forbidden to return to Cuba. See also Arrival of Miguel y Perico Gonzalez in St. Augustine, April 14, 1812, EFP, microfilm reel 12, PKY.

48. Franco, *Las conspiraciones,* 19; Childs, *The 1812 Aponte Rebellion,* 156.

49. José Luciano Franco, *La conspiración de Aponte* (Havana, 1963); Howard, *Changing History;* Childs, *The 1812 Aponte Rebellion.*

50. Childs, *The 1812 Aponte Rebellion,* 21, 47, 120, 154.

51. Memorial of Nicolás Lane to Captan General Juan Ruiz de Apodaca, April 25, 1812; Troops of the Batallon de Morenos de la Habana going to St. Augustine as a result of the invasion there, May 13, 1812, and Memorials of the Captains and Officials of the Batallon de Morenos, May 28, 1812; June 18, 1812; August 13, 1812; September 14, 1812; October 22, 1812; December 17, 1812, Cuba 1798, AGI. Miguel Porro complained regularly about the poor conditions in Florida and his troops' lack of clothing and was imprisoned in the Castillo de San Marcos in St. Augustine in 1813. Miguel Porro to the Governor, March 29, 1813, To and From the Commander of the Negro Militia, 1812–1821, EFP, microfilm reel 75, PKY.

52. Memorial of Francisco de Montalvo to Captain General Juan Ruiz de Apodaca, April 29, 1812, Cuba 1798, AGI.

53. Roque E. Garrigo, *Historia documentada de la conspiración de los soles y rayos de Bolívar* (Havana, 1922), 100.

54. Asuntos Politicos (hereafter cited as AP), Legajo 214, Signatura 118, Archivo Nacional de Cuba (hereafter cited as ANC), in Deschamps Chapeaux, *El negro en la economía habanera,* 18.

55. Francisco Montalvo to Captain General Juan Ruiz de Apodaca, October 19, 1812, Cuba 1798, AGI.

56. Jensen, *Children of Colonial Despotism,* 47–49.

57. Garrigo, *Historia documentada,* 102–103.

58. *El Negrito,* vol. 1, no. 1, March 28, 1821, *http://digital.library.miami.edu/chcdigital/negrito/negrito_main.shtml* (accessed 12/31/06).

59. *Félix Varela y Morales, El Habanero, Papel Político, Cientiífico y Literario* (Miami, 1997).

60. Relation of the Florida Exiles, August 22, 1821, Cuba 357 and 358, AGI.

61. See Landers, *Black Society;* Schafer, *Anna Madgigine Jai Kingsley;*

Anna Ruth B. Barr and Modeste Hargis, "The Voluntary Exile of Free Negroes of Pensacola," *Florida Historical Quarterly* 17 (1938): 3–14.

62. Petition of Prince Whitten, July 31, 1819, EFP, microfilm reel 14, PKY.

63. Relation of the Florida Exiles, August 22, 1821, Cuba 357 and 358, AGI.

64. Among the Florida families leaving Havana for Matanzas were those of Corporal Sandy Embara (Sergeant Felipe Edimboro's son), Corporal Pedro Yznardi (the mulatto son of Florida's Treasurer) and the extended Aysik, Zamorano, Rivas, and Rait families. Emigrados de Florida, Cuba 358, AGI.

65. Garrigo, *Historia documentada.*

66. Varela also established schools and nurseries and served in various parishes. See *Félix Varela y Morales;* "Memorial que demuestra la necesidad de extingur la esclavitud de los negros de la isla de Cuba, atendiendo a los intereses de sus propietarios," *Obras de Félix Varela y Morales,* vol. III (Havana, 1944).

67. Deschamps Chapeaux, *Batallones de Pardos y Morenos,* 33, 54–55. On Afro-Colombian politics of the day, see Marixa Lasso, "Race War and Nation in Caribbean Gran Colombia, Cartagena, 1810–1832," *The American Historical Review* (April 2006), *www.historycooperative.org/journals/ahr/111.2 /lasso.html* (accessed 6/24/09), and "Revisiting Independence Day: Afro-Colombian Politics and Creole Patriot Narratives, Cartagena, 1809–1815," in Mark Thurner and Andrés Guerrero, eds., *After Spanish Rule: Postcolonial Predicaments of the Americas* (Durham, N.C., 2003), 223–247.

68. Deschamps Chapeaux, *El negro en la economía,* 5–6, 8–16.

69. Real Junta de Fomento, Agricultura y Comercio, legajo 144, no. 7126, cited in Deschamps Chapeaux, *El negro en la economía,* 20.

70. Comisión Militar series (hereafter CM), ANC. It is worth noting that white soldiers who expressed sympathy for the Liberal Constitution of 1812 were also being investigated and charged by these commissioners.

71. All material on the Prieto case is found in CM, Legajo 11, no. 1, fo-

lios 194–334, ANC. A terrible fire destroyed much of the Jesús María neighborhood in 1828 and the *cabildo*'s original license was destroyed, but Prieto secured a replacement.

72. Ibid. The records on Prieto's *cabildo* and many others investigated by the Military Commissions in Havana and Matanzas are located in the National Archives of Cuba in Havana, and with lesser frequency, the Archive of the Indies in Seville. Possibly because of the divide between church and state in Cuba, the records of secularly authorized *cabildos* and religiously sanctioned *cofradías* have long been deposited in different repositories. Few scholars have examined the records in the Archbishopric archives in Havana.

73. For more on Kongo *nkisi* and European misunderstandings of African religious practices, see Wyatt MacGaffey, "Dialogues of the Deaf: Europeans on the Atlantic Coast of Africa," in *Implicit Understandings: Observing, Reporting, and Reflecting on the Encounters between Europeans and Other Peoples in the Early Modern Era*, ed. Stuart B. Schwartz (Cambridge, 1994), 249–267, and *Art and Healing of the Bakongo Commented by Themselves: Minkisis from the Laman Collection*, Kikongo texts trans. and ed. by Wyatt MacGaffey (Stockholm, 1991).

74. CM, legajo 11, no. 1, folios 194–334, ANC. Despite the repression of the 1830s and 1840s, black *cabildos* survived, as did black confraternities. The Swedish writer Frederika Bremer wrote of her visit to several black *cabildos* in 1851, all concentrated outside of the city walls. At the *cabildo* of Our Lady, Saint Barbara of the Lucumí Alagua [*sic*] nation, an elected king and queen sat on thrones beneath a canopy while another woman danced under a canopy supported by four attendants. Other women and men danced, but only with their own gender, while musicians rattled gourds and beat out rhythms on drums and with sticks on benches and doors. Bremer was flattered when one shirtless male danced up in a red skirt and hat, decorated with strings of glittering beads, to pay her a compliment. Saint Barbara was the patron saint of the Artillery and the Yoruba counterpart of Shango, the *orisha* of war. Alagua/Elegua was the Yoruba trickster god of the crossroads

who shaped the future for good or ill. According to Bremer's local companions, the Lucumíes had become wealthy by winning lotteries and used their winnings to buy the freedom of their enslaved kinsmen, as Juan Nepomuceno Prieto's *cabildo* also had. Frederika Bremer, *The Homes of the New World: Impressions of America*, trans. Mary Howitt, vol. 2 (New York, 1853), 379–383; Robert Farris Thompson, *Flash of the Spirit: African and Afro-American Art and Philosophy* (New York, 1984), 17–38.

75. On Monzón see CM, legajo 23, no. 1, ANC, cited in Deschamps Chapeaux, *Batallones de pardos y morenos*, 79–84, and AP 40/1, ANC, cited in García, *Conspiraciones y revuletas*, 107–117. In her careful examinations of the vast Military Commission records, Gloria García has discovered a number of "secret societies" with names like the Danish Society, Moon Dwellers, and the Academy of Our Lady of Dolores. See also Franco, *Conspiraciones*. On Margarita Blanco and the work and organization of stevedores, see López Valdés, *Pardos y morenos, esclavos y libres*, 255, 309–330. Comparable organization can be seen among the Hausa stevedores in Salvador de Bahia. See Stuart B. Schwartz, "Cantos and Quilombos: A Hausa Rebellion in Bahia, 1814," in Landers and Robinson, eds., *Slaves, Subjects, and Subversives*, 247–272.

5. Black Seminoles: A Nation Besieged

1. Abraham to General Jesup, Fort Deynaud, April 30, 1838, Miscellaneous Manuscripts, Box 5, PKY.

2. Landers, *Black Society*, 171–172.

3. Mark F. Boyd, "Events at Prospect Bluff on the Apalachicola River, 1808–1818: An Introduction to Twelve Letters of Edmund Doyle, Trader," *Florida Historical Quarterly* 16:2 (October 1947): 55–96.

4. A peso was about equivalent to the U.S. dollar of the day.

5. List of the blacks belonging to the inhabitants of Pansacola [*sic*], May 4, 1815, SD 2580, AGI. Sierra's own slaves were Moises, Harry, Simon, and Lucas.

6. The Seminole town is variously spelled also as Latchaway or Ala-chua. Many Southeastern indigenous groups spoke languages of the Mus-kogean linguistic family. English traders designated those living along the Chatahoochee and Flint Rivers as Lower Creeks, while the so-called Up-per Creeks lived on the Alabama, Coosa, and Tallapoosa Rivers. J. Leitch Wright, Jr., *Creeks and Seminoles: The Destruction and Regeneration of the Muscogulge People* (Lincoln, Neb., 1986), 1–40.

7. John K. Mahon and Brent R. Weisman, "Florida's Seminole and Mic-cosukee Peoples," in *The New History of Florida*, ed. Michael Gannon (Gainesville, Fla., 1996), 183–206; Weisman, *Like Beads on a String: A Cul-ture History of the Seminole Indians in North Peninsular Florida* (Tuscaloosa, Ala., 1989).

8. *William Bartram on the Southeastern Indians*, ed. Gregory A. Wasel-kov and Kathryn E. Holland Braund (Lincoln, Neb., 1995), 52.

9. Daniel L. Schafer, "St. Augustine's British Years, 1763–1784," *El Escribano* 38 (2001): 76–77. Schafer argues that by tightly controlling Indian traders, Governor Grant avoided disastrous wars like those his fellow En-glishmen had experienced in Carolina and Georgia.

10. *Bartram on the Southeastern Indians*, 52.

11. James W. Covington, *The Seminoles of Florida* (Gainesville, Fla., 1993), 29.

12. Brent R. Weisman, "The Plantation System of the Florida Seminole Indians and Black Seminoles during the Colonial Period," in Jane G. Land-ers, ed., *Colonial Plantations and Economy in Florida* (Gainesville, Fla., 2001), 136–149.

13. Abraham's wife was said to be "the widow of the former chief of the nation," meaning Bowlegs, and may have been the woman Hagar, whose son, Renty, Abraham formally freed in 1839. Abraham also had at least one other son, named Washington, and a daughter married to a young man named Juan. Kenneth Wiggins Porter, "The Negro Abraham," *Florida His-torical Quarterly* 25 (July 1946): 1–43.

14. Cimarrones visited St. Augustine on January 4, 1786, on February

28 and July 31, 1787, and on August 31, 1788. Caleb Finnegan, "Notes and Commentary on The East Florida Papers: Lists of Gifts to Indians, 1785–1788," unpublished research notes drawn from EFP, microfilm reel 160, PKY.

15. Collins's mother was of African descent and a native of Le Cap in Saint Domingue. His father was a French planter from Nagitoches, Louisiana. Landers, *Black Society,* 90–93.

16. On the Seminole cattle economy, see Susan R. Parker, "The Cattle Trade in East Florida, 1784–1821," in Landers, *Colonial Plantations,* 150–167; Juan Bautista Collins against Don José Antonio Yguíniz, Notarized Instruments, January 16, 1810, EFP, microfilm reel 167, PKY; Suit of Bukra Woman, December 15, 1824, Box 174, Folder 59 and Box 176, Folder 28. The case dragged on until 1844. St. Johns County Circuit Court, Minute Book B and Box 117, Folder 44, St. Augustine Historical Society. I am indebted to Charles Tingley for copies of these documents.

17. Susan R. Parker, "Success through Diversification: Francis Philip Fatio's New Switzerland Plantation," in Landers, *Colonial Plantations,* 69–82; Testimony of Peter B. Cook, *American State Papers* (hereafter *ASP): Military Affairs* (hereafter *MA),* 1: 727. http://memory.loc.gov/cgi-bin/ampage (accessed 6/7/09).

18. Alcione M. Amos, T*he Life of Luis Fatio Pacheco, Last Survivor of Dade's Battle* (Dade City, Fla., 2006), 2; Landers, *Black Society.*

19. Catalina Satorios to Andrew Jackson, April 16, 1822, in James Parton, *Life of Andrew Jackson,* vol. 1 (New York, 1860), 174; Catalina Satorios to Fernando, June 14, 1822. Renamed "Polydore," Fernando married one of Jackson's slaves at the Hermitage, and when his Spanish owner sought his recovery, Jackson paid $500 to retain him in Tennessee. Catalina Satorios to Andrew Jackson, June 7, June 14, and July 8, 1822, and Andrew Jackson to Catalina Satorios, May 16 and May 22, 1822. I am indebted for this reference to my neighbor, Dr. Larry McKee, former archaeologist at the Hermitage, and to Sharon Macpherson of the Andrew Jackson Papers Project at the University of Tennessee, Knoxville.

20. List of the blacks belonging to the inhabitants of Pansacola [*sic*], May 4, 1815, SD 2580, AGI.

21. Colonel D. L. Clinch gave an eyewitness account of the destruction. August 2, 1816, in John Grant Forbes, *Sketches Historical and Topographical of the Floridas* (New York, 1821), 200–205.

22. Kenneth Wiggins Porter, *The Black Seminoles*, rev. and ed. Alcione M. Amos and Thomas P. Senter (Gainesville, Fla., 1996).

23. Testimony of John Lewis Phenix, April 26, 1818, *ASP, MA.*

24. Joshua R. Giddings, *The Exiles of Florida* (Columbus, Ohio, 1858); Kenneth Wiggins Porter, *The Negro on the American Frontier* (New York, 1971) and *The Black Seminoles;* George Klos, "Blacks and The Seminole Indian Removal Debate, 1821–1835," in *The African American Heritage of Florida,* ed. David R. Colburn and Jane L. Landers (Gainesville, Fla., 1995), 128–156; Landers, *Black Society,* 235–237.

25. *ASP,* Foreign Relations, 4: 586–597, cited in Porter, *Black Seminoles,* 20.

26. Porter, *Black Seminoles,* 19.

27. The Humble Representation of the Chiefs of the Creek Nation to his Excellency Governor Cameron (of the Bahamas), cited in *Narrative of a Voyage to the Spanish Main in the Ship "Two Friends,"* facsimile of 1819 edition (Gainesville, Fla., 1978), 219.

28. Ibid., 20.

29. In English sources Heijah's name is spelled variously as King Hadjo, King Hachy, Kenhache, Kenhagee, Kinhache, or Kinhajo. His indigenous name appears on documents as Cappichimico (*mico* designating a chief). Heijah, in fact, did have blacks among his people. General Edmund P. Gaines to the Seminoly Chief, and King Hachy to General Gaines, August 1818, cited in *Narrative of a Voyage to the Spanish Main,* 221–222.

30. Letters of Arbuthnot and of the Seminole Chiefs presented as evidence at Arbuthnot's trial, cited in *Narrative of a Voyage to the Spanish Main,* 216–239.

31. George Perryman to Lt. Richard Sands, February 24, 1817, *ASP: In-*

dian Affairs, 2:155. See also "East Florida," *National Intelligencer*, in *Niles Weekly Register* 13 (November 13, 1817): 190. Testimony of Peter B. Cook, *ASP: MA*, 1:727

32. Andrew Jackson to Governor of West Florida, April 6, 1818, cited in Parton, *Life of Andrew Jackson*, 451.

33. Alexander Arbuthnot to John Arbuthnot, April 2, 1818, cited in *Narrative of a Voyage to the Spanish Main*, 216–218.

34. Testimony of Peter Cook, cited in ibid., 258–259.

35. Robert Ambrister to Edward Nicolls, 1818, cited in ibid., 260.

36. J. Leitch Wright, Jr., "A Note on the First Seminole War As Seen by the Indians, Negroes, and Their British Advisors," *Journal of Southern History* 34 (November 1968): 565–575; Coker and Watson, *Indian Traders of the Southeastern Spanish Borderlands*, chap. 15; Andrew Jackson to Governor Rabun of Georgia, April 20, 1818, cited in *Niles Weekly Register*, May 23, 1818.

37. Porter, *Black Seminoles*, 26.

38. Andrew Jackson to Catherine Satorios, February 1822, cited in Parton, *Life of Andrew Jackson*, 483.

39. Jackson wrote back that he did not want to separate Polydore from the wife and children he had at the Hermitage, and he paid Catalina Satorios $500 for her runaway. In 1846, when Polydore was approximately fifty years old, Jackson sent him to Mississippi, and in 1861, when he was almost sixty-five, Jackson conveyed Polydore to his grandson Samuel in Louisiana. Parton, *Life of Andrew Jackson*, 483–484.

40. Richard Ivy Easter to Andrew Jackson, Nashville, May 10, 1821, in Parton, *Life of Andrew Jackson*, 39–41.

41. Andrew Jackson to Secretary of War, cited in Mahon and Weisman, "Florida's Seminole and Miccosukee Peoples," in Gannon, ed., *The New History of Florida*, 183–206.

42. Canter Brown, Jr., *Florida's Peace River Frontier* (Orlando, Fla., 1991), 42.

43. "The Defences of the Floridas: A Report of Captain James Gadsden, Aide-de-Camp to General Andrew Jackson," *Florida Historical Quar-*

terly 15 (April 1937): 248. Creeks and Seminoles traditionally migrated to hunting grounds in southern Florida from November to March of each year, and because the Seminole hunters traveled with their families, they established permanent villages around Tampa Bay. Brown, *Florida's Peace River Frontier,* 4–5.

44. Brown, *Florida's Peace River Frontier,* 9–10; Canter Brown, Jr., "The 'Sarrazota,' or Runaway Negro Plantations: Tampa Bay's First Free Black Community, 1812–1821," *Tampa Bay History* 12 (Fall-Winter 1990), 5–19; Department of Archives, *The Bahamas in the Age of Revolution, 1775–1848* (Nassau, 1989), 16.

45. United States Secretary of War John C. Calhoun denounced the raid and blamed it on the Creek nation. *Nassau Royal Gazette and Bahama Advertiser,* March 20, 1822, cited in Brown, "'Sarrazota,' or Runaway Negro Plantations."

46. Most English language-accounts assume that Abraham's leadership begins in this period, but Spanish accounts document his long record of resistance. Porter, *Black Seminoles,* 26–27.

47. *ASP: Indian Affairs,* 2: 241, cited in Porter, *Black Seminoles,* 27.

48. Howard F. Klein, *Florida Indians, Provisional Historical Gazeteer with Locational Notes on Florida Colonial Communities* (New York, 1974). Klein worked from lists created by the Mikasuki chief, Neamathla, and by Captain John Bell at an Indian conference convened by Andrew Jackson on September 18, 1821.

49. Horatio Dexter visited a number of Seminole villages, including Pilaklikaha, in 1823. Horatio Dexter's Report on South Florida, August 20, 1823, in James David Glunt Papers, PKY. Terry Weik, of the Department of Anthropology, University of South Carolina, has conducted surface collections at this site.

50. Porter, *Black Seminoles,* 27–29.

51. *ASP: Military Affairs,* 6: 454, 458, 464, 465, cited in Porter, *Black Seminoles,* 33.

52. *New York Observer,* January 30, 1836, Newspaper Article Database, 1762–1885, PKY. *http://web.uflib.ufl.edu/Goza/* (accessed 6/5/09).

53. John K. Mahon, *History of the Second Seminole War, 1835–1842* (Gainesville, Fla., 1967). One soldier in that war, Henry Prince, described several meetings between Army officials and Seminoles in which Abraham served as negotiator. Diary of Henry Prince, Box 33, PKY. Prince heard of the Dade Massacre on January 21, 1836; *ASP: MA* 7: 820–822, cited in Porter, *Black Seminoles,* 67.

54. Abraham to Cae/Coa Hadjo, Tampa, September 11, 1837, Miscellaneous Manuscripts, Box 5, PKY.

55. Abraham to General T. S. Jesup, Tampa, April 30, 1838, Miscellaneous Manuscripts, Box 5, PKY. Porter, "The Negro Abraham."

56. M234, roll 290, frames 164–168, *www.african-nativeamerican.com /freesem.htm* (contributor Lance Hall, Creek researcher; accessed 6/7/09).

6. Atlantic Creoles in Matanzas, Cuba

1. Quoted in Frederick S. Stimson, "Cuba's Romantic Poet: The Story of Plácido," University of North Carolina, *Studies in the Romance Languages and Literature* 47 (1964).

2. Escoto Collection, Conspiracies, 710–719, Documentos de la Conspiración de Negros, 1844, Houghton Library, Harvard University; José L. Franco, *Plácido, una polémica que tiene cien años* (Havana, 1964).

3. Allan J. Kuethe, "Havana in the Eighteenth Century," in *Atlantic Port Cities: Economy, Culture, and Society in the Atlantic World, 1650–1850,* ed. Franklin W. Knight and Peggy K. Liss (Knoxville, Tenn., 1991), 13–39.

4. Childs, *Aponte Rebellion,* 49.

5. Laird W. Bergad, Fe Iglesias García, and María del Carmen Barcia, *The Cuban Slave Market, 1790–1880* (Cambridge, Mass., 1995), 23–37.

6. David Murray, *Odious Commerce: Britain, Spain and the Abolition of the Cuban Slave Trade* (Cambridge, 1980). A British traveler described the ongoing trade in Cuba in the 1820s; see Robert Francis Jameson, *Letters from the Havana: During the Year 1820, Containing an Account of the Present State of the Island of Cuba* (London, 1821), 23–37.

7. List of ships, owners, and captains, 1811–1812, in Varios, EFP, microfilm reel 84, Bnd 298 C16, LC; EFP, microfilm reel 133, PKY.

8. José Luciano Franco, *Comercio Clandestino de Esclavos* (Havana, 1996), 97.

9. Anne Farrow, Joel Lang, and Jennifer Frank, *Complicity: How the North Promoted, Prolonged, and Profited from Slavery* (New York, 2005), 110–112.

10. Franco, *Comercio Clandestino*, Lino Novás Calvo, *Pedro Blanco, El Negrero* (Madrid 1979); Blanco offered to provide as proof of his allegation his correspondence with customers in Florida, Louisiana, and Arkansas. *The Maryland Colonization Herald* cited in *The Provincial Freeman*, Toronto, Canada West, September 16, 1854.

11. Franco, *Comercio Clandestino*, 132–135.

12. Joseph C. Dorsey, *Slave Traffic in the Age of Abolition: Puerto Rico, West Africa, and the Non-Hispanic Caribbean, 1815–1859* (Gainesville, 2003); Luis Martínez-Fernández, *Fighting Slavery in the Caribbean: The Life and Times of a British Family in Nineteenth-Century Cuba* (Armonk, N.Y., 1998).

13. Robert Francis Jameson visited Matanzas in 1818 and said its revenues totaled $249,023, a fourfold increase in just over fifty years. Jameson, *Letters from the Havana*, 90–91.

14. Laird W. Bergad, *Cuban Rural Society in the Nineteenth Century: The Social and Economic History of Matanzas* (Princeton, N.J., 1990), chap. 1.

15. Matanzas was trading with Boston, New York, Philadelphia, Charleston, New Orleans, Mobile, Baltimore, Wilmington, Savannah, Providence, and Salem in the United States. European trading partners included Hamburg, Antwerp, Barcelona, Bristol, and Bath. Despatches from U.S. Consuls in Matanzas, 1820–1899, vol. 1, U.S. State Department General Reports, U.S. National Archives, TR 339, microfilm reel 1; *La Aurora de Matanzas*, February 19, 1838, included in TR 339, microfilm reel 1, Latin American Collection, University of Florida Libraries, Gainesville, Fla.

16. For extensive material on Cuban railroad construction, see Ultra-

mar, Cuba Fomento, legajo 37, Archivo Histórico de la Nación, Madrid (hereafter cited as AHN).

17. Bergad, Iglesias García, and Barcia, *Cuban Slave Market*, 23–37; Kuethe, "Havana in the Eighteenth Century."

18. A large force of maroons also attacked coffee plantations in Cuba's eastern provinces. This triggered major retaliatory expeditions against two of the largest eastern *palenques*, Toa and El Frijol, a well-fortified settlement of over 400 people. Saul Vento, *Las rebeldías de esclavos en Matanzas* (Havana, 1976), 16–18.

19. Bergad, *Cuban Rural Society*, 80–83.

20. Memorial to reform the Hermandad de la Santíssima Virgen del Rosario, March 26, 1736, Matanzas Cathedral Archive, ESSS, DSCN 1081.

21. Captain Gabriel Dorotea Barba asked that the Company of Pardos and Morenos from Matanzas be incorporated into the Havana Battalion so that they would then be covered by the *fuero*. He wrote that the "poor individuals [of that unit] despite much work and fatigue, which has not ceased since the creation [of their unit], still do not enjoy the *fuero militar*." Memorial of Gabriel de la Dorotea Barba, May 25, 1812, Cuba 1798, AGI.

22. Franklin W. Knight, "The Caribbean in the Age of Enlightenment, 1783–1837," paper delivered at Vanderbilt University.

23. *Diario del Gobierno de la Habana*, December 13, 1817, EFP, microfilm reel 109.

24. Criminal charges against the *pardo* Manl José Blond, Escoto Collection, Conspiracies, bMS Span 502 (700), Causas políticas en Matanzas por subversión y sedición, 1821–1822, folder 3, Houghton Library, Harvard University.

25. Francisco J. Ponte y Domínguez, *Matanzas: biografía de una provincia* (Havana, 1909), 94–97, 104.

26. Los emigrados de Florida, Cuba 358, AGI.

27. All material on the Sevillán case comes from Comisión Militar de Matanzas (hereafter cited as CMM), Legajo 9, número 24, ANC. See also Comisión Militar Ejecutiva y Permanente, Legajo 9, numero 25, ANC, cited in García, *Conspiraciones y revueltas*, 93–94.

28. CMM, Legajo 9, número 24, ANC.

29. For other discussions of contemporary free black subscription associations, dances, and balls, see Landers, *Black Society,* 147–148, and Hanger, *Bounded Lives,* 132–133, 144–147. This was probably an adaptation of Shakespeare's work translated from the French and published in Havana in 1833 as *Otelo o El Moro de Venecia.* Friol, *Suite para Juan Francisco Manzano,* 72. See also Howard Johnson, "Slave Life and Leisure in Nassau, Bahamas, 1783–1838," paper presented at the Association of Caribbean Historians, San Germán, Puerto Rico, 1994.

30. Another person arrested at Sevillán's house was Antonio Bernoqui, who was later executed in the La Escalera conspiracy. García, *Conspiraciones y revueltas,* 94–96.

31. Some escaped slaves from St. Ann's had also found religious sanctuary in Cuba. Scott, "A Common Wind."

32. All materials on the Davison case can be found in CMM, Legajo 17, número 1, ANC. Several authors cover this case briefly, among them Philip Howard, *Changing History,* and Gloria García, *Conspiracions y revueltas,* 104.

33. CMM, Legajo 17, número 1, ANC.

34. William A. Gibbs reporting from Matanzas, September 20, 1837, "A Caution to Travelers in General," in *The Colored American,* New York, October 21, 1837, *www.accessible.com/accessible* (accessed 6/20/08). Gibbs had, in fact, been briefly detained and interrogated by the Military Commission of Matanzas, who reported that he was a black carpenter from New York without a passport to travel to Matanzas. The Captain General approved his detention. Captain General Miguel Tacón to the Governor of Matanzas, September 7, 1837, Esclavos, Legajo 23, no. 23, Archivo Historico Provincial de Matanzas (hereafter cited as AHPM).

35. *The Colored American,* New York, June 16, 1838, *www.accessible.com/accessible* (accessed 6/20/08).

36. Ibid., October 24, 1840, and April 24, 1841.

37. Bergad, *Cuban Rural Society,* 83.

38. Vento, *Las rebeldías de esclavos en Matanzas,* 44. Gabino La Rosa

Corzo, *Los palenques del oriente de Cuba: resistencia y acoso* (Havana, 1988) and "Los palenques en Cuba: Elementos para su reconstrucción histórica," in *La esclavitud en Cuba* (Havana, 1986), 86–123.

39. Gabino La Rosa Corzo, ed., *Cazadores de esclavos: Diarios* (Havana, 2004); Garrigo, *Historia documentada,* 98–100; Gloria García, *La esclavitud desde la esclavitud* (Havana, 2003), 171–177.

40. García, *Conspiraciones y revueltas,* 83–87; García, *La esclavitud desde la esclavitud,* 178–183; Israel Moliner Castañeda, "Las sublevaciones de esclavos en Matanzas," *Islas* 85 (1986): 24–48.

41. Bergad, *Cuban Rural Society,* 84–85.

42. Vento, *Rebeldías de esclavos,* 25–31. Manuel Barcia Paz has found that in this same period at least some slaves from Matanzas plantations filed successful legal protests against maltreatment, which may have also helped to diffuse some conflict. Manuel Barcia Paz, *La resistencia esclava en las plantaciones Cubanas* (Havana, 1998), 14–18.

43. CM, Legajo 29, no. 5, 1842, ANC, cited in Moliner Castañeda, *Sublevaciones de esclavos,* 38–45; Robert L. Paquette, *Sugar Is Made with Blood: The Conspiracy of La Escalera and the Conflict between Empires over Slavery in Cuba* (Middletown, Conn., 1988), 209–211, 214–215; García, *Conspiraciones y revueltas,* 127–132; García, *La esclavitud desde la esclavitud,* 187–199.

44. Paquette, *Sugar Is Made with Blood,* 220–232. There are sixty-three folders of documents from this lengthy investigation in the Escoto Collection, Conspiracies, Documents 1844, bMS Span 52 (708–719), Houghton Library, Harvard University.

45. Paquette, *Sugar Is Made with Blood,* 227.

46. Ibid., 219–229; *The North Star,* Rochester, N.Y., July 7, 1848, reporting an article from *The New York Evangelist,* Havanna [*sic*], March 1848, *www.accessible.com/accessible/text/freedom/00000111/00011162.htm* (accessed 10/14/2007).

47. Apprehensions of free people of color, Escoto Collection, Conspiracies, Documents 1844, bMS Span 52 (715), folder 3, Houghton Library, Harvard University. These documents list the person on whose testimony the

I intend to fulfill my purpose to teach and delight humanity through my writing.

I intend to give and receive love with a good man who will be my life long companion.

others were arrested, some descriptions of the suspects, sometimes their occupations, and sometimes where they lived.

48. Lt. Nicolás Lanes did not take his name but left Father Valdés more than $3000 in his will. Deschamps Chapeaux, *El negro en la economía,* 70.

49. Paquette, *Sugar Is Made with Blood,* 2–26, 233–266. On Plácido's transnational impact, see Ifeoma Kiddoe Nwankwo, *Black Cosmopolitanism: Racial Consciousness and Transnational Identity in the Nineteenth-Century Americas* (Philadelphia, 2005), 29–47.

50. Deschamps Chapeaux, *El negro en la economía,* 157–165; Paquette, *Sugar Is Made with Blood,* 227–229. Plácido's testimony to the Military Commissioners, and that of his fellow poet, Juan Francisco Manzano, are found in CM, Legajo 52, no. 1, ANC. These declarations show that the two men met often in homes of the elite, at celebratory dinners, and at cock fights and taverns. Friol, *Suite para Juan Francisco Manzano,* 188–212.

51. Governor of Matanzas to the Military Commission, July 9, 1844, Escoto Collection, Conspiracies, Documents 1844–45, bMS Span 52 (716), Houghton Library, Harvard University.

52. Burials for June 28, 1844, Cathedral of San Carlos de Matanzas, *ESSS,* Andres José Dodge, entry no. 152, Santiago Pimienta, Entry no. 153, Gabriel de la Concepción Valdés, alias Plácido, entry no. 154. In addition to the executed leaders are many others whose entries describe them as "prisoners in the Royal Jail who died in the Charity Hospital of this city."

53. Juan Pérez de la Riva, *Para la historia de las gentes sin historia* (Barcelona, 1976), 143–174; Rodolfo Sarracino, *Los que volvieron à Africa* (Havana, 1988).

54. Libro de pasaportes, Misc. No. 10714, ANC, cited in Deschamps Chapeaux, *El negro en la economía,* 25–26.

55. Schafer, *Anna Madgigine Jai Kingsley.*

56. AP, legajos 140/38 and 141/6, ANC.

57. Petitions of foreign blacks that they not be deported, 1844, legajos AP 141/6 and 140/38, ANC. I am grateful to Manuel Barcia Paz for these references.

58. Rebecca J. Scott, *Slave Emancipation in Cuba: The Transition to Free Labor, 1860–1899* (Princeton, N.J., 1985); Aline Helg, *Our Rightful Share: The Afro-Cuban Struggle for Equality, 1886–1912* (Chapel Hill, N.C., 1995); Bergad, García, and Barcia, *The Cuban Slave Market*.

Epilogue

1. Petition of José Manuel Rivas, June 10, 1844, AP 141/6, ANC.

2. Lists of Families Emigrating from East Florida, August 23, 1821, Cuba 358, AGI.

3. AP 141/6, ANC. José Manuel Rivas's case begins on May 4, 1844, and concludes June 10, 1844. Adam Rayt's case begins May 10, 1844, and concludes June 4, 1844.

4. Dubois, *Avengers of the New World*, 160.

Index

Kongo (African kingdom and people), 7, 147, 157, 172, 259n15

Lambert, Jean-Pierre, 76
Lame Cudjo, 198
Langueste, 176
Las Casas, Luis de, 80–82, 84–85
Latin America, 15, 111, 128
Laurens, Henry, 17, 19, 23, 26–27, 239, 262n43
Laveaux, Etienne, 68
Lenormand de Mézy plantation (Saint Domingue), 60
Leonardy, John, 116–119
Leonardy, Roque, 250
Lesley, Net, 247
Leslie, Gen. Alexander, 31
Leslie, Juan, 49, 272n118
Leslie, Prince, 247
Liberty, 4, 13, 14; absolute, 211; British law against slavery, 121; French revolutionary influence and, 51; revolutionary rhetoric of, 9, 24
Literacy, 14, 43, 152, 192
Literature, subversive, 215
Little Ephraim Robin John, 4, 16
Llorente, Col. Tomás, 249, 250
Long Warrior (Seminole head man), 182
López, Jorge, 215
Loubel, Juan Luis, 247–248
Louis XVI, king of France, 69, 94, 233; arrested by revolutionaries, 59, 60; Counter-Revolutionary beliefs of rebel slaves and, 62; execution of, 68, 240; Saint Domingue insurgents devoted to, 68, 276n23
Louisiana, 11, 53, 112; Barataria pirates,

124; purchased by United States, 110, 166, 241
Loyalists (Tories), 9, 10, 26; Bowles's supporters, 102–103; Rangers in South Carolina, 28, 29, 30; retreat to Florida, 33, 36, 239
Lucumí nation. *See Cabildos de nación* (Lucumí nation)

Macaya (slave rebel), 72, 147, 233
MacGregor, Gregor, 131–133, 135, 189, 242
Madan, Joaquín, 208–209
Madison, James, 110, 129
Mandinga people and culture, 1, 2, 19, 39
Mañes, Marcelino, 229
Mangourit, Citizen Michel-Ange, 51
Manucy, Albert, 4
Margarita (dependent of Whitten family), 49
María Dolores (slave ship), 206
María Luisa, queen of Spain, 48
Marie Antoinette, queen of France, 59
Marie-Séraphique, La (slave ship), 57
Marines, U.S., 54, 114, 157, 241
Marion, Francis ("Swamp Fox"), 28, 29, 30, 32, 263n55
Maroon settlements, 96, 103; in Cuba, 169, 220, 316n18; at Negro Fort, 124, 127; Savannah River community, 97–98; Seminoles' alliance with, 179. *See also Palenques*
Maroon War, Second, 53
Marronage, 5, 170
Martineau, Harriet, 217
Matanzas (Cuba), city and province of, 12, 142, 315n15; La Escalera